THE CONSTRUCTION OF WHITENESS

UNIVERSITY PRESS OF MISSISSIPPI • JACKSON

THE CONSTRUCTION OF
WHITENESS

An Interdisciplinary Analysis
of Race Formation and the
Meaning of a White Identity

Edited by Stephen Middleton,
David R. Roediger, and
Donald M. Shaffer

www.upress.state.ms.us

The University Press of Mississippi is a member of the Association of American University Presses.

First printing 2016

∞

Library of Congress Cataloging-in-Publication Data

Names: Middleton, Stephen, editor. | Roediger, David R., editor. | Shaffer, Donald M., 1974– editor.
Title: The construction of whiteness : an interdisciplinary analysis of race formation and the meaning of a white identity / edited by Stephen Middleton, David R. Roediger, and Donald M. Shaffer.
Description: Jackson : University Press of Mississippi Jackson, [2016] | Includes bibliographical references and index.
Identifiers: LCCN 2015031980 (print) | LCCN 2015047396 (ebook) | ISBN 9781496805553 (cloth : alk. paper) | ISBN 9781496805560 (ebook)
Subjects: LCSH: Whites—Race identity—United States. | United States—Race relations.
Classification: LCC HT1575 .C66 2016 (print) | LCC HT1575 (ebook) | DDC 305.800973—dc23
LC record available at http://lccn.loc.gov/2015031980

British Library Cataloging-in-Publication Data available

In Memory of
Stephen Middleton II

CONTENTS

ACKNOWLEDGMENTS

OBVIOUSLY, *THE CONSTRUCTION OF WHITENESS* IS THE RESULT OF contributions made by many people. While a separate list of contributors to this collection appears in this anthology, the editors wish to express appreciation for their professionalism during the process of bringing this book to completion. The editors also wish to thank Craig Gill, Editor-in-Chief at the University Press of Mississippi, for his confidence in this interdisciplinary project from the start. We are grateful for the services of Katie Keene, editorial associate, and Shane Gong Stewart, senior project editor, at the Press, for their help with the project. Surely, the anonymous readers for the Press did their job in vetting the manuscript. We tried to heed their advice as much as possible without giving up the integrity of our scholarship. This volume benefitted from their comments.

Specifically, Stephen Middleton wishes to thank his co-editors for joining him on this journey. David Roediger is well known to most historians, especially those interested in the study of whiteness. My interest in whiteness studies led me to invite Dave to Mississippi State University to give a lecture in 2008. I am pleased that he agreed when I invited him be a co-editor and contributor to this volume. I am also pleased that Donald Shaffer, my colleague at Mississippi State University, joined our team. I also want to thank a few of the many scholars who made helpful suggestions on my manuscript. Michael Les Benedict, my professor from my days at Ohio State University, remains as generous to me as when I was a student. Bernie Jones, Lyndsay Campbell, Joshua D. Rothman, and Jack N. Rakove made helpful suggestions on ways to improve my work.

David Roediger wishes to thank John Carlos Marquez, his research assistant, for supporting his work expertly. He is also grateful for the generous support of the Illinois Program for Research in the Humanities. Roediger's research assistant at the University of Kansas, Hannah Bailey, contributed greatly to the final preparation of the manuscript, and staff members Pam

LeRow and Paula Courtney drafted the index. Donald Shaffer wishes to thank his wife, Venessa, for her love and support and his research assistant, Jermaine Thompson, for the careful way he read some of the essays in this collection. Many people and institutions also provided valuable assistance to the writers for this anthology. We cannot thank you all here, but please know that we are grateful for your service in helping to make this a better anthology.

The Editors

THE CONSTRUCTION OF WHITENESS

INTRODUCTION

APPROXIMATELY A CENTURY AGO, RENOWNED HISTORIAN W. E. B. Du Bois insisted that the very existence of "personal whiteness" was a problem American scholars needed to explain. Du Bois was suggesting that whiteness is not a naturally occurring fact of human life. The sense that some people claimed a cherished racial identity was, Du Bois argued, applicable only during a tiny sliver of human history. Du Bois theorized that whiteness was about 250 years old.[1] He characterized it as an exception in world civilization and asserted that it requires critical investigation and analysis. Hence, African American intellectuals like Du Bois suggest that whiteness is anything but normal or natural, from slave folk tales to Ida B. Wells, James Baldwin, and Toni Morrison. However, it is only recently that whiteness has received a hearing in mainstream academic disciplines, such as the humanities and social sciences, where it seemed less of a problem to reckon with by scholars.[2]

The exception to this pattern began in the 1990s. The election of consecutive leaders like Ronald Reagan and George H. W. Bush to the presidency in 1980, 1984, and 1988 saw each garner unprecedented numbers of white working-class votes. Thus, whiteness suddenly seemed like a problem threatening the whole of American liberalism as it had existed since the New Deal. A new cadre of prolific, widely read and reviewed writers now engage whiteness studies. Their work illustrates the connections between a white racial identity and reactionary politics. These authors include Vron Ware, Neil Foley, Alexander Saxton, David Roediger, Noel Ignatiev, Cheryl Harris, Karen Brodkin, and Theodore Allen.[3] Their passionately argued and critically analyzed hypotheses crack open a window for a new generation of scholars to engage the study. Even as conservative critics try to reduce the field to a caricature, it continues to blossom. Margaret Talbot's 1997 *New York Times Magazine* article, for example, cast attempts to study whiteness as the equivalent of "porn studies" and "Madonna studies." Other critics share her disdain for whiteness studies and set the regrettable pattern of arguing that mainly white scholars advance the field. Nevertheless, the *Times* article inadvertently gave rare publicity to scholarship appearing mostly from university presses.[4] In 1997 and 1998 alone, no fewer than seven weighty anthologies assaying the critical study of whiteness appeared.[5]

Talbot prematurely pronounced the work she reported on as "ill-equipped to stand the test of time."[6] Nearly twenty years later her comment has proven to be a grave misstatement; the leading work critically studying whiteness remains oft-cited and hotly debated. Such studies also continue to be a bane and, indeed, incomprehensible to some conservative commentators in their fundamental arguments. The African American economist and columnist Walter Williams, for example, recently reacted to a scholar invoking Du Bois's idea that "personal whiteness" was a latecomer to the world's stage with at least feigned puzzlement. If there were no white people before 1681, he asked rhetorically, were Plato, Locke, Newton, and Shakespeare "people of color," or did they "not exist"?[7]

If critical studies of whiteness have survived such attacks, as well as those mounted from time to time by liberal scholars, the field has matured in ways at odds with its stormy rise in the 1990s.[8] It no longer announces itself with such certainty that the fate of left politics in the United States rides on its wisdom. The restraint and clarity in Nell Irvin Painter's exemplary 2010 volume *The History of White People,* a study in which one of America's leading black historians tackles whiteness, typifies the change.[9] Painter's audacious and transnational work establishes that the field surely is not a fad or a peculiar area of scholarship. However, scholars of critical whiteness studies are wary of developing institutions like those organized in the wake of the civil rights movement. They have not pursued or created academic departments at universities, nor published professional journals or a lengthy book series. (The Australian Critical Race and Whiteness Studies Association and its estimable journal *Critical Race and Whiteness Studies* are exceptions.) Scholars of whiteness no longer convene the spectacular academic conferences once held in the 1990s. Instead, they produce scholarship that folds naturally into inquiries about other important matters, including gender, management, disability, mixed-race studies, Indian policy, and more. The editors of this anthology agree that scholars have produced excellent collections in whiteness studies into this century, though we believe they are infrequent. Thus, this volume offers us an opportunity to take measure of this fascinating and provocative field of study by weaving this multidisciplinary body of knowledge into the conversation.[10]

The Construction of Whiteness: An Interdisciplinary Analysis of Race Formation and the Meaning of a White Identity joins the discussion by approaching what it means to be "white" from an interdisciplinary perspective. The collection brings together scholars from the humanities and social sciences, representing fields including history, law, American studies, communication, English, and sociology. Our intention is to offer an anthology that pushes beyond the border of one discipline as we challenge existing scholarship and open new vistas for investigation. Readers will also likely enjoy the wide array of perspectives and methodologies in this single volume. In addition to its breadth in methodology and depth in analysis, this multidisciplinary study provides an assessment of whiteness across two hundred years. Readers will see how whiteness surfaced under slavery, then traveled through the tumultuous Civil War and the Jim Crow era. From this trajectory, it metastasized during the long civil rights movement, and into modern times. The contributors maintain that our society will continue to suffer from the malady of racial suspicion and conflict as long as we adhere to a "white" racial classification. Whereas a white racial category assumes that Caucasians are entitled to certain privileges and immunities, it mandates the existence of a racial other, including people of color. African Americans, Hispanics, and Indians in particular are frequently marginalized because they are not white. Furthermore, mixed-race individuals who may self-identify as "white" are sometimes rejected by the majority for not being "white" enough for acceptance under legal or community standards.

Stephen Middleton and Erica Cooper tackle the embryonic development of the one-drop rule from different vantage points. Middleton looks at the origins of the one-drop theory under community standards before its codification by southern legislatures. Moreover, he analyzes how the one-drop rule germinated in culture and gradually gained acceptance by local prosecutors and trial judges. He makes the bold assertion that appellate judges in Ohio gave the one-drop rule judicial recognition in 1859. Middleton makes it clear that the Ohio Supreme Court established the racial category of Negro to include individuals who looked white, but had known African lineage. He maintains that appellate judges applied the one-drop rule to education cases, but he concedes that they allowed racial migration in voter registration. The court, Middleton contends, could consign all mixed-race children to the segregated colored school system. However, legislators could not create a dual system of voting, and judges deliberately chose to err on the side of protecting the civil rights of Americans who appeared to be white. Middleton agrees that the codification of the one-drop rule was a twentieth-century phenomenon but argues that it is faulty logic to assume that white Americans allowed people whom they believed to be black to openly pretend that they were white.

Erica Cooper examines the one-drop rule in Louisiana in the late nineteenth and twentieth centuries. She emphasizes the way state courts endorsed or rejected its legitimacy during this period. Cooper analyzes how Louisiana judges in particular slowly chipped away its broad construction of whiteness in the nineteenth century. Louisiana courts eventually established that individuals with one drop of African blood were black, regardless of their near white complexion. Furthermore, she shows how the one-drop rule hardened over time and how judges initially waffled over enforcing it. Finally, Cooper shows how this seemingly rigid classification of race began to collapse after 1980. However, even though Louisiana eventually moved away from the one-drop rule in jurisprudence, Cooper argues that it survives in American culture. An unspoken one-drop rule, she maintains, is now the norm under societal standards throughout the United States.

Robert Westley and David Roediger offer novel interpretations and perspectives of the history of American slavery. Westley challenges conservative and mainstream approaches to temporal dimensions of race relations. He insists that whites historically have been of two minds about America's material prosperity in comparison to nations in the rest of the world. The white majority takes pride in their assumed exceptionality, Westley argues; yet, they often overlook the role that involuntary African workers played in the growth and prosperity of the republic. Westley deploys the philosophy of "double standard" to show how courts reviewed differently property claims made by blacks and whites. He contends that judges refused to recognize legitimate restitution claims filed by African American litigants based on the color of their skin. Westley also intimates that whites frown on public policy conversations today that argue for reparation for the descendants of enslaved African Americans.

David Roediger invokes the concept of "emancipation from whiteness" to show that white workers benefitted from the emancipation of enslaved African Americans in 1865. Karl Marx has argued that the emancipation of enslaved blacks energized other groups seeking justice in the United States.[11] Specifically, the emancipation of enslaved African Americans ignited the national labor movement by challenging a race-based identification of workers with their employers as free, able, white men. The essay further argues that the wholesale increase in disability among white Civil

War soldiers contributed to a rethinking of race, gender, and ability in the country.

Our two literary scholars, Donald Shaffer and Tim Engles, explore the construction of whiteness through the writings of two prominent novelists. Shaffer examines the representation of whiteness and "the problem of citizenship" in *The House Behind the Cedars* by Charles W. Chesnutt. He argues that Chesnutt contested the discourse of racial difference in the post-Reconstruction era through his portrayal of figures passing as white. By using the racial passer, Chesnutt interrogates racial migration and the solidity of the color line. A malleable color line, Chesnutt suggested, raised questions about the legitimacy of racial boundaries that limited citizenship. If concepts about "race" existed in nature, Chesnutt intimates, the racial passer would not have been able to vanish into the white world. Shaffer makes it clear that Chesnutt uses the trope of the mulatto figure in his writing. While mulatto historically meant half white, Chesnutt applied it broadly to incorporate all mixed-race people, which was likely the way whites viewed them under community standards.

Tim Engles approaches whiteness through Louis Begley, a Holocaust survivor. Begley established a successful legal career in New York City but gained renown as a novelist.[12] Using one of Begley's prominent novels, *About Schmidt*, which sheds light on the inner lives of wealthy white American men, Engles exposes the construction of white masculinity as emotionally reactionary. He is not alone in making the case that white American masculinity induces a typical conservative response. Sally Robinson, for instance, argues that white men anxiously viewed their group as a besieged social state being forced to expand opportunities for undeserving minorities.[13] Begley depicts this perspective by deploying the trope of white male victimhood. He does so less to sympathize with white men as many other writers in the United States have done; rather, Begley tries to diagnose the emotional turmoil of white men and the consequences of their mindset on others. He claimed that the assumed superior social status of white men depended on the denigration and subordination of the racial other in order to bolster their own image.

The contributors in the social sciences—Mathew Hughey, Sadhana Bery, and coauthors Becky Thompson and Veronica Watson—engage whiteness through their disciplinary perspective. Hughey argues that white racial identity has gone through many stages since the dawn of the twentieth century. He states that sociologists had initially seen whiteness as one-dimensional, that is, as an ideology of power and privilege. That view changed when they began to see whiteness as a synonym for social invisibility and normality. Ultimately, Hughey explains, sociologists see whiteness as heterogeneous, whereby it intersects class, gender, various political ideologies, and even local customs. He calls the last stage the "third wave" because it emphasizes the changing and fluid character of whiteness. Hughey adds the caution that this body of work tends to divide "structure" and "agency" into rigid independent and dependent variables.

Sadhana Bery examines the "reproduction" of white supremacy and white epistemologies and ontologies in the afterlife of slavery. She centers her analysis on white reenactments of slavery, specifically their reenactment of slave auctions and the Underground Railroad. Bery suggests that these amateur actors have made slave plantations into living history museums. She argues that staging reenactments allow whites to engage in dialogue involving slavery on their terms. They can sanitize and legitimize slavery by seeing it from the perspective of slaveholders. Thus, reenactors can discuss slavery without making anyone accountable for it.

Becky Thompson and Veronica Watson explore whiteness as a form of trauma that affects contemporary white culture. Building on the foundational work of African American race scholars like Du Bois, Chesnutt, James Baldwin, and many others, Watson and Thompson seek to expose the psychological and emotional consequences of racism on whites, recognizing, as Laura van Dernoot Lipsky argues, that "bearing witness to others' suffering" affects the observer.[14] They suggest that whiteness does not demand that the privileged class confront itself, and that many whites deny and discredit anyone suggesting that they do so. As such, the form of trauma white Americans suffer extends beyond acts of commission to moments of violence, denial, and institutionalized racism done in their name. The repressed and ignored mental anguish felt by the dominant white culture, they suggest, has consequences.[15] This chapter tries to isolate specific traumas due to a shared belief in whiteness. Thompson and Watson further explain how trauma can manifest in everyday life.

These essays illustrate that whiteness was woven into the fabric of American culture at the founding and blossoms in our society today. White people early believed they could read the body of a racial other to deny them the benefits of white-skin privilege. Caucasians act on the belief that only "pure" whites deserve benefits associated with white skin. Whiteness is not benign; judges, employers, and legislatures have created and re-created it. In showing how whiteness harms whites, these essays also show the possibilities associated with emancipation from it. Since whiteness is ever-present in our legal and cultural imagination, the essays suggest that the day of jubilee will continually be under siege as long we recognize it. The very existence of a white race and the temptation for some people to claim this identity induces separation and conflict in society. In order to realize the potential of what James Baldwin called the "suffering and dancing" humanity, we must rid our society of the ideology of white supremacy.[16]

NOTES

1. W. E. B. Du Bois, *Darkwater: Voices from Within the Veil* (New York: Harcourt, Brace, and Howe, 1920), 29.

2. For the long roots of African American inquiry into whiteness, see David Roediger, ed., *Black on White: Black Writers on What It Means to Be White* (New York: Schocken, 1998); see also Stephanie Li, *Playing in the White: Black Writers, White Subjects* (New York: Oxford University Press, 2015); Veronica T. Watson, *The Souls of White Folk: African American Writers Theorize Whiteness* (Jackson: University Press of Mississippi, 2013); Marvin McAllister, *Whiting Up: Whiteface Minstrels and Stage Europeans in African American Performance* (Chapel Hill: University of North Carolina Press, 2011).

3. On the genesis of critical whiteness studies and for discussion of these authors, see David R. Roediger, "Accounting for the Wages of Whiteness: U.S. Marxism and the Critical History of Race," in *Wages of Whiteness and Racist Symbolic Capital*, ed. Wulf D. Hund, Jeremy Krikler, and David Roediger (Berlin: Lit Verlag, 2010), 16–36; see also David Roediger, *The Wages of Whiteness: Race and the Making of the American Working Class* (1991; London and New York: Verso, 2007); David Roediger, *Working Toward Whiteness: How America's Immigrants Became White: The Strange Journey from Ellis Island to the Suburbs* (New York: Basic, 1998); Noel Ignatiev, *How the Irish Became White* (New York: Routledge, 1995); Karen Brodkin, *How Jews Became White Folks and What That Says About Race in America* (New Brunswick: Rutgers University Press, 1998); Theodore Allen, *The Invention of the White Race*, 2 vols. (New York: Verso, 1994). The most provocative three works of the 1990s remain Toni Morrison, *Playing in the Dark: Whiteness and the Literary Imagination* (New York: Vintage, 1990); Cheryl Harris, "Whiteness as Property," *Harvard Law Review* 106 (1993): 1709–95; and George Lipsitz, "The Possessive Investment in Whiteness: Racialized Social Democracy and the 'White Problem,'" *American Quarterly* 47 (September 1995): 369–87.

4. Margaret Talbot, "Getting Credit for Being White," *New York Times Magazine* (November 30, 1997), 116–19.

5. Ruth Frankenberg, ed., *Displacing Whiteness: Essays in Social and Cultural Criticism* (Durham and London: Duke University Press, 1997); Noel Ignatiev and John Garvey, eds., *Race Traitor* (New York: Routledge, 1998); Michelle Fine, Lois Weis, Linda C. Powell, and L. Mun Wong, eds., *Off White: Readings and Race Power and Society* (New York and London: Routledge, 1997); Joe L. Kincheloe, Shirley R. Steinberg, Nelson M.

Rodriguez, and Ronald E. Chennault, eds., *White Reign: Deploying Whiteness in America* (New York: St. Martin's, 1998); Matt Wray and Annalee Newitz, eds., *White Trash: Race and Class in America* (New York and London: Routledge, 1997); Mike Hill, ed., *Whiteness: A Critical Reader* (New York: New York University Press, 1997); Richard Delgado and Jean Stefancic, eds., *Critical White Studies: Looking Behind the Mirror* (Philadelphia: Temple University Press, 1997).

6. Talbot, "Getting Credit for Being White," 116–19.

7. Walter Williams, "White Privilege" (May 27, 2014), *Front Page*, www.frontpagemag.com/2014/walter-williams/white-privilege/.

8. Eric Arnesen, "Passion and Politics: Race and the Writing of Working-Class History," *Journal of the Historical Society* 6 (2006): 323–56; and "Whiteness Studies and the Historians' Imagination," *International Labor and Working Class History* 60 (2001): 3–32.

9. Nell Irvin Painter, *The History of White People* (New York: Norton, 2010).

10. George Yancy, ed., *What White Looks Like: African American Philosophers on the Whiteness Question* (New York: Routledge, 2004). For another exemplary anthology that speaks to the role of the most ambitious conference of the 1990s, see Birgit Brander Rasmussen et al., eds., *The Making and Unmaking of Whiteness* (Durham: Duke University Press, 2001). The best transnational work includes Marilyn Lake and Henry Reynolds, *Drawing the Global Colour Line: White Men's Countries and the International Challenge of Racial Equality* (Cambridge: Cambridge University Press, 2008); and Aileen Moreton-Robinson, *White Possession and Indigenous Sovereignty Matter: Essays in Social and Cultural Criticisms*, forthcoming. See also Jerry Davila, *Diploma of Whiteness: Race and Social Policy in Brazil, 1917-1945* (Durham: Duke University Press, 2003).

11. For Marx, see International Workingmen's Association, "Address to the National Labor Union" (May 12, 1866), found at www.marxists.org/archive/marx/iwma/documents/1869/us-labor.htm.

12. Allan Hepburn, "Lost Time: Trauma and Belatedness in Louis Begley's 'The Man Who Was Late,'" *Contemporary Literature* 39 (1998): 380; James Atlas, "Louis Begley: The Art of Fiction," *Paris Review* 162 (Summer 2002), www.theparisreview.org/interviews/392/the-art-of-fiction-no-172-louis-begley.

13. Sally Robinson, *Marked Men: White Masculinity in Crisis* (New York: Columbia University Press, 2000), 3, 2.

14. Laura van Dernoot Lipsky with Connie Burk, *Trauma Stewardship: An Everyday Guide to Caring for Self While Caring for Others* (San Francisco: Berrett-Koehler, 2009), 3.

15. We use the term *schizophrenic* here to invoke the recognized symptoms of the genetic illness of schizophrenia. However, we diverge from the medical discourse of the disease most notably in our assertion that white schizophrenic subjectivity is a social construct that can be healed through specific knowledge and actions.

16. James Baldwin, *The Fire Next Time* (1963; New York: Vintage, 1993), 96.

THE BATTLE OVER RACIAL IDENTITY IN POPULAR AND LEGAL CULTURES, 1810–1860

STEPHEN MIDDLETON

THE ACTUAL CODIFICATION OF THE ONE-DROP RULE BY STATE LEG-islatures in the early twentieth century is indisputable. Tennessee enacted a law in 1910 stating that "Persons of color . . . having any African blood in their veins" were black.[1] Louisiana followed and classified "colored persons" as mixed-race individuals "with any applicable mixture of Negro blood."[2] Texas and Arkansas adopted their variations of the one-drop rule in 1911; Mississippi did so in 1917 and North Carolina in 1923. Virginia passed its comprehensive Racial Integrity Act in 1924, which classified a white person as someone who had "no trace whatsoever of any blood other than Caucasian."[3] Alabama and Georgia adopted their versions of the one-drop rule in 1927, and Oklahoma followed suit in 1931. Thus, it is irrefutable that statutory recognition of the colloquial one-drop rule is a twentieth-century development. These laws gave credence to the belief that white-looking individuals with documented or visual evidence of African heritage were black.[4]

There is an obvious orthodoxy among some legal scholars regarding the one-drop rule. Modern scholars in particular deny that the one-drop rule was applied to establish racial identity before the Jim Crow era.[5] Others purport that "racial migration" (crossing over from black to white) went on in broad daylight. These scholars further suggest that whites understood that some of their neighbors had minimal traces of African ancestry that did not matter to them.[6] They suggest the malleability and fluidity of whiteness in the nineteenth century and its rigidity and inflexibility one century later.

However, legal scholars are not unanimous in their interpretation of the one-drop rule. Nathaniel Gates maintains that the one-drop rule continued to be malleable and fluid after its codification.[7] He suggests that racially mixed individuals had their way of crossing the color line without opposition, just as they had done in the prior century. As restrictive as the Virginia Racial Integrity Act of 1924 appeared, Gates argues, it classified Native Americans as white if they had one-sixteenth or less Indian ancestry. He contends that this was clearly contrary to a rigid application of the one-drop rule. Furthermore, the Virginia legislature moderated its one-drop rule and later classified a "colored" "person" as someone "in whom there is ascertainable any negro blood."[8] The revised statute did not endorse invisible blackness—the automatic classification of a white-looking person as black regardless of his or her European traits. Invisible blackness undergirds the modern one-drop rule.

Although historians and social scientists mark the emergence of the one-drop rule in the nineteenth century, they recognize its codification a century later. Nell Irvin Painter maintains that the "myth of tainted blood and a belief in invisible ancestry" had become the national racial conviction in the white mind before 1860. Patrick Rael agrees, bluntly asserting "all people of African descent generally were considered 'black,' regardless of their apparent degree of European heritage."[9] Jerrold Packard in *American Nightmare* stated that as "long as a person's physical black heritage—one's African roots—could be detected, either by his or her appearance or from general knowledge that he or she had been born of non-wholly white parentage, that person was considered and treated as black."[10] Other scholars assert that the one-drop rule was a well-known phenomenon in American culture since at least the early nineteenth century.[11] Long before southern legislatures enacted one-drop statutes, therefore, the white community had its way of enforcing a relatively rigid color line throughout the United States.[12]

This essay illustrates that nearly-white people frequently contested their racial classification as black or Indian in antebellum America. It argues that the community established standards to determine who was white or black in the 1800s, and by default Native Americans also were seen as not being white. Furthermore, this chapter will illustrate that the lived experiences of white-looking people of African or Indian ancestry belie the belief that it did not matter to whites if some of their neighbors had non-European ancestors. Certainly, they did not apply a codified one-drop rule; nevertheless, whites understood and practiced a one-drop creed that hardened over time. Ultimately, southern state legislatures implemented the standard for a white identity in the early twentieth century.

CROSSING THE COLOR LINE

There undoubtedly was occasional seepage across the color line in the nineteenth century. Having a white identity in the nineteenth century was predicated on appearance, community acceptance, and performance as a citizen with legal rights. Now and then, the individual who ostensibly looked Caucasian and deported himself or herself as a white of European descent could withstand a challenge to his or her white racial identity. The people in this category were often phenotypically European and had indiscernible African or Indian features. Judges who secured their whiteness believed they were protecting whites from mistakenly being deprived of civil rights. Some whites believed they could successfully read bodies to determine their race. They presumed that if a community of whites had accepted a person as white and allowed them to enjoy civil rights, they most certainly must have been white people. South Carolina judge William Harper maintained this perspective in *State v. Cantey* (1835), stating, "The condition of the individual is not to be determined solely by the distinct and visible mixture of negro blood." The racial identity of an individual, he continued, could be established by a competent jury that used community standards as their guide. On the other hand, Harper seemed to recognize the existence of an informal one-drop rule when it involved enslaved people. "It is hardly necessary to say that a slave cannot be a white man," he wrote. Judge Harper obviously believed slave status would trump white-looking skin, even if the enslaved person looked like a pure white.[13]

Most assuredly, individuals with remote African lineage clandestinely crossed the color line and lived as whites in the nineteenth century. However, "passing" seldom went on without controversy. As I noted earlier in this essay, there was a difference between the lived experiences of white-looking people and the passage of statutes that established a black racial identity. Moreover, it was commonly believed in the United States and widely practiced in society that "white" implied someone solely of European ancestry. Benjamin Franklin held this point of view, once stating, "the English make the principal body of white people on the face of the earth."[14] Of course, he was pointing out that Anglo-Saxons were white people, but Franklin would not have disputed that French and German people are white. Alexis de Tocqueville specifically classified white Americans as Europeans, while adding that Anglo-Saxons particularly were proud of their white racial heritage.[15] Stephen A. Douglas agreed and asserted in the Lincoln-Douglas Debates in 1858 that whites were people of "European birth and descent."[16] Believing a white could recognize nonwhites, some whites attempted to enforce the idea that one drop of African blood made an individual wholly black.[17] These whites agreed that knowledge of someone's ancestry was sufficient proof of his or her race. Moreover, they endeavored to prevent racial interlopers from benefiting from white-skin privilege before 1860. Complaints of racial passing frequently forced the accused to contend for a white identity in state courts.

Racial identity case transcripts are the most reliable sources to evaluate the lived experiences of nearly-white people with known African or Indian lineage. They illustrate that plaintiffs who believed they were unfairly deprived of a white racial identity felt compelled to litigate their whiteness. These cases frequently arose in the free states of the North, where courts were accessible to them. It is not surprising that litigation often surfaced in the Northwest Territory. In a free state, the racial passer could live as white for years, provided that they did not draw undue attention to themselves. Challenges to a white identity usually came to the surface when a white-looking person allegedly violated a state law or broke a social convention. They were a minority, and prosecutors did not take an interest in them until an inquiry into their racial identity was initiated. While the legislatures in the North had not yet enacted a system of racial classification, state policy seemingly fostered it by imposing rigid racial qualifications for accessing civil rights or enjoying the privileges and immunities of citizenship.[18] Zealous whites believed that the legislature required them to enforce the color line. They believed state laws authorized them to challenge white-looking people of known African or Indian "blood." They believed they were also obligated to oppose anyone whose appearance gave away clues of a nonwhite heritage.

Among the midwestern states, Ohio was the leader in developing laws to deprive mixed-race people of their civil rights. The state legislature withheld the vote in local elections to blacks and mulattoes, and denied them a public education. Legislators deprived blacks and mulattoes of the ability to protect themselves when on trial by closing both the jury box and the witness stand to them in all cases in which white people were parties. The intention of the legislature in barring mulattoes explicitly as opposed to individuals who were above their grade—those who were three-quarters white or more—left open a puzzling question: Did the legislators also intend to deny white privilege to mixed-race people who had a preponderance of European ancestry? The defenders of white purity would rarely stop to figure out whether someone they accused of having African "blood" was actually white enough to be considered wholly white. These self-appointed guardians of the white race frequently used one-drop arguments to separate white-looking people from those whom they presumed were "pure" white. They would also sabotage romantic relationships between white-looking individuals and "pure" whites. Invariably, local prosecutors and judges would back local whites in their presumptions about white purity, with lawyers also using one-drop arguments and judges one-drop reasoning in their opinions.[19] The white community, therefore, had advanced the theory that white-looking people could be black or Indian decades before formal adoption of the one-drop rule. By the eve of the Civil War, even progressive Supreme Court justices in Ohio had switched sides and had begun to apply the one-drop rule in selective racial identity cases, especially in public education.[20]

In contrast to locally influenced judges, appellate courts typically did not openly advance racial purity. However, some appellate judges occasionally broke rank with the court to articulate the grand European American vision that it was the manifest destiny of the United States to become a country of purely white people. Ohio Supreme Court justices Nathaniel C. Read and William V. Peck candidly expressed their beliefs in the purity of the white race.[21] Justice Read fervently rejected racial migration in *Thacker v. Hawk* (1842), arguing that the courts had created the judicial concepts of "partly white" and "more white than black." Read believed these categories were inconsistent with state law. The Ohio constitution in particular meant "pure white" when it addressed suffrage, Justice Read explained, and so did various other legislative acts: "The word 'white' means pure white, unmixed" in every context where they used it. "A mixture of black and white is not white," he continued.[22] Read pressed his colleagues to endorse his construction of whiteness by arguing that one drop of African blood automatically denied a person of color a white racial identity.

Almost two decades later Justice William Peck wrote candidly about the racist ideology of the state of Ohio in *Van Camp v. Board of Education* (1859). Whites had subordinated African Americans for generations, he admitted. Justice Peck listed various provisions in the Ohio Black Laws to illustrate his point.[23] He explained that the legislature had denied African Americans civil rights solely because of the color of their skin. The "natural repugnance of whites to communion and fellowship with" blacks had hardened over time.[24] Given this background, Peck proposed two ways of looking at racial identity. First, he believed Americans could view race in a strictly "*legal sense.*" State law may regard a mixed-race person as white; however, Peck questioned whether such a classification would make a person white by societal standards.[25]

Second, Justice Peck postulated that Americans can also look at racial identity in the "*ordinary*" way, that is, under community standards or in popular culture. He surmised that a shared belief among whites of European heritage was that the word "colored" was synonymous with "black," "Africans, or their descendants, *mixed* or *unmixed.*"[26] While the Supreme Court of Ohio had initially considered mixed-race individuals with a preponderance of European traits as white, Justice Peck concluded, it had done so only to secure their civil rights in particular circumstances. He explained that community standards for a white identity were even stricter than this: "In affixing the epithet 'colored,' we do not ordinarily stop to estimate the precise shade, whether light or dark."[27] Peck conceded that some African Americans might have been considered "light-colored"; nevertheless, he insisted that they were still Africans. He affirmed that some people were "entirely white," or, as Justice Read put it in *Thacker v. Hawk*, "pure white." Only those individuals could legally claim a white racial identity, he said. Whites at the time embraced these sentiments in virtually every American city and hamlet in the country. The white community proceeded to enforce the statutes that denied anyone with known black or Indian ancestors a white racial identity. "This feeling of prejudice," Justice Peck concluded, "had been fostered by long years of hostile legislation and social exclusion."[28] Under this rubric, therefore, it is self-evident that the pure white ideology was a quality of American racism and culture in the antebellum era.

AMERICAN ORIGINS OF WHITENESS

It is well known among historians that the American custom of seeing mixed-race people as the racial other began in the colonial period in the nineteenth century with the idiom *mulatto.*[29] Following Independence, the states relegated mulattoes to the African race for legal and social purposes. State legislatures passed statutes that denied mulattoes white privilege, notwithstanding their half-white status. Over time, most whites began to use mulatto as a catchall phrase to classify all mixed-race individuals, regardless of their complexion or degree of white-looking skin. Appellate courts north of the Mason-Dixon Line would diverge from community standards on grounds that lexicographers defined the term precisely as someone who was a descendant of a white and a black parent. Using that definition, these judges questioned whether the offspring of a mulatto and a white couple should be considered black.[30] However, appellate judges stood virtually alone in applying this elastic construction to whiteness. Their application of this rule was never standardized by states anywhere in the country, nor was it given recognition under community standards.[31]

Appellate judges in the South disagreed when deciding whether the children of a mulatto and a Caucasian were white. South Carolina judges defined a mulatto as a person of "whatever proportions the blood of the two races may be mingled in the individual."[32] However, in 1850 the Alabama Supreme Court accepted the definition of lexicographers and conferred a white identity on the offspring of an octoroon and a white.[33] Alabama appellate judges complained that the judiciary was not the proper authority on whiteness. They believed legislators could rightly decide that question, and they urged them to adopt uniform standards.

The majority of whites probably construed mixed-race people under the South Carolina construction of whiteness. The white community believed a mixed-race person was black or Indian, notwithstanding their genetic proximity to a European ancestor. As historian Winthrop Jordan bluntly asserted, "Americans [typically of European descent] lump together both socially and legally all persons with perceptible admixture of African ancestry."[34] Scholars may quibble about what Jordan meant, but it is doubtful that his use of "perceptible" did not imply the one-drop rule. State legislators evidently saw it this way when they added the phrase "and mulattoes" to nineteenth-century statutes that subordinated mixed-race people. Furthermore, legislators perceived mulatto and black as synonyms and subordinated them equally.[35] It is problematic to presume that antebellum whites automatically stopped to perform a shade-of-color test to figure out if someone with known African ancestry was white enough for civil rights.

Racial passing has entered our colloquial language to indicate that some biracial people had become so white that they could clandestinely vanish into white society. The term suggests that the racial passer was aware of his or her African lineage, yet rejected his or her blackness to secretly live as white.[36] Surely there were persons who concealed their black identity in the nineteenth century to escape the legal restrictions imposed upon mulattoes. As Winthrop Jordan concluded, the rigid color line in the United States had made racial passing an obligatory accommodation to people "with so little African blood that they appeared to be white."[37] Racial migration is the modern term, which essentially means the same thing as passing; however, it also suggests that whites did not mind if some people with minimal black ancestry lived openly as white.[38] Passing in this context implies that whites believed "superior" European "blood" expunged "inferior" African "blood." Once enriched by "white blood" they supposedly could no longer be considered black.[39] However, most whites did not see passing in this way; knowledge of a person's black or Indian heritage would automatically trump a white-looking complexion. Such an allegation frequently provoked the accused to fight to affirm their white identity in state courts. Without the assertion that someone was pretending to be white and the accused taking umbrage to it, there would not have been any litigation over a white racial identity in the nineteenth century.

There was obviously implicit acceptance of the one-drop rule among antebellum whites; that is to say, they presumed that no one with African or Indian "blood" could transcend their lineage to become fully white. Indeed, Americans grafted European ethnic groups, including Jewish and Irish immigrants, into the "white" race, but not persons with perceptible African or indigenous lineages. The racial passer's claim to whiteness was precarious at best because they could only *pretend* to be white in the European sense of the word. By "passing," they intentionally concealed their African or Indian lineage in a society that would have deprived them of fundamental civil rights.

THE MANY MEANINGS OF WHITENESS

To accept the argument that the white community in the nineteenth century endorsed racial passing without dissent would suggest that they likewise rejected "invisible blackness" until the twentieth century. However, there is compelling evidence that white Americans had considered their whiteness to have been a normative construct long before their enslavement of African peoples in British America. As Benjamin Isaac asserts in *The Invention of Racism in Classical Antiquity*, "there is a consensus that [scientific racism] originated in the nineteenth century and has its intellectual roots in that century."[40] However, Isaac insists that racism is even older and that this "proto-racism" provided the embryonic qualities for the bigotry that developed in the nineteenth century. The majority of whites in this period believed that people with a dark complexion were subhuman. It is faulty logic, therefore, for us to assume that these whites made exceptions for people with known or perceptible African or Indian ancestry.

On the contrary, the belief in a pure white race made it obligatory for Caucasians also to assume that they could identify nonwhite outliers, notwithstanding their nearly white complexions. American whites in the 1800s increasingly faced a population of mixed-race people who were no longer merely half white and half black living among them. Given this reality, it was inevitable that lawyers, judges, and legislators throughout the country were called upon to grapple with the meaning of white racial identity. While many of these "new people," as historian Joel Williamson inferred, appeared white in appearance, they had African lineage, and racial identity disputes entered antebellum courtrooms.[41]

State legislators in the United States did not extend civil rights to nonwhites. Ohio explicitly barred blacks and mulattoes from attending public schools, voting, and serving as jurors and acting as witnesses at trial along with whites. However, the Ohio legislature did not create precise racial categories for mixed-race people. Without clear guidance from lawmakers, appellate judges occasionally recognized mixed-race plaintiffs as white. While the government expressly gave white children access to public schools, judges opened these institutions to mixed-race youths nearer to the white race than the black. Parents who classified their children as white protested the hubris of their neighbors. When they sued in county courts for relief, they discovered that local prosecutors and trial judges were in agreement with the community. On appeal, the plaintiffs found a panel of judges who believed it was possible for someone to have remote African ancestry and no longer be recognizable as black. However, appellate judges allowed this minority population to cross over into whiteness only when they had found acceptance in the white community and had long severed any ties they might have had with their black or Indian relatives. Mixed-race people could not openly live in two racial categories and still enjoy the privileges of being white.

Unlike the racial passer, the plaintiffs in racial identity cases did not feel they had family secrets to conceal. Being socially white, they did not associate or identify with African Americans or Indians and believed they were as white as any person of European descent. They were white both in body and mind, and took offense when self-appointed guardians of whiteness brought up a past they had long forgotten or had never known.[42]

Slavery complicated classifying people by race. White men had begun to cross the color line for sex in the seventeenth century. Legislators immediately faced the challenge of determining how to classify their mixed-race children. To secure their investment in slaves, colonial legislators made the children follow the status of their enslaved mothers no matter their complexion. Initially, the white community as a whole did not seem to be bothered by a minority of light-skin slaves. As light-skin women became more appealing to white men, who made them mistresses, by the nineteenth century their children had become whiter and whiter. Slave owners were in a quandary, as their descendants had become nearly white. They could change the matrilineal line for determining slave status; or they could redefine whiteness by enforcing the idea that one drop of African "blood" made a person black. Because of their pecuniary interest in slavery, they came to accept the logic that white-looking people could be slaves in perpetuity.[43] Southerners conflated mulatto to include all mixed-race individuals. Under its guise, biracial people, including those who looked white, could be considered black if they were slaves.

White-looking individuals contested the way local whites classified them as black. They filed racial-identity lawsuits to confirm their claim of being white. Historians face many difficulties when exhuming judicial controversies involving whiteness. State court transcripts are readily available; however, they often do not provide a clear visual portrait of plaintiffs. Without photographs, we will never know how white these people appeared. Scholars also face the difficulty of trying to determine whether plaintiffs suffered racial discrimination in their communities before litigation commenced. Furthermore, they have the challenge of figuring out whether white-looking people were passing in their communities because they were not solely of European descent. One strategy for getting at the core of this phenomenon is to extract cultural records from European travelers. These visitors frequently used different lenses from those of American whites, so their commentaries can often provide a useful entrée into the struggle over who was white in America.

Gustave de Beaumont, the French novelist, frequently created characters in his writings to unveil the injustices he observed while on his American tours in the 1830s. His characters are deployed to express their surprise to learn of the racial hierarchy they encounter in this country. In his foreword to *Marie*, Beaumont explicitly states that his fiction mirrored real life in the United States. To make the point, he describes an event in painful detail from his direct observations:[44]

The first time I attended a theater in the United States, I was surprised at the careful distinction made between the white spectators and the audience whose faces were black. In the first balcony were whites; in the second, mulattoes; in the third, Negroes. An American, beside whom I was sitting, informed me that the dignity of white blood demanded these classifications. However, my eyes being drawn to the balcony where sat the mulattoes, I perceived a young woman of dazzlingly beauty, whose complexion, of perfect whiteness, proclaimed the purest European blood. Entering into all the prejudice of my neighbor, I asked him how a woman of English origin could be so lacking in shame as to seat herself among the Africans; the American answered:

'That woman,' he replied, 'is colored.'

What? Colored? She is whiter than a lily!

'She is colored, he repeated coldly; 'local tradition has established her ancestry, and everyone knows that she had a mulatto among her forebears.'

At the same moment I made out in the balcony for whites a face which was very dark. I asked for an explanation of this phenomenon.

'The lady who has attracted your attention is white.'

What? White! She is the same color as the mulattoes.

'She is white,' he replied; 'local tradition affirms that the blood which flows in her veins is Spanish.'[45]

The "colored" woman apparently possessed a quality of invisible blackness, even though her body appeared to be white. The translation for invisible blackness in this case was that whites were only aware of her African lineage and would not allow her to be white, notwithstanding her skin color. However, the white-looking woman with a darker hue had been accepted as white by community standards. Once taken as white, they could not reclassify her as black.

The claim that a person was a dark-skinned European became a common defense for Americans wrongly accused of possessing an African racial identity. On the other hand, a white-looking individual with known black ancestry was not given the same benefit, despite his or her light skin color. Thus, under the ideology of invisible blackness, the fear of hidden African ancestry lurking in a seemingly "pure" white individual was a commonly held belief among whites.

Beaumont then deploys characters in the novel to further illustrate what he had observed in real life. He introduces a romantic relationship involving Marie and Ludovic, who arrive in Baltimore and suddenly fall madly in love with each other. Marie initially resists his romantic advances, Beaumont wrote, "because she is in possession of a dark 'mystery.'" The French traveler is undeterred because he sees a woman of such refined qualities that he would never imagine she was not of European descent. Marie not only has a lily-white complexion; Ludovic considers her "even whiter than the swans of the Great Lakes." Subsequently, he learns that Marie's father had married a woman whose ancestors had included a mulatto. Also, he discovers that Marie has inherited the invisible "taint" of African "blood" and her known past in Baltimore has made her black under community standards. Ludovic is undeterred and carries Marie to New York, hoping she will be able to cross over into whiteness, but even there the taint of invisible blood follows her. A rumor spreads throughout the city that the amalgamation of the races was about to take place, and a white mob organizes to challenge the couple. Fearing for their lives, they flee the city, later arriving in Michigan, where Marie dies of a mysterious fever.[46] Marie never crosses over, even though she has a white-looking complexion and refined cultural manners all suggestive of her whiteness.

While Beaumont's story is fictitious, he could have easily written about a real-life illicit romance in Indiana circa 1820. James Flint, a Scottish traveler, witnessed the drama occurring under community standards. In one of his letters back home, the Scotsman recounts the time in Indiana when an African American appeared before a justice of the peace with a white woman. He intended to marry her, only to have the magistrate turn them away under the marriage act. The official immediately had a change of heart as he looked at the crestfallen couple to whom he had denied the covenant. Thereupon, he recalled them to unveil a scheme commonly used to accomplish interracial marriages. The woman only needed to "swear that there was black blood in her."[47] Hoosiers understood that no matter how white the bride appeared, she could have conceivably been black under community standards. "The loving bride drank the blood, made the necessary oath, and his honor joined their hands, to the great satisfaction of all parties," Flint writes. Of course, the bride did not drink the groom's blood; she merely professed blackness, and this made her "black in the eyes of the law."[48] Naturally, nothing short of the one-drop rule could render such a subterfuge plausible.

The Indiana magistrate understood that in American culture, white Hoosiers did not elevate white-looking people merely because of their quantity of white blood. It was plausible to most whites that someone who looked like them could still belong to the African race. Whites at the time commonly believed that a white woman would not marry an African American or even associate with blacks as equals. Community standards for whiteness and legal norms were virtually the same. As Winthrop Jordan explained it, legislators did not develop a racial hierarchy; the racial category of mulatto gave all blacks the same social rank.[49] No one in the nineteenth century would have assumed that a person who looked white could not also have been an African American under community standards. Thus, drinking her fiancé's blood, as Flint reported, represented a white person's ability to be identified as an African American.

Another real-life episode involving the workings of invisible blackness took place in Indianapolis. John Wilson, whom historian Peggy Pascoe called a "nearly white" man, was the catalyst for the melee. Wilson had been a faithful servant to Sophia Spear's family. While on his deathbed, Mr. Spear asked John to take care of his family upon his demise, and Wilson discharged the responsibility flawlessly. Whites had come to accept white-looking people living as caretakers in their homes. However, Wilson presented a problem when he fell in love with Sophia and asked her to marry him. Sophia's mother had full confidence in John's character and approved of the relationship. Local whites, however, believed John had crossed the line and immediately organized a mob that sent him into hiding.[50] Most appellate judges in the North would have likely considered Wilson legally white, but under community standards, whites saw him as an African American merely because he had known black ancestors. Wilson had "one drop" of African blood, so to speak, and this made him black. Once the fracas ended, the Indiana legislature apparently endorsed this construction of whiteness by criminalizing all interracial marriages, regardless of whether the defendant was white in appearance.[51]

In 1855 the charge of invisible blackness raised its head again in Illinois, where William Dungey learned firsthand how tenuous a white racial classification was for people who had a slightly dark complexion. Merely an unsubstantiated charge that he was black was enough to embroil Dungey in a legal fight to preserve his white identity. He evidently had a falling out with Joseph Spencer, his brother-in-law, who publicly gave him the moniker of "Black Bill," apparently suggesting that Dungey was passing as a white man.[52] Dungey had performed whiteness by marrying a white woman, negotiating contracts, and voting in state elections. Spencer was aware that his assertion could deprive Dungey of white-skin privilege; however, he did not anticipate the extent to which Dungey would go to affirm his white racial identity. He hired a prominent lawyer and politician who would later become the sixteenth president of the United States. Abraham Lincoln cleverly endorsed the plaintiff's assertion that his client was dark-skinned; then he added that Dungey was a European. Americans realized that there were various shades of Europeans, and the litmus test for a white racial identity was acceptance in the white community. Dungey had met that standard, which was enough to satisfy the jury.[53]

By mid-century community standards for a white racial identity were indeed in flux. White-looking people throughout the country undoubtedly hoped to gain greater rights by aligning themselves with whites. As the crisis involving freedom and slavery accelerated, they were pushed into building alliances with black people. South Carolina is an example of this "changeover," as historian Joel Williamson calls it. Andrew and Maria Chesnutt illustrate this metamorphosis taking place in the Palmetto State and the rest of the South. Their "white blood went back several generations," Williamson noted, with "kin [including] substantial yeoman farmers in the Old North State" (Williamson, *New People*, 76). Both were freeborn offspring of mixed-race mothers and elite white slaveholding fathers. During the 1850s, white-looking people frequently found themselves in a precarious situation, with their safety and civil rights subject to the whims of white society. They left the South for greater economic and social security in the North, even though northern states limited their political rights unless they successfully passed as white. Hundreds of white-looking people in this class fled Louisiana after 1830 for Haiti, hoping to escape the "lash of public opinion." Andrew and Maria Chesnutt ultimately migrated to Oberlin, Ohio. They soon became the proud parents of the famous novelist Charles Chesnutt, whose direct experience became a subject in his writings.[54] White-looking people like the Chesnutt family made the Midwest even "whiter." As controversies arose about what privileges and immunities they were due, they litigated their claims to white privilege.

TRIAL COURTS AND RACIAL IDENTITY CASES

The elements in racial identity cases were similar. A white-looking person would attempt to exercise a right that was legally restricted to whites. More often than not, the white-looking person had been regarded as socially white and had been allowed to enjoy white privilege. Litigation inevitably followed when an event caused whites to have a change of heart about the racial identity of someone previously regarded as white. A sudden shift in the outlook of the community typically followed the attempt by the white-looking person to expand his or her scope of benefits, violate a social convention, or commit a crime. Courts all over the country faced this persistent problem from time to time. Trial judges frequently joined towns and cities in withholding white privilege. Unlike appellate judges, many local judges did not see whiteness as malleable and routinely used one-drop reasoning in their opinions. There can be little doubt that it was well established in American culture that "white" meant a person who did not have any admixture of nonwhite "blood." Prosecutors and judges give us a glimpse of the application of community standards for whiteness, even though it was not laid down in state law.

Racial identity cases frequently originated in common pleas courts in the county where the parties resided. They went before a circuit court on appeal, and sometimes went to the state supreme court for final disposition. The prosecutor "read" the body of the defendant and, in most instances, disregarded any phenotype that implied a white racial identity. Local prosecutors readily identified mixed-race defendants as black and denied them the privileges and immunities typically given to whites. For example, Elizabeth George looked white and apparently had been received as white in the state of Ohio. She could have probably lived her entire life under the radar, so long as there was no trigger to arouse the hostility of whites against her. George came under fire because she allegedly murdered a white person. While court records are not available from Jefferson County; *Liberty Hall and the Cincinnati Gazette* reported on the case when it came before the circuit court in 1821.

The newspaper transcript illustrated that racial identity was the central issue in the proceedings. The *Gazette* reported that community standards determined ancestry in Ohio. The prosecutor, therefore, had no doubts about George's background as a black. As he understood it, the "term white person, in common parlance, meant one who had no mixture of black blood."[55] The prosecutor called Mary Cooper as a witness, fully knowing that the testimony law prohibited blacks from being a witness in a case where a white person was a party. He ran into a problem when the defense attorney objected to Cooper being called as a witness. The testimony law, the defense argued, prevented her from giving evidence against his client. The prosecutor apparently did not see the defendant as a "pure" white person. "There was no instance in any dictionary of the English language," he argued, "where the term white person was not limited to those who were pure white." Since the testimony law, he continued, "did not authorize the placing of quadroons in the same class with the whites," Elizabeth George could only be regarded as black.[56] If legislators intended to classify quadroons as white, they would have written this language into the statute explicitly. The prosecutor, therefore, advanced the one-drop rule, thereby suggesting that Elizabeth George was black under community standards.

County judges evaluated racial identity in the same way, and frequently applied community standards to deny white-looking people white privilege. Polly Gray, who lived in Hamilton County, looked white; yet in *Gray v. Ohio* (1831), the common pleas judge accepted the argument that she was not white.[57] The county prosecutor agreed that the testimony law was a penal statute and required a strict interpretation. Strictly applied, the act would have empowered white-looking people to give evidence against a party who was white, but this would not have made them white. It would mean "the prohibition of the statute does not extend to them."[58] The statute "is silent, as it regards persons of the prisoner's color." The prosecutor responded by claiming that "Common law rules must . . . apply," because Gray was black under community standards. From his perspective, the state had a legal right to enroll a black witness to testify against her. The common pleas judge sided with the prosecutor and admitted the witness, thereby enforcing the standard for whiteness found in their culture.[59]

White-looking people were undeterred by the judgments of trial courts. For one thing, lower court holdings were subject to appeal, and as will be shown, appellate judges frequently did not agree with them. Understanding the law in this way, plaintiffs sued whenever the state denied them white privilege. Mr. Williams and his family faced that problem in Hamilton County. They lived in the tight-knit Whitewater Township, where everyone seemed to know their neighbors. Williams was initially white enough for acceptance in the community. He had performed whiteness by paying taxes and marrying a white woman.[60] The Ohio legislature would not outlaw interracial marriages until 1861, so Williams and his bride had not broken any laws.[61] They faced few known difficulties in Hamilton County until they attempted to enroll their children in the state-funded white school. School directors acted on their own volition and denied the children admission on grounds that they were black.[62]

The Williams family had self-identified as white, and they had many reasons to believe they had properly done so. The children were at least seven-eighths white and did not acknowledge an African lineage at all. Only their known African ancestry through their father made them vulnerable. Williams sought relief in court but discovered that the state attorney had accepted community standards by calling him, and his children, black people.

The Hamilton County common pleas judge made the same determination about them. The judge made it clear to the jury that if Williams had any black blood in him whatsoever, he "could not sustain his action." The jury, being charged in this way, had no alternative but to apply community standards in the case. The court transcript tersely states, "the jury without retiring found for the defendants."[63] Thus, the trial judge accepted community standards of racial identity and ruled that Ohio law barred persons with any degree of African ancestry from attending public schools with white children.

Native Americans also endeavored to affirm their white identity. Parker Jeffries was the son of a white father and a "half-breed" mother, which made him three-quarters white under the blood formula or ratio of that day. Many American Indians had the phenotype of Europeans, sharing such traits as straight hair and a light complexion. Parker Jeffries had evidently assimilated into American culture and lived his life as a white man. It is not surprising, therefore, that Jeffries presented himself to vote in Greene County, where his background was well known among election workers.[64] The Ohio constitution had given the right to vote to "white male inhabitants above the age of twenty-one."[65] The jury saw Jeffries as "a person of color . . . without more than one-fourth Indian blood."[66] This measurement, of course, was not scientific—we do not know what percentage of Indian "blood" he had. Nevertheless, the trial judge did not distinguish a person of color from an Indian. Thus, even though Jeffries looked white, the judge denied him a white identity.

The trial judge in Gallia County faced the same issue when Edwill Thacker came before him. Thacker had imperceptible African ancestry, but appeared white in body. The community accepted him as white until he went to vote. Thacker complained that the registrar had illegally rejected his vote. Election trustees refused his ballot based on their knowledge that he had black relatives. During the trial, Thacker asked the court to tell the jury that since he "was nearer white than a mulatto, or half blood, he was entitled to vote." The court, however, refused to instruct the jury in this way, instead telling them: "if the plaintiff had in him any Negro blood whatever, he was not entitled to vote."[67] The judge applied one-drop reasoning by charging the jury that African ancestry, though imperceptible, meant that the plaintiff was not white.

A trial judge in Russell County, Alabama, viewed racial identity in exactly the same way. Edward Thurman had lived as a white in Russell County his entire life. His mother was white, and the court would later determine that his father was at least three-quarters white.[68] Thurman had no reason to self-identify as an African American since he had the body of a white. Moreover, Alabama had been silent on what constituted a white racial identity. Under slavery, the state considered a white-looking slave to be a person of African ancestry; however, Thurman was a free man, and the population of people of his color was too small to have concerned the state legislature. His parents had few reasons to worry about their children, and Edward had gone unmolested by anyone until he crossed the racial boundary in a romantic affair with Mary Mann. Whites in Russell County familiar with his background invoked the one-drop rule. They asserted Thurman's African "blood" canceled his white "blood." They rejected the alleged fluidity of the color line as appellate judges elsewhere conceived it.[69]

White men felt obliged to protect white womanhood upon learning that Thurman had a romantic relationship with Mary Mann. Without any prompting from her, they filed a cause of action against Thurman, alleging that he had raped a white woman. The solicitor in the Ninth Judicial Circuit of Russell County, Johnson J. Hooper, asked that a grand jury review the allegation. Hooper immediately labeled Thurman as "a free negro or mulatto." Recognizing that Thurman's phenotype provided visible evidence that he could have been white, the solicitor gave Thurman the traditional, though not universally agreed-upon identity of a mulatto, which would have automatically made him an African American.[70]

Judge Nathaniel Cocke convened the grand jury on March 25, 1850, to decide the validity of the charge that Edward Thurman had "fornicated against the peace and dignity of the State of Alabama." It takes little imagination to read "fornicated" as a euphemism for rape, since white men did not believe a white woman would voluntarily engage in sexual intercourse with a black man.[71] The solicitor wrote the indictment so Thurman would be given the death penalty upon conviction under Alabama law. "Every slave, free Negro or mulatto, who shall commit, or attempt to commit, the crime of rape on any white female, and be therefore convicted, shall suffer death."[72] The grand jury accepted the state's argument that Thurman was a mulatto and formally charged him with the crime of rape. Thurman pleaded not guilty, conceding only that Mary Mann and he had engaged in a consensual sexual relationship.[73]

Defending white womanhood was a serious matter, and the judge promptly put the case on the docket. Once it got the case, the jury quickly found Thurman guilty. The judge gave Thurman the death penalty, with orders that the authorities execute the sentence expeditiously. James Belser appealed the conviction on grounds that his client's racial identity as a black was inconclusive. If Thurman was not black or mulatto, his relationship with Mann would not have been criminal. Judge John J. Woodward in the Circuit Court of Russell County granted a stay of execution to hear arguments.[74]

The state maintained its argument that Thurman was not white because he had "the kinky hair and yellow skin of a mulatto."[75] Since Alabama had not yet classified mixed-race persons, the defense objected to the state's argument that the mere presence of African ancestry had made Thurman black. If "they were satisfied from the testimony that the prisoner was the offspring of a white mother and a mulatto father," Belser told the jury, Thurman could not be a free "negro" or mulatto as charged in the indictment.[76] However, Judge Woodward used one-drop language in his charge to the jury. If "they believed from the evidence that the defendant was a colored person of mixed blood between the African and white race in any degree he was such a mulatto as the state contemplated."[77] Given the way Judge Woodward construed race, the jury found Thurman guilty for having a sexual relationship with a white woman.

There can be little doubt that under community standards for whiteness, local prosecutors and trial judges were in agreement about racial purity. Their opinion did not immediately become state law; yet, appellate courts that overruled them did so because the statutes under review were vague. As will become apparent, state Supreme Court judges throughout the country reversed trial judges. They used the technicality that legislatures had not classified the races. Thus, it was plausible that someone nearer to the white race than African or Indian was entitled to white privilege. Appellate courts would later come to agree with trial judges that white-looking skin did not mean that a person of African ancestry was white.

RACIAL IDENTITY CASES IN APPELLATE COURTS

The foregoing appellants endeavored to legally establish a white identity. They were not, however, seeking to enlarge whiteness to include people of the black or Indian race. They belonged to a growing population of mixed-race people who were becoming whiter, and they identified as white. Further complicated by the ideological construct of the one-drop rule, their contested identities reflect underpinning cultural beliefs and social practices based on the idea of whiteness as signifying purity and blackness as signifying contagion. Some of them had emigrated from the South or had fled from slavery for a new life in the free Midwest.[78] If the state had classified them as black, they would have faced repressive laws and been subordinated as descendants of Africans. A desire to possess political and civil rights motivated Polly Gray, Elizabeth George, Mr. Williams, and others to litigate their whiteness.[79] Their lives were undoubtedly confusing to them and their families. The states had indeed not formally developed the one-drop rule; nevertheless, it was emerging under community standards. Whites did not agree that a white-looking complexion should trump their knowledge of a person's African or Indian heritage.[80]

As a first step in classifying race, state legislators would draw upon the English common law practice of calculating the proportion of "blood" to settle disputes involving lineage.[81] At various times, antebellum legislators adopted the ratios of one-half to one-thirty-second "blood" to place individuals in a racial category. States north or south of the Mason-Dixon Line never developed uniform standards for classifying race. Hence, community standards became the norm, and they frequently diverged from state to state. Nearly-white people throughout the country continued to argue for recognition of their white racial identity in the courts. They did not attack the legitimacy of the system that assigned privilege based on skin color alone. In fact, they separated themselves from blacks because they believed they had been wrongly consigned to the "degraded race." As Alexis de Tocqueville observed, "when quarrels originating in differences of color take place, mulattoes generally side with the whites."[82] In their legal fight to preserve their claim to white privilege, they discovered a receptive audience among appellate judges who assigned white identity on a case-by-case basis.

Appellate judges followed a different construct for a white racial identity from the one in existence in the community. They had at least three motives for developing this standard. First, they did not agree that racial identity formation should be left to the predilection of judges. "This discretion," Judge Silas Parsons of the Alabama Supreme Court unequivocally stated in *Thurman v. State* (1850), "belongs to the Legislature."[83] Second, prominent nineteenth-century scholars who wrote on jurisprudence frequently urged appellate judges to apply a strict construction of laws that take away civil rights. Fortunatus Dwarris, an English lawyer and author, admonished judges to be sure that they were always carrying out the intent of the legislature when interpreting laws that restricted civil rights.[84] Appellate judges believed denying people white privilege solely because of an allegation of blackness was wrong. The Indiana Supreme Court in *Doe v. Avaline* (1856) acknowledged that appellate judges, particularly those in the state of Ohio, were troubled by laws that abridged civil rights but had no corresponding benefit.[85] Third, appellate judges did not want to extend a rigid racial classification to the point where it would affect the reputations of people who had successfully established a white identity. Judge Silas Parsons asked: "If we take the first step by construction, are we not bound to pursue the line of descendants, so long as there is a drop of negro blood remaining?"[86]

Judge Ebenezer Lane expressed a similar concern in *Jeffries v. Ankeny* (1842). Lane considered it robbery for the state to deny white privilege to people who had already established a white racial identity under community standards. Judge Lane was suspicious of racial purists, lamenting that they might unfairly target white individuals in a witch hunt. After all, the white community had already accepted many of the plaintiffs as white. They had successfully voted in state elections and served in state offices where they had "worthily discharged their duties." "One such is now a clerk of this court, and two are now members of this bar, and disfranchisement, for this cause, would be equally unexpected and startling."[87] Appellate judges wanted to protect the minority of "white" citizens whom racial purists might accuse of being black or Indian.

Free states with repressive laws were fertile with racial identity cases, and a rich body of case law is available in the Midwest and the North. Appellate courts in Massachusetts, Ohio, Indiana, Illinois, and Michigan faced such cases. Although some of these tribunals gave white identities to mixed-race litigants, it is clear that these judges were not necessarily progressive. Furthermore, appellate courts were not unanimous on the question. They applied a strict construction of disabling laws because they affected people who might have had a reasonable claim to vote, offer testimony in court against whites, or gain a public education. Southern states, on the other hand, looked at slave status, not color, to determine racial identity. Believing that a slave could not be white, they disregarded a white appearance so long as the person was a legal slave. Plaintiffs in racial identity cases in the South needed to produce convincing genealogical evidence to prove that their freedom had been stolen under the guise of blackness in order to sustain their claim to a white racial identity.

It is important to remember that their desire to protect Caucasians motivated appellate judges to give a white identity to white-looking plaintiffs.[88] The mere suggestion that a person presenting himself or herself as white was actually related to the African race could cause a plethora of personal and legal problems, including the loss of property and revocation of contracts. The South Carolina Supreme Court held that calling a white person a mulatto was actionable under the common law. Chief Justice John Rutledge explained that "if true, the party would be deprived of all civil rights . . . and would be liable to be tried in all cases, under the Negro Act, without the privilege of a trial by jury."[89] The Mississippi Supreme Court ordered Peebles to pay damages of $500 for impugning the character of the plaintiff in *Scott v. Peebles*. Peebles had made the unsubstantiated claim that Scott "had negro blood in him."[90] An Ohio court held the defendant liable for telling someone: "I understand that you are going to marry [Polly Barrett]; I am sorry you should, for they are akin to negroes."[91] The charge of blackness in libel cases hinged on an informal one-drop rule. The plaintiffs were all white, but under community norms, remote African ancestry was enough for some people to call a neighbor black.

When Massachusetts, reputedly a progressive colony and ostensibly the first state to abolish American slavery, faced the racial identity problem, it made securing a white identity a priority. *Medway v. Natick* (1810), on the surface, might seem like a public welfare case; however, it had all the elements of a racial identity dispute. Ultimately, the Supreme Court would establish a standard followed by appellate judges elsewhere. It held that only the legislature could decide the ratio of "blood" required to classify race. It also concluded that, when a person was nearer to the white race than black, that person should be regarded as legally white.

There were specific circumstances that led to this decision. First, Massachusetts never had a dense African American population, and the legislature had neither developed nor enforced racially repressive laws. The legislature had outlawed interracial marriages in 1786, and whites did not ordinarily marry outside of their race.[92] The statute, however, was not prohibitive in practice. Some people were apparently white enough to be left alone, and when Ishmael Coffee married a white woman, local whites did not complain, and the state had no reason to prosecute them. While the Supreme Court would later describe Coffee as "half white and half black," this characterization of him only tells us that he had remote African ancestry. As has been shown in this essay, Americans lumped all mixed-race people into the mulatto category. However, this does not mean that Coffee was not white in appearance. Given the era in which he lived, it is more reasonable to assume that he was virtually white, and that is why he did not encounter resistance when he presented himself as white in the community. Coffee and his family had been living as white people for many years. Their daughter Roba was even whiter than her father. She openly dated white men and eventually married Christopher Vickons. Their wedding took place in a white church where Reverend Stephen Badger performed the ceremony.[93] Christopher took his bride most likely never concerned about her questionable racial identity, undoubtedly because he too believed he had married a white woman.

Trouble lay ahead for Roba upon her husband's premature death. Unable to support herself and her child in Natick, the widow returned to Medway and became a ward of the town. The most compelling issue facing townsmen was that they did not want to provide welfare to Roba. Medway sued Natick to collect the payments they had already made. The governments in both communities agreed to make the prohibition against interracial marriages the key issue to determine liability. The statute had banned the marriage of a black or mulatto and a white person. Medway would be responsible if the marriage were valid, and Natick would be liable if it were void. The court focused on the racial identity of Roba. Under the common law, a mulatto was the offspring of a black and a white parent. The Supreme Court held that since her father was not black, and her mother was white, Roba could not have been black. Thus, the court rejected the strict construction of race as advanced by Medway that one drop of African blood had made Roba black.[94]

In *Elizabeth George v. Ohio* (1821), circuit court judges Calvin Pease and Peter Hitchcock saw racial identity in the same way. The Ohio circuit court departed sharply from the verdict of the trial judge, who saw Elizabeth George as black, notwithstanding her white-looking appearance. The circuit court extended the immunity in the testimony law to persons above the grade mulatto—that is, to people who looked white, because the statute did not explicitly grant blacks and mulattoes testimony against them.[95] While the Supreme Court would follow the ruling in *Elizabeth George*, the circuit court's opinion was not binding. It did not appear in the official record, and the Ohio Supreme Court would never cite it. Nevertheless, like the *Medway* case, *Elizabeth George* set up the judicial paradigm for evaluating laws that undermined civil rights. Appellate courts gave a strict interpretation to state statutes that explicitly identified blacks and mulattoes, and would not extend the prohibition to them to parties closer to the white race than black or Indian.

The Ohio Supreme Court formally established its position in the *Polly Gray* case (1831). Gray was "nearer white than a mulatto [and] should partake in the privileges of whites," the majority said, which included immunity from a black witness.[96] In *Williams v. School District* (1833), it again stated that individuals "nearer white than a mulatto or half-blood (Indian) were entitled to the privileges of whites."[97] The Supreme Court used the same language in *Jeffries v. Ankeny* (1842) and *Thacker v. Hawk* (1842). Persons "nearer white than black ... were entitled to enjoy every political and social privilege of the white citizen."[98] The Ohio court had accommodated these plaintiffs for one reason only: the court did not want to deprive white-looking people of civil rights when they had a reasonable claim to them. The court followed the admonition of Fortunatus Dwarris and limited the application of state laws that took away rights to the people the legislature had intended to deprive of such rights. Judge William Peck made the same observation in *Van Camp* (1859), explaining that the Supreme Court had made these decisions because the laws under review were disabling and exclusive.[99]

By 1859 the situation had changed dramatically in Ohio, especially in education cases. Before 1848 Ohio followed an exclusionary public school policy, with only whites benefiting from state-funded institutions. That same year, the legislature made provisions for the education of black youths.[100] Mixed-race residents who had once been identified as legally white now faced a new and discomforting state regime when the state Supreme Court gave recognition to the one-drop rule. Enos Van Camp and his family discovered that they had lost the protections the court had once granted to people in their racial class.

The Ohio Supreme Court decision in *Van Camp* marked the gradual ascendance of the one-drop rule in public education cases. Since the segregated school was available to blacks, the Supreme Court began to use broader language to identify people of African ancestry. It followed the legislature, which no longer used the limiting terms of black and mulatto, and added to its statutes "colored" or "persons of color." These phrases, the court believed, "bear its ordinary and popular signification." The Supreme Court concluded that the "decisions in regard to the right of persons more than half white to testify, and to attend the common schools, have had their day."[101] Since the statutes to which they had applied had been repealed for slightly more than a decade, and new state laws had been passed to classify people by race, they were no longer acts of racial exclusion. Under the school law, therefore, white children would attend public schools with children of their race. All of the other pupils "who have any visible taint of African blood" would attend the segregated schools for blacks.[102] The court believed it was now appropriate for school leaders to exclude white-looking pupils from white schools because they had the power to classify people by race. In prior years, the school law was not exclusionary, and the reason the court once used (to allow pupils with a preponderance of white "blood" to attend schools with white youths) was outdated. Although the Van Camp children looked white, they did not have the legal right to go to school with white children.[103]

Supreme Court judges in Indiana, however, rejected the way their peers in Ohio had initially construed race. The court reviewed the legislation that established criteria for the way Native Americans disposed of real property, requiring buyers and sellers to get prior legislative approval. Catherine had made a will turning over land to her white husband, which her Indian heirs disputed upon her death. Counsel for the defendant claimed that the state had applied a disabling act, which required a strict interpretation. The court agreed to an extent but concluded that the state legislature had passed the law to protect Native Americans. The only question it would consider was the racial identity of Catherine Lasselle. The court acknowledged that she was only three-eighths Indian under their standards. Nevertheless, whites, the state and federal governments, and her tribe considered her an Indian. They could not, the Supreme Court decided, set aside these considerations in favor of the preponderance of white-blood theory.[104]

COMMUNITY STANDARDS FOR WHITENESS

By the 1850s, Americans in the North and South were aware of white slavery. In 1850 Dennis Framell, a professional slave catcher from Arkansas, went looking for white slaves in New Albany, Indiana. The *New Albany Daily Ledger* captured the buzz about a family going on around town, as did the *North Star* in its reprint and editorial about the incident. The community learned that the alleged slaves included a fifty-five-year-old woman and her thirty-five-year-old daughter with her eight-year-old son. Upon request, the sheriff arrested the family until Justice of the Peace Jared C. Jocelyn arranged a hearing. The *North Star* editorialized that the seizure shows how "complexion is no security for freedom even in the nominally free states of our country. What is singular about this case," the editor continued, "is that the so-called fugitives are, to all appearances, white persons. No trace of Negro or Indian blood is discernable in the oldest woman or in the boy. Some few of those who have seen the other woman think there is a slight resemblance to the Indian in some of her features, but a large majority is of the opinion that she also is of purely white origin."[105]

In 1850 Fredricka Bremer, a well-known Swedish writer at the time, went on tour to the American South. She reported on a trade in "fancy girls," or white-looking women forced into prostitution. These highly sought-after women had one drop of African blood that made them slaves. Bremer was further dismayed by the "white children of slavery" when she saw them in the nation's capital. A "slave lady" had apparently been trained to please white aristocrats in conversation as well as in the cult of domesticity. In Richmond, Virginia, she found a white boy "with cheeks as red as roses" in the company of these "fancy girls." Bremer lamented when she later learned that the boy "was indeed a Negro [and] had been sold away from his mother." Moreover, one of her companions reported on a "negro jail" in Lexington, Kentucky, which amounted to a brothel. The proprietor of the "house" displayed the women "to show to advantage their finely developed and graceful forms." New Orleans was also well known for its white-looking women, from whom slave owners picked their mistresses.[106]

Ella Thomas recorded her outrage in her diary about how white society allowed their men to have their way with enslaved women in Georgia, many of whom were the offspring of white men. Undoubtedly some white-looking women used their color for personal gain for themselves and their children. In 1858 Thomas noted her family's white-looking slave, whose daughter was "as white as any child." Thomas also pointed out how a young man carried his slave off to the North in order to marry her, only to have his father threaten to disinherit him. Like Bremer, she was offended by the way men made use of "fancy girls." The trade in white slaves had become so popular in the country that New Orleans and Lexington, Kentucky, had gained notoriety as centers for "fancy girls."[107]

While southern courts recognized that white skin would not automatically free a slave, they were not immune to racial identity litigation. The Alabama Supreme Court overturned three lower courts to identify Edward Thurman as white under state law. On the surface it might have seemed that the high court had expanded the meaning of a white racial identity; however, the court used the Thurman case to make a clarion call for the legislature to catalogue the races. The Supreme Court acknowledged that the judge had applied one-drop language in his charge to the jury. It was also significant that Thurman was not the offspring of a black and white parent, which would have made him black under the strict definition of a mulatto. Since he had a white-looking father and a white mother, Justice Parsons wrote, there was nothing in Alabama law "to authorize a conclusion" that he was a mulatto: "Penal statutes are not to be extended by construction. If this rule is violated the fate of [the defendant would be] decided by the arbitrary discretion of judges, and not by the express authority of the laws."[108] The court was not willing to create and subordinate a new caste of people under disabling statutes. Justice Parsons believed this discretion belonged to the legislature.

Studying racial identity disputes in the antebellum period illustrates that whites had long thought that one drop of African "blood" made an individual black, and that the line between white and black in the United States has always been impenetrable.[109] Local circumstances and the year or decade of the dispute had a great deal to do with the fluidity of the color line. Nevertheless, there is compelling evidence that an informal one-drop rule was conceptualized under community standards as soon as mixed-race people became visible. Trial judges and county prosecutors recognized these standards and used one-drop language in judicial proceedings. Appellate courts took exception to the application of the one-drop rule but did so because they wanted legislative guidance. Appellate judges also believed disabling laws should receive a strict construction. Once legislatures began to classify people more precisely, appellate judges quickly put people of color in the same racial class as blacks.

By the Civil War, virtually everyone in the United States recognized an informal one-drop rule. Booker T. Washington summed it up this way: "It is a fact that, if a person is known to have one percent of African blood in his veins, he ceases to be a white man. The ninety-nine percent of Caucasian blood does not weigh by the side of the one-percent of African blood. The person is a Negro every time."[110] Washington, a mixed-race person, had himself lived under the informal one-drop rule. Apparently he thought the one-drop rule had germinated in American culture before Tennessee codified it into law in 1910. In other words, its tacit application in formal legal matters had been a reflection of various ways in which the increasingly polarized racial climate of American society rested on this pervasive biological myth.

NOTES

1. Gilbert T. Stephenson, *Race Distinctions in American Law* (New York: D. Appleton, 1910), 15; Nathaniel Gates, *Racial Classification and History*, ed. (New York: Garland, 1997), 2110.

2. Pauli Murray, *States' Laws on Race and Color* (Athens: University of Georgia Press, 1997), 173–74.

3. *An Act to Preserve Racial Integrity*, Chapter 371, Section 5, 1942, *Va. Sess. Laws*, 534, 535; Stephenson, *Race Distinctions in American Law*, 15; Gates, *Racial Classification and History*, 2110.

4. Murray, *States' Laws*, 22, 237, 443–44.

5. Ariela J. Gross, *What Blood Won't Tell: A History of Race on Trial in America* (Cambridge: Harvard University Press, 2010), 88.

6. Daniel J. Sharfstein, "Crossing the Color Line: Racial Migration and the One-Drop Rule, 1600-1860," *Minnesota Law Review* Vol. 91 (2007): 594.

7. Gates, *Racial Classification and History*, 2110, note 240.

8. Acts of the General Assembly of the Commonwealth of *Virginia*, 6 vols. (Richmond: Division of Purchase and Printing, 1930), 1: 96–97; Gates, *Racial Classification and History*, 2110; A. Leon Higginbotham and Barbara Kopytoff, "Racial Purity and Interracial Sex in the Law of Colonial and Antebellum Virginia," *Georgetown Law Journal* 77 (August 1989): 2021.

9. Neil Irvin Painter, *The History of White People* (W. W. Norton & Co., 2010), 131; Patrick Rael, *Black Identity and Black Protest in the Antebellum North* (Chapel Hill: University of North Carolina Press, 2002), 14.

10. Jerrold M. Packard, *American Nightmare: The History of Jim Crow* (1982; New York: Scribner, 2002), 96.

11. Erica Faye Cooper, "One 'Speck' of Imperfection—Invisible blackness and the one-drop rule: An Interdisciplinary Approach to Examining *Plessy v. Ferguson* and *Jane Doe v. State of Louisiana*," PhD diss., Indiana University, 2008, 25; Frank W. Sweet, *Legal History of the Color Line: The Rise and Triumph of the One Drop Rule* (Palm Coast: Backintyme, 2005), 168; Nikki Khanna, *Biracial in America: Forming and Performing Racial Identity* (Lanham, MD: Lexington, 2011), 31.

12. Nell Irvin Painter, "'Who We Are': Lawrence Levine as William Jamesian Pragmatist and Gustave de Beaumont," *Journal of American History* Vol. 93, no. 3 (December 2006): 766.

13. *State v. Cantey*, 2 Hill's Law, 617 (S.C. 1835); Sweet, *Legal History of the Color Line*, 314; Joel Williamson, *New People: Miscegenation and Mulattoes in the United States* (New York: Free Press, 1980), 18–19, 71; John G. Mencke, *Mulattoes and Race Mixture: American Attitudes and Images, 1865-1918* (Ann Arbor: UMI Research Press, 1979), 20; Helen Tunnicliff Catterall, *Judicial Cases Concerning American Slavery and the Negro*, 5 vols. (New York: Octagon, 1968), vol. 2: 269; Gross, *What Blood Won't Tell*, 54.

14. Quoted in Matthew Frye Jacobson, *Whiteness of a Different Color: European Immigrants and the Alchemy of Race* (Cambridge: Harvard University Press, 1998), 40; Peter Kolchin, "Whiteness Studies: The New History of Race in America," *Journal of American History* 89, no. 1 (June 2002): 158.

15. Alexis de Tocqueville, *American Institutions and Their Influence* (New York: A. S. Barnes, 1873), 378.

16. *The Collected Works of Abraham Lincoln*, 8 Vols., ed. Roy P. Balser (New Brunswick, NJ: Rutgers University Press, 1953–55), vol. 3: 12; Abraham Lincoln and Stephen A. Douglas, *The Lincoln-Douglas Debates* (New York: Dover, 2004), 35; *The Civil War and*

Reconstruction: A Documentary Collection, ed. William E. Gienapp (New York: W. W. Norton, 2001), 71–72; quoted in Kolchin, "Whiteness Studies," 165; Brian R. Dirck, *Abraham Lincoln and White America* (Lawrence: University of Kansas Press, 2012), 78, 79.

17. Packard, *American Nightmare*, 96; Monica McDermott and Frank L. Samson, "White Racial and Ethnic Identity in the United States," *Annual Review of Sociology* 31 (2005): 247.

18. Stephen Middleton, ed., *The Black Laws in the Old Northwest: A Documentary History* (Westport, CT: Greenwood Press, 1993), 15–24; Stephen Middleton, *The Black Laws: Race and the Legal Process in Early Ohio* (Athens: Ohio University Press, 2005), 49–54.

19. Middleton, *The Black Laws in the Old Northwest*, 15–24.

20. Adrienne D. Davis, "Identity Notes Part One: Playing in the Light," 45 *American University Law Review* 695 (1996): 702.

21. Elliott Howard Gilkey, *The Ohio Hundred Year Book: A Hand-book of the Public Men and Public Institutions of Ohio from the Formation of the North-West Territory (1787) to July 1, 1901* (Columbus, OH: Fred J. Heer, 1901), 467, 472.

22. *Edwill Thacker v. John Hawk*, 11 Ohio 377 (1842), 380–81; *Parker Jeffries v. John Ankeny*, 11-12 Ohio 372 (1842), 376.

23. Middleton, *The Black Laws in the Old Northwest*, 15–18; Middleton, *The Black Laws: Race and the Legal Process in Early Ohio*, 47–51.

24. *Enos Van Camp v. The Board of Education*, 9 Ohio (Critchfield), 407 (1859), 411.

25. Ibid., 411.

26. Ibid., 412.

27. Ibid.

28. Ibid.

29. Edward Byron Reuter, *The Mulatto in the United States: Including a Study of the Role of Mixed-Blood Races Throughout the World* (New York: Negro University Press, 1918; Reprint, 1968), 109–13.

30. *Medway v. Natick*, 7 Massachusetts 87 (1810).

31. Winthrop D. Jordan, "American Chiaroscuro: The Status and Definition of Mulattoes in the British Colonies," *William and Mary Quarterly* 19, no. 2 (April 1962): 183–84; William Q. Lowe, "Understanding Race: The Evolution of the Meaning of Race in American Law," *Albany Law Journal* 72 (2009): 1122; Christine B. Hickman, "The Devil and the One Drop Rule: Racial Categories, African Americans, and the U.S. Census," *Michigan Law Review* 95, no. 5 (March 1997): 1161; Penelope Bullock, "The Mulatto in American Fiction," *Phylon* 6, no. 1 (1945): 78.

32. *The State v. Davis*, 18 South Carolina 558 (1831); *State v. Cantey*, 20 South Carolina 614 (1835).

33. *Thurman v. The State*, 18 Alabama 276 (1850).

34. Winthrop Jordan, *White Man's Burden: Historical Origins of Racism in the United States* (Oxford: Oxford University Press, 1974), 84.

35. Middleton, *The Black Laws in the Old Northwest*, 15, 17–18.

36. Randall Kennedy, "Racial Passing," *Ohio State Law Journal* 62 (2001): 1145; Jordan, *White Man's Burden*, 85; Packard, *American Nightmare*, 97.

37. Jordan, *White Man's Burden*, 85; Mencke, *Mulattoes and Race Mixture*, 20.

38. Sharfstein, "Crossing the Color Line," 594.

39. Jordan, *White Man's Burden*, 85.

40. Benjamin Isaac, *The Invention of Racism in Classical Antiquity* (Princeton: Princeton University Press, 2004), 1.

41. Williamson, *New People*.

42. Packard, *American Nightmare*, 97.

43. Ibid., 96; Mencke, *Mulattoes and Race Mixture*, 20–21; "White and Colored Slaves," *Harper's Weekly*, (January 30, 1864): 71; Joseph R. Washington Jr. *Marriage in Black and White* (Boston: Beacon Press, 1970), 42–46; Mary Niall Mitchell, "Rosebloom and Pure White," *American Quarterly* 54, no. 3 (September 2002): 369–75.

44. Gustave de Beaumont, *Marie, ou l'Esclavagea ux Etats-Unis, Tableaud e Moeursa Mdricaines* (*Marie, or Slavery in the United States: A Portrait of American Custom*, trans. Barbara Chapman (1835; Baltimore: Johns Hopkins University Press, 1958), 4.

45. Ibid., 4–5; Also quoted in Nell Irvin Painter, *The History of White People* (W. W. Norton, 2010), 130.

46. Beaumont, *Marie*, xiii–xiv; Louis J. Kern, "Beaumont and Tocqueville Confront Slavery and Racism," in *National Stereotypes in Perspective: Americans in France, Frenchmen in America*, ed. William L. Chew (Amsterdam: Rodopi Press, 2001), 162; Aurelian Crăiutu and Jeffrey C. Isaac, ed., *America Through European Eyes: British and French Reflections on the New World from the Eighteenth Century to the Present* (University Park: Pennsylvania State University, 2009), 149–52.

47. James Flint, *Flint's Letters From America: Containing Observations on the Climate and Agriculture of the Western States, the Manners of the People, the Prospects of Emigrants*, ed. Reuben Gold Thwaites, (Carlisle, MA: Applewood Books, 1822), vol. 33: 197; Sharfstein, "Crossing the Color Line," 592; Paul Finkelman, "Color of Law," 87 *Northwestern University Law Review* (1993), 954.

48. Sharfstein, "Crossing the Color Line," 592. Edna Ferber's novel and Broadway musical *Show Boat* portrays the same idea, when a white-looking woman and her lover were accosted in the play for breaking the miscegenation law of Mississippi, the man pricked his lover's finger and sucked out some blood. Turning to the sheriff coming to arrest them he asked, would you call a man with black blood in him white? The sheriff replied, "One drop of nigger blood makes you a nigger in these parts." *Show Boat* (New York: Doubleday, 1926), 90–91, 134–45; Williamson, *New People*, 1.

49. Jordan, "American Chiaroscuro," 185.

50. Peggy Pascoe, *What Comes Naturally: Miscegenation Law and the Making of Race in America* (New York: Oxford University Press, 2009), 51–52.

51. Ibid., 53. The fines ranged from $100 to $1,000 for ordinary citizens who gave counsel to marry, $500 to $10,000 for ministers, and $500 to $5,000 to clerks who issued such licenses.

52. *William Dungey v. Joseph Spencer*, Dewitt County Circuit Court, May 15, 1855, www.papersofabrahamlincoln.org/Briefs/briefs23.htm; Stacy Pratt McDermott, "Black

Bill' and the Privileges of Whiteness in Antebellum Illinois," *Journal of Illinois History* Vol. 12, No. 1 (Spring 2009): 2.

53. McDermott, "'Black Bill,'" 17.

54. Williamson, *New People*, 62, 75–76; Mencke, *Mulattoes and Race Mixture*, 16–17, 20–21; Joseph R. Washington Jr., *Marriage in Black and White* (Boston: Beacon Press, 1970), 99–100; Joshua D. Rothman, *Notorious in the Neighborhood: Sex and Families Across the Color Line in Virginia, 1787-1861* (Chapel Hill: University of North Carolina Press, 2003), 206.

55. *Liberty Hall and the Cincinnati Gazette*, December 5, 1821; Ervin H. Pollack, *Ohio Unreported Judicial Decisions Prior to 1823* (Indianapolis: Allen Smith, 1952), 187.

56. *Liberty Hall and the Cincinnati Gazette*.

57. *Gray v. Ohio*, 3 Ohio (Hammond) 353 (1831), 353.

58. Ibid.

59. Ibid.

60. *Williams v. School District No. 6* (Wright), 578 (1834), 578–79; Middleton, *The Black Laws: Race and the Legal Process in Early Ohio*, 86–88.

61. Irving G. Tragen, "Comment: Statutory Prohibitions Against Interracial Marriages," *California Law Review* 32, no. 3 (1944): 270; Carter G. Woodson, "The Beginnings of the Miscegenation of the Whites and Blacks," *Journal of Negro History* 3, no. 4 (October 1918): 335–53.

62. *Williams v. School District*, 578–79; Middleton, *Black Laws: Race and the Legal Process in Early Ohio*, 86–88.

63. *Williams v. School District*, 578–79; An Act to provide for the better regulation of common schools, *Laws of Ohio*, Section 1, February 10, 1829; Middleton, *The Black Laws: Race and the Legal Process in Early Ohio*, 34.

64. *Jeffries v. Ankeny*, 375.

65. *Constitution of Ohio*, 1802, Article IV, Section 1 (Article V Section 1 of the revised constitution of 1851 maintained that stipulation); Middleton, *Black Laws: Race and the Legal Process in Early Ohio*, 12.

66. *Jeffries v. Ankeny*, 373.

67. *Thacker v. Hawk*, 377; *Anderson v. Millikin*, 9 Ohio (Critchfield) 568 (1859), 570.

68. Alabama Supreme Court Records, June Term 1850, 6 vols. These volumes are not indexed and were not online as of 2009. Researchers will need to consult a reference librarian to locate and retrieve these sources. Alabama Department of Archives and History, Montgomery, 120. The Michigan Supreme Court concluded that it was proven that Edward Thurman was the son of a mulatto father and a white mother, which made him a quadroon. See *People v. Dean* 14 Michigan 406 (1866), 418.

69. Cheryl I. Harris, "Whiteness as Property," *Harvard Law Review* 106, no. 8 (1993): 1724–37.

70. Alabama Supreme Court Records, 1850, 118.

71. Ibid.

72. C. C. Clay, *A Digest of the Laws of the State of Alabama: Containing all the Statutes of a Public and General Nature* (Tuscaloosa, AL: Marmaduke J. Slade, 1843), Chap. XV,

Sec. 4, 472. The Alabama statute was also cited by the Michigan Supreme Court in *People v. Dean*, 412.

73. Alabama Supreme Court Records, 1850, 119.

74. Ibid., 120.

75. Ibid., 121.

76. Ibid.

77. Ibid.

78. Williamson, *New People*, 58; also see Eugene H. Berwanger, *The Frontier against Slavery: Western Anti-Negro Prejudice and the Slavery Extension Controversy* (1967; Urbana-Champaign: University of Illinois Press, 2002).

79. Rael, *Black Identity and Black Protest*, 13.

80. Ibid., 12.

81. Paul Spruhan, "A Legal History of Blood Quantum in Federal Indian Law to 1935," *South Dakota Law Review* 51, no. 1 (2006); Melissa Meyer, *Thicker than Water: The Origins of Blood as Symbol and Ritual* (New York: Routledge, 2005).

82. Alexis de Tocqueville, *Democracy in America* (New York: George Adlard, 1839), 1:371; *Alexis de Tocqueville on Democracy, Revolution, and Society*, ed. John Stone and Stephen Mennell (Chicago: University of Chicago Press, 1980), 334; Jordan, "American Chiaroscuro," 185; Khanna, *Biracial in America*, 29–30.

83. *State v. Thurman*, 279.

84. Ibid.

85. *Van Camp v. Board of Education*, 411; *Doe on the Demise of Lafontaine and Another v. Avaline*, 8 Indiana 6 (1856).

86. *State v. Thurman*, 374–75.

87. Ibid., 375.

88. *Gray v. Ohio*, 355.

89. *Eden v. Legare*, 1 Bay (South Carolina) 171 (1791), 172.

90. *Scott v. Peebles*, 2 Smedes (Mississippi) 546, (1844).

91. See notes in *Aspinwall v. Williams*, 1 Ohio 84 (1823).

92. "Act for the more orderly consummation of marriages," Massachusetts, 1 Statute 1786, Chapter 3, Section 7; *Medway v. Natick*; Charles S. Mangum Jr., *The Legal Status of the Negro* (1940; New Orleans: Quid Pro Books, 2014), 238.

93. *Medway v. Natick*; Mangum, *The Legal Status of the Negro*, 238.

94. *Medway v. Natick*; Louis Ruchames, "Race, Marriage and Abolition in Massachusetts," *Journal of Negro History* 40 (July 1955): 250–73; Pascoe, *What Comes Naturally*, 40.

95. Pollack, *Ohio Unreported Judicial Decisions*, 187; Middleton, *The Black Laws: Race and the Legal Process in Early Ohio*, 17.

96. *Gray v. Ohio*, 355; *Chalmers v. Stewart*, 11 Ohio 386 (1842), 387–88; *Doe v. Avaline*, 14.

97. *Williams v. School District*, 579.

98. *Jeffries v. Ankeny*, 376.

99. *Van Camp v. The Board of Education*, 413; *Lane v. Baker*, 11 Ohio 238 (1843), 238–43.

100. Middleton, *The Black Laws: Race and the Legal Process in Early Ohio*, 34, 38–45.

101. *Van Camp v. Board of Education*, 414.

102. Ibid.

103. Ibid., 414–15.

104. *Doe v. Avaline*.

105. *North Star*, December 5, 1850; Mitchell, "Rosebloom and Pure White," 375–76; Carol Wilson and Calvin D. Wilson, "White Slavery: An American Paradox," *Slavery and Abolition* 19 (Apr. 1998), 1-23; "A White Woman Sold into Slavery," *New York Tribune*, reprinted in *The National Anti-Slavery Standard* (January 3, 1863.)

106. Fredricka Bremer, *The Homes of the New World: Impressions of America*, trans. Mary Howitt, 3 vols. (London: A. Hall, 1853), 1: 492–93, 2: 534–35; Williamson, *New People*, 67–69; *National Antislavery Standard*, February 21, 1863; Mitchell, "Rosebloom and Pure White," 397.

107. Diary of Ella Gertrude (Clanton) Thomas, January 2, 1858, Manuscript Division, Duke University Library, Durham, NC; Williamson, *New People*, 67–69; Frederic Bancroft, *Slave-Trading in the Old South* (Baltimore: J. J. H. Furst, 1931), 131, 315, 321; Reuter, *The Mulatto in the United States*, 140.

108. *Thurman v. The State*, 279.

109. Howard Bodenhorn, "The Mulatto Advantage: The Biological Consequences of Complexion in Rural Antebellum Virginia," *Journal of Interdisciplinary History* 33, no. 1 (Summer 2002): 26; Carl N. Degler, *Neither Black nor White: Slavery and Race Relations in Brazil and the United States* (New York: Macmillan, 1971), 102.

110. Quoted in Mencke, *Mulattoes and Race Mixture*, 37; Lowe, "Understanding Race," 1122–23.

2

RESTITUTION CLAIMS FOR WRONGFUL ENSLAVEMENT AND THE DOCTRINE OF THE MASTER'S GOOD FAITH

ROBERT WESTLEY

I. CONTEMPORARY LEGAL STANDARDS FOR PERSONS WHO WERE FREE, I.E. WHITES, VS. ENSLAVED PERSONS

> Had the learned Chief Justice lived to try this case, he would have
> been compelled to admit that at least one exception to the rule
> that we are not faithless to the dead exists, and that the objection
> is not in every case imaginary.
> —CHIEF JUSTICE JOSEPH BROWN[1]

A. Slave Law's Racial Double Standard

The political interdependence of white democratic institutions and black slavery has been well established in historical literature on the subject, as has the reliance of modern capitalism on slavery.[2] Americans frequently tout the United States as the wealthiest nation on Earth, yet whites hardly ever acknowledge the contribution of black slavery both to the creation of that wealth and to the opportunities that flow from it. The purpose of this essay is to show the regularity of the legal double standard between blacks and whites in antebellum property claims. This double standard set the stage for diminished expectations with respect to property claims by blacks, such that the most that blacks could typically hope for was their freedom from bondage, but rarely—if ever—could they hope for compensation for their exploitation and abuse by whites. Since whites enjoyed a presumption of freedom, their expectations of compensation in property disputes, even if sometimes disappointed, were routinely validated as a central focus of their legal claims.

The case of *James v. Carper* is exemplary of this double standard.[3] In that case, a white woman, Mrs. James, brought suit for compensation on a claim of trespass against an innkeeper to whom she had rented her slave Bill. James sued to be personally compensated for the injuries inflicted when the innkeeper severely whipped Bill under the assumption that he had stolen money from one of the guests at the inn. At trial, the jury was instructed that the employer of an enslaved person had the same right as the owner to inflict punishment on the slave. The only limit on such punishment under Tennessee law at that time was to refrain from taking life or limb, or the infliction of great or unnecessary torture. Nevertheless, the Supreme Court of Tennessee found that the transfer of the right to punish a slave from the owner to a temporary employer could not arise by legal implication in a case that involved allegations of criminal wrongdoing on the part of the slave, as opposed to insubordination toward a superior or wanton misconduct that was not criminal in nature. Such a rule would interfere with the court's own authority to punish a slave. Thus, the court granted James a new trial and a fresh opportunity to prove her claim before a jury, which could include, according to the court, payment of exemplary damages by the defendant to the slave owner.

By contrast, consider the much more notorious case of *Dred Scott v. Sandford*, decided by the Supreme Court of the United States in the same year as *James v. Carper*.[4] The *Dred Scott* case involved a much more complex set of facts, raised matters of national importance, and traversed a much more circuitous path to resolution of its underlying issues.[5] In a technical sense, *Dred Scott* was a freedom suit, in contrast to litigation for damages.[6] Nevertheless, when Scott and his wife filed suit under Missouri law, they alleged the intentional torts of battery and false imprisonment. If successful, the suit would have entitled them to claim monetary damages.[7] Such damages would not have been paid by the defendant in the freedom suit, but would have derived from the labor of the plaintiff who was typically hired out to an employer by the court during the pendency of his freedom claim.[8] On the other hand, if the plaintiff was unsuccessful in proving that he had been wrongfully enslaved, the fund created by his labor would be paid to his master. This procedure ensured that even slave masters who had wrongfully enslaved blacks would not be required to make restitution to the persons they enslaved. Whereas the worst outcome for the slave master would be the loss of a slave, the most that blacks could typically hope for in such suits was to win their freedom from bondage. Antebellum slave law ensured that even these uncompensated victories were rare and difficult to achieve. The Scotts, for instance, fought for their freedom in the courts for over eleven years. In the end, Justice Taney, writing for the majority, concluded that the Scotts were not free persons wrongfully enslaved, and that even if they had been free, they could not be citizens and had "no rights that the white man was bound to respect."[9]

If there is a bottom line to be drawn in the comparison between the white as litigant seeking to enforce property rights and the black as litigant seeking both freedom and restitution under antebellum slave law, it is that the law overwhelmingly favored the white litigant over the black litigant. In a dispute among whites—the owner, the hirer, the jury, the court—over who could exercise an unfettered right to inflict physical punishment and humiliation on a black man—in *James v. Carper* the description of the court held that the defendant claimed to be within his rights when he "stripped the slave and bucked him over a wheelbarrow, took out his knife, and threatened to castrate the slave if he did not give up the money"—the black man who has been battered, beaten, and threatened with emasculation, even if it turned out to be an unjust or wrongful act, would have no standing to claim any violation of his rights; only his white owner had a legal right to claim damages under the law.[10]

B. Defining Just and Unjust Enslavement through the eyes of Slave Masters

From a modern perspective, perhaps, the racial double standard is not odd or unusual; the ability of slaves to file freedom suits at all might be considered unusual, since Black slaves were generally treated as persons without legal rights and mere objects of property.[11] However, it must be kept in mind that the law of slavery was as instrumental in preserving freedom as it was in perpetuating slavery. Under the law of slavery the state regulated who may rightfully be enslaved, thereby articulating a pro-slavery ideology. The state was also obliged to recognize that others are rightfully free under this reasoning. A person with legal rights in a slave society possesses probably the most valued property of all. However, this was still not the only property that mattered to the slave owner. As Andrew Fede points out, "slaves were unique property because they could commit crimes."[12] Thus, in the primary forum where the law recognized black slaves as persons rather than property, it was for the purpose of imposing special burdens on them without the ordinary protections of the common law. Indeed, the course of development of the common law bears the mark of slavery's institutional presence, as lawmakers and judges over the course of many years sought to accommodate the preservation of slavery and social hierarchy within an existing legal framework that rhetorically valorized equal and inalienable human rights.

Blacks were afforded some means of challenging the legality of their status in court, even if it required the intervention of a white advocate.[13] The substantive grounds for claiming wrongful enslavement and the legal process to be followed in making the claim were set by social elites who were themselves typically slave owners. Far from being a threat to the institution of slavery, recognition of the claim of wrongful enslavement acted as a concession to the master's property interest in the enslaved person, therefore reinforcing the legitimacy of slavery generally. The ability of masters to manumit or free their slaves corresponded with their ability to alienate or dispose of ordinary property. Recognition of a cause of action for wrongful enslavement also functioned as a protection against encroachment on the racial and territorial boundaries of slavery that the law established.

However, the master's power to free his slaves was hardly absolute. There were always restrictions based on substantive concerns about the implications of a "racial" democracy and the economic impact of freeing slaves on the white community. For instance, the slave owner had full responsibility for maintaining his chattels during the duration of their bondage; however, once emancipated, the poor laws made taxpayers responsible for the needy among the free population.[14] Manumission of elderly, incompetent, or handicapped slaves under these circumstances could just as easily reflect a slave owner's unscrupulous calculation of his personal financial interest as any benevolence toward his slaves, or second thoughts about slavery. Moreover, manumission by will or testamentary disposition was sometimes ineffective in the absence of legislation, and such legal prescriptions frequently required freed slaves to migrate to another jurisdiction within a prescribed period of time or risk re-enslavement.[15] Thus, while manumission was not invariably seen as an institutional threat to slavery, the presence of free blacks in a society based on racial slavery was often viewed as a threat to the verity of that institution and accordingly tightly circumscribed by the law.[16]

Whether based on a deed, contract, or testamentary disposition, successful claimants in a manumission suit had to show that their freedom was consistent with their master's wishes or intentions. By contrast, freedom suit claimants such as the Scotts sought to free themselves in opposition to the wishes of their purported owners based either on travel to a free state or territory, or the local law of the slave state.[17] In the late antebellum period, as the nation approached civil war, the comity that had once been extended traveling slave owners seeking passage through a free state had become increasingly tenuous. Justice Taney's decision in the *Dred Scott* case possibly meant to restore repose on this issue among slave owners; however, his opinion had the effect of inflaming sectional tensions against slavery among free soilers (those who wanted to keep slavery out of their states) and abolitionists.[18]

Based on the foregoing considerations, wrongful or unjust enslavement should be seen as a homeostatic device deployed by slave owners to maintain the legitimacy of "rightful" or just slavery. By means of a wrongful enslavement claim, persons who would otherwise have no chance to become free were [sometimes] able to gain their freedom. However, their freedom was never meant to be a reproach to slave owners, and therefore rarely included compensation paid by the alleged slave master to the person wrongly enslaved. However, this anomaly in the law, created by the exigencies of slavery based on white supremacy, meant that even when there were no procedural barriers to court-ordered restitution for enslavement, the substantive commitment of antebellum southern courts was against it. If we then ask the post-emancipation question of when was the proper time to seek reparations for slavery, the resounding response that comes down through ages of resistance to racial oppression is not yet, perhaps never.[19]

C. The Perils and Scope of Comparative Examination of Slave Law: Developments/Reform

Although this essay relies on a comparative analysis of slave law restitution doctrine in the United States South, focusing on developments in the common law states rather than Louisiana or Spanish-controlled Florida, the work of mapping this legal history has already been done by many others who are likely better trained than the author in historiography.[20] The primary purpose of retracing the maps already drawn by others is to link this history to contemporary debates over racial reconciliation and social justice. As demonstrated by Ariela Gross, conservative and liberal political discourses on race and social justice often incorporate competing histories of slavery in ways that fail to engage the historical premises of conservatives' arguments against the redress of slavery's harms.[21] This essay is about examination of the historical premise that there was a time for the redress of slavery's harms in the American justice system, but that time has come and gone. Just as Gross questions whether the time of slavery has passed, I continue to question whether the time of slavery redress has yet arrived.[22]

If the time of slavery's redress has come and gone, it is vital to 1) choose the date when redress was made and list the elements of such redress, or 2) if the possibility of meaningful redress was lost, identify the date of its occurrence and outline the reasons for the loss.[23] Stephen Best and Saidiya Hartman choose the second path, observing that by 1787 it was already too late to undertake reparations for slavery. As Best and Hartman conclude, "the incommensurability between grief and grievance, pain and compensation" had become an unbridgeable chasm by the end of the eighteenth century, suggesting that abolition was the most enslaved blacks could reasonably expect. Unfortunately, conservative critics of reparations for slavery implicitly hold that the time of slavery's redress has passed, and explicitly count policies such as affirmative action or fair housing laws or abolition itself as elements of redress, but these critics refuse to specify any date on which redress occurred. As Gross points out, conservative histories of slavery are linked to a narrative in which freedom was inevitable, slavery and Jim Crow were transient deviations from the American creed, the Republican party is the champion of civil rights whose true meaning rests on a timeless principle of colorblindness embodied in the federal Constitution, and finally, that American slavery, resembling slavery in the ancient world or other parts of the world, was not a racial institution.[24] This tableau of commitments permits some conservatives to conclude that "'no single group' (i.e. whites) clearly benefitted from slavery, that few whites owned slaves or benefited from slavery, that most blacks did not suffer from slavery, and therefore, that whites as a group do not 'owe' blacks anything."[25]

In *In re African American Slave Descendants Litigation*, the court invokes the narrative device of slavery as a transient stage toward inevitable freedom, while refusing to hear the plaintiffs' arguments on the merits, and dismissing their lawsuit for reparations on procedural grounds.[26] In the course of constructing its own narrative of redress for slavery, the court makes plain in dicta its belief that slaveholders who lost their property as a result of the Civil War, Union soldiers who lost their lives in the war, and subsequent generations who suffered social, political, and financial losses due to the war, paid the nation's debt to the slaves.[27] In the zero-sum approach of the court, it seems, any loss suffered by white Americans linked to the abolition of slavery, regardless of any consideration of legal or even moral entitlement, represents restitution for slavery.

In the analysis that follows a more rigorous methodology will be applied to the question of restitution for enslaved persons. Despite the perils of analogous reasoning, comparisons can and should be made between the treatment of restitution under slave law for white litigants and black litigants. Other fruitful points of comparison can be drawn between the so-called Deep South and border states, early colonial slave law and late antebellum slave law, the North and the South, and of course, the traditional comparative law framework of international developments. These are distinctions that the following analysis seeks to observe, rather than points to be developed. For present purposes, the argument will outline the grounds for skepticism and critique of conservative histories of slavery, beginning in the next section with the relatively substantial archival foundation for believing that American slavery was a racist institution almost from the start.

II. THE ARCHITECTURE OF SLAVE LAW: DEVELOPMENT, INTERPRETATION, AND REFORM

As with most bodies of law, the development of slave law reflected its cultural precursors. Since the publication of *Slave Law in the Americas*,[28] however, it has become a commonplace in the comparative historiography of slavery to observe that the English colonies that later became the slaveholding states of the United States differed from their European counterparts in that the English legal tradition neither had any slave law of its own, nor did it borrow from ancient Roman law sources on the subject as the continental powers did. In the absence of an existing body of law governing slavery under the common law, the English colonists who took possession of Africans as enslaved persons simply made up their own slave laws as they developed the institution over time.

A. The Absence of Slavery from the Common Law Tradition

According to Alan Watson, lawmaking in the Western world, especially private law and its sources, developed in the space created by the neglect and indifference of rulers and governments. The case of English common law is no exception to this pattern; from its origins until the second half of the nineteenth century, Watson argues, the common law was left to be developed mainly by judges who followed judicial precedent. Although judges, unlike Roman jurists, were officially appointed, no ruler actually gave judges the power to make law, which gave rise to the enduring conceit that judges were "finders," not "makers" of law. Moreover, the discursive practices invoked by the judges describe law as an autonomous field of judgment, self-reliant and impermeable to other concerns or discourses, such as politics or morality, which are considered external to legal logic. Legal decision making and development conceived of in this way is most often a slow, accretive process in which desuetude does not necessarily lead to repeal or reform.

To make good that part of his thesis concerning the operation of legal logic, Watson examines the exchange between the majority and the lone dissent in the case of *Commonwealth v. Turner*, where the court held that a Virginia slave master was permitted under the common law to beat his slave "cruelly, immoderately and excessively," so long as no homicide resulted from the beating.[29] Writing for the court, Judge William A. G. Dade asserts, "In coming to a decision upon this delicate and important question, the Court has considered it to be its duty to ascertain, not what may be expedient, or morally, or politically right in relation to this matter, but what is the law."[30] Arguing in favor of judicial restraint and the greater authority of the legislature to make law, Judge Dade makes a number of assertions that Watson finds to be either incorrect, surprising, or contrary to the much vaunted judicial value of restraint in its lawmaking capacity. Judge Dade writes:

> It is said to be the boast of the common law, that it continually conforms itself to the ever-changing condition of society. But, this conformity keeps on pari passu with those changes. Like them it is slow and imperceptible: so that society may easily conform itself to the law. When great changes take place in the social order, a stronger hand, that of the Legislature, must be applied. Thus, when slavery, a wholly new condition, was introduced, the common law could not operate on it. The rules were to be established, either by the positive enactments of the law-making power, or to be deduced from the Codes of other countries, where that condition of man was tolerated.[31]

As Watson observes, the second source of law mentioned by Judge Dade—legal rules from countries where slavery once existed or now exists—is surprising given that no foreign system is a source of law if it was not accepted as authoritative. Moreover, such legal borrowing by the court would itself constitute lawmaking, especially when the foreign systems had different rules.

From his initial premise that slavery was a stranger to the common law, Judge Dade moves on to assert that slavery has no connection to the English institution of villenage (an institution whereby subjects in medieval England paid dues and rendered services to his lord), and therefore no arguments could be made by analogy to it. But if such an analogy was permitted, Judge Dade argues that it would still not be a crime for a slave master to beat his slave. As a commercial practice with no ties to English custom or law, and introduced into the colony "at the mere will of the buyers and sellers," Judge Dade concludes, "the condition of the slave was that of uncontrolled and unlimited subjection to the will of the master."[32]

Judge William Brockenbrough disagrees with the court on the question of slavery's complete discontinuity with the common law, as well as the implication that the slave's humanity may be ignored in deference to the master's property right in the slave. He writes:

> It is true, that to the common law, slavery, except in the modified form of villenage, was unknown. But, the relations of superior and inferior, had their rules well established by that law. A master had the power to correct his servant; a parent, his child; and a tutor, his pupil; but the moment either of these persons transcended the bounds of due moderation, he was amenable to the law of the land, and might be prosecuted for the abuse of his authority, for his cruelty and inhumanity. When slaves were introduced, although the power conferred on the master by that relation, was much greater than that conferred by either of the others, yet the common law would easily adapt itself to this new relation. . . . The slave was not only a thing, but a person, and this well-known distinction would extend its protection to the slave as a person, except so far as the application of it conflicted with the enjoyment of the slave as a thing.[33]

Judge Brockenbrough believed not only that the proper course was to argue by analogy from other branches of the common law, as Alan Watson notes, but also that slavery was continuous with other human relationships recognized by the common law. His views clarify that the court's holding relies on the belief that slavery was anomalous from other human relationships. This disagreement over the fundamental nature of slavery continues until the present day.[34]

B. The Desultory Introduction of Slavery into the English Colonies Through Social Practice[35]

Although the first African settlers in North America arrived in Jamestown, Virginia, in 1619 where their official status within the colony, according to English colonial custom at that time, should have been as indentured servants, their arrival as "cargo" on a Dutch man-of-war seems to indicate that they were probably originally taken by the Dutch as slaves, possibly from Portuguese slave merchants.[36] In any event, the Dutch captain traded these Africans in exchange for food to the English governor of the Virginia colony, Sir George Yardley, who was also the proprietor of the thousand-acre Flowerdew Hundred plantation.[37] At the time of the arrival of these Africans, no slavery existed in the English colonies of North America, although the African slave trade had already been flourishing among the Portuguese and the Spanish for over a hundred years, since prior to the start of the sixteenth century. The English colonies used indentured servitude initially to supply their labor needs. Indentured servants were free persons who were either convicts sentenced to labor for a term of years, or the poor who contracted to labor for a term of years in order to pay their passage to the colonies, and sometimes included persons who had been kidnapped. For the next twenty years after the arrival of these African servants, no legal distinction was made between European and African indentured servants.

Statutory recognition of slavery in the English colonies of North America began first in Massachusetts in 1641,[38] followed by Connecticut, 1650; Virginia, 1661;[39] Maryland, New York, and New Jersey, 1664; South Carolina, 1682; Rhode Island and Pennsylvania, 1700; North Carolina, 1715; and Georgia, 1750. Prior to these enactments, there are indications that African slavery had already become part of the architecture of American colonial life, as well as the practice of treating Africans as an order of beings inferior to Europeans, and deserving of harsher treatment under the law than Europeans. For instance, in Virginia in 1630 a white man, Hugh Davis, was sentenced to be publicly whipped "for abusing himself to the dishonor of God and the shame of Christians by defiling his body in lying with a Negro," despite the fact that no legislation would be passed in the Virginia colony prohibiting sexual relations between whites and blacks until 1662.[40] It is also telling that in another Virginia case involving three runaway servants in 1640, the two European runaways, in addition to a whipping, were sentenced to serve out their indentures, but the African runaway was sentenced to serve his master for the time of his natural life.[41] And in 1639 Virginia passed legislation prohibiting blacks from bearing arms.[42]

Statutory recognition of the commercial practices of colonists who engaged in the traffic in slaves, however, was not equivalent to acceptance of all aspects of the trade as legitimate, much less the legislation of a comprehensive framework for the regulation of slavery and the slave trade. Indeed, the absence of a basis in law for determining who could be held as a slave (or for how long and with what consequences for civil liberties or progeny) led to some surprising reversals at the outset of establishing slave law in the English colonies of North America. For instance, in 1646 Massachusetts ordered the return to Africa at the public's expense of two enslaved persons who had been kidnapped from the Guinea coast by John Smith, a colonist.[43] In 1652 Rhode Island passed a statute that purported to limit the period of slavery for both blacks and whites to no more than ten years, although it seems that this law was never enforced.[44] In Virginia in 1655 Elizabeth Key, the daughter of an enslaved woman and an influential planter, successfully sued for her freedom on the grounds that 1) her father was a free man, and by common law she inherited her father's status; 2) she had been baptized as a Christian, asserting that no Christian could be a slave for life; and 3) she had been sold as a slave beyond the nine-year period of her indenture.[45]

In his study of this period, John Hope Franklin finds that the English colonists came to realize that white servants were unsatisfactory, and African slaves were preferable, for a number of reasons.[46] In his analysis Franklin concludes that the supply of white labor was insufficient to the demands of plantation crops such as tobacco, rice, and indigo. Additionally, the terms of service under indenture were a constant source of irritation since they often led to litigation against masters and ship captains for illegal detention. Finally, many indentured servants ran away to unsettled lands, making it difficult and expensive to apprehend them. On the other hand, because of their color, Africans who ran away were much easier to apprehend. Moreover, a planter could purchase enslaved Africans outright, and this helped to stabilize the labor supply in the colonies. It was easier to impose authoritarian and rigid controls on African slaves as they were outsiders to English cultural norms and moral beliefs. Still, an additional aspect in the preference for African slave labor was that they were cheaper to purchase, and the supply seemed inexhaustible in a period when economic considerations were vital.[47] In the end, it seems that the outsider status of Africans—who were both a minority among the colonists and perceived by them to be non-English, non-Christian, nonwhite, and without kinship ties within the community of settlers—led inexorably toward their oppression and exploitation.[48] But whatever the cause-and-effect relationship between anti-black prejudice and slavery, the historical record is clear that within the English colonies, legal enactment of slavery followed social practice rather than vice versa.

C. Formalization of the Relationship Between Master and Slave Through Legislation

The formal legal reduction of enslaved African persons to mere objects of property with no or few civil rights was accomplished slowly over the course of years through the passage of several statutes and court decisions. The period beginning near the middle of the seventeenth century through the start of the eighteenth century was an extremely active period for legislation, as European competition in an increasingly profitable slave trade flourished. In 1657 Virginia passed a statute authorizing the establishment of a militia to apprehend runaway servants, and another in 1659 reducing import duties on merchants bringing slaves into the colony. In 1660 Virginia made indentured servants who ran away with slaves liable for the loss of the slaves. In that same year, Maryland and Virginia passed laws under which white servants could buy their freedom, but African slaves could not. Additionally, Virginia passed a law limiting taxes on the sale of slaves in which enslaved Africans were referred to as "chattels."

Possibly in response to the Elizabeth Key's successful freedom suit, Virginia was the first colony to pass legislation reversing the common law rule that the status of children, whether slave or free, followed the status of their father. In 1662 Virginia enacted legislation requiring children to take on the status of their mothers. The so-called doctrine of *partus sequitur ventrem*, literally translated as "that which is brought forth follows the womb," was derived from Roman civil law, and while probably not an inherently racist mode of reckoning kinship, its invocation in the context of the expanding number of children born in the Virginia colony to enslaved African women and European men provided an inchoate racial definition of slavery. Because the admixture of African heritage was treated legally as an irredeemable deficiency in order to promote European commercial interests, this doctrine permitted white slave masters to increase their property in slaves by enslaving their own children born of enslaved African mothers. By the beginning of the eighteenth century, the doctrine of *partus sequitur ventrem* was the law in all the English colonies of North America.

In partial completion of the project of defining African heritage as racial deficiency, Maryland became the first colony in 1664 to pass legislation prohibiting marriage between men of African descent and freeborn English women.[49] Under the statute, the children of such marriages were to be considered slaves. Similar so-called anti-miscegenation laws followed in Virginia (1691), Massachusetts (1705), North Carolina (1715), South Carolina (1717), Delaware (1721), and Pennsylvania (1725). The same Maryland statute that prohibited interracial marriages between black men and white women declared that every black person currently residing in the colony and any who might enter in the future should be considered slaves *durante vita* (meaning for his or her lifetime).[50]

In 1667 Virginia passed a law declaring that conversion to Christianity did not alter a person's condition of bondage. And two years later, Virginia enacted a law that exempted from felony both masters and overseers who killed a slave while administering punishment to the slave.[51] The legislation of the Carolina colony in 1669 mirrored the path set by Virginia in declaring that "Every Freeman of Carolina shall have absolute power and authority over Negro slaves of what opinion or Religion soever."[52] In 1671 Maryland, New York, and New Jersey also passed laws negating any effect of Christian conversion on slave status.[53]

Virginia further codified black subordination in 1682 when it passed a law that prohibited the possession of weapons by slaves and restricted slaves from leaving their owner's premises without permission or attempting force, even in self-defense, against any white person. Under this law, runaway slaves could be killed without penalty if they refused to surrender themselves. As a leader in the codification of slave law, Virginia's law was copied by Maryland, Delaware, and North Carolina. By the end of the seventeenth century, the demand in the colonies for African slaves was so great that in 1698 the colonists were successful in lobbying the British Parliament to revoke the slave trading monopoly of the Royal African Company.[54] Thus, it became possible for colonial entrepreneurs to legally enter the slave-trading business and supply the needs of the colonies for more slaves.

The slave codes of the New England colonies were somewhat milder than their southern counterparts. By 1690 Massachusetts, Rhode Island, and Connecticut, for example, had codified the need for slaves to have written permission to leave their owner's premises, but no colony in New England denied the right of slave owners to manumit their slaves, although several did impose some restrictions on manumission. In all colonies, an enslaved person who struck a white person was severely punished, and the northern slave laws typically prohibited the sale of alcoholic beverages to slaves, as well as trading with slaves and harboring runaways. But unlike in the South, slaves and free white persons were subject to the same procedures in cases that involved the death penalty, and in Massachusetts and Connecticut enslaved persons and free whites were governed by the same courts and procedures in all criminal matters. Massachusetts even recognized the right of enslaved persons to own property and to sue their masters if it was taken away.

Virginia slave laws, by contrast, could not have been more intrusive on the prerogatives of slave owners, more subordinating of enslaved persons, or more racially provocative. In 1691 Virginia passed a law that prohibited any slave owner from freeing enslaved Africans without paying a bond for their transportation out of the colony, and in 1692 passed additional legislation that imposed banishment from the colony on any free white man or woman who married a black, a mulatto, or a Native American. The penalty was later changed to imprisonment for six months plus a fine of ten pounds. Under the same law, slaves were forbidden to keep horses, cattle, or hogs. Finally, slaves charged with a capital offense were to be tried without any jury, and could be convicted on the testimony of two witnesses under oath. Maryland, Delaware, and North Carolina eventually copied the Virginia laws of 1682 and 1692.

In 1702 New York passed a slave code that followed the pattern established in the English colonial slave law of the previous century by infringing on the prerogatives of slave owners in order to enforce criminal sanctions against rebellious enslaved persons. Its code provided that no more than three slaves could assemble without the consent of their owners, and that while slave owners retained broad discretion in punishing their slaves, an enslaved person who struck any free person could be confined for fourteen days and whipped. The slave population in New York City at this time was so numerous that a census showed as many as 43 percent of all whites in the city owned one or two slaves. In 1705 New York prescribed the death penalty for any slaves caught beyond a forty-mile line north of Albany. By 1706 New York had likewise adopted legislation enforcing *partus sequitur ventrem* for "all and every, Negro, Indian, Mulatto or Mestee" and denying slaves the right to testify in any case involving whites.[55]

As part of its law reform efforts, in 1705 Virginia collected all of its laws dealing with blacks under the title "Act Concerning Servants and Slaves." The act purported to define those who could be slaves under Virginia law. Its definition stated that servants "who could not make due proof of their being free in England, or any other Christian country, were to be accounted slaves."[56] The act included provisions that restricted the movement of blacks within the colony, prohibited intermarriage, and disqualified black persons for civil or military office. The act further defined slaves as attached to the soil, so that the heir to the plantation was entitled to purchase the inherited interests of others in the slaves. Under this Virginia law all slaves, at the time including Indian slaves, were considered to be real estate. In the same year, Virginia placed legal restrictions on the purchase of white servants by free blacks. The statute not only restricted black ownership of white Christian servants, but also declared automatically free any white Christian servant whose master married a black. Thus, Virginia law imposed a racial restriction on the property rights of free blacks in the colony: blacks could only own other blacks.[57]

In 1712 South Carolina revised its model slave code of 1690 that was mostly borrowed from the 1688 slave code written for the English settlement in Barbados.[58] Although revised several times thereafter, it remained the basic law of slavery in South Carolina until abolition. Other English colonies used this slave code as a model even as they modified it to suit their needs. In 1755 Georgia adopted the South Carolina slave code, and later Florida adopted the Georgia code. By contrast, the Virginia slave code, whose elements were somewhat different and reflect its ad hoc development over the course of decades, served as the model in the tobacco colonies of Maryland, Delaware, and North Carolina. The model slave code of South Carolina included the following provisions:

> Baptism in the Christian faith does not alter the status of a slave.
>
> Slaves are forbidden to leave the owner's property without written permission, unless accompanied by a white person.
>
> Every white person in the community is charged to chastise promptly any slave apprehended without permission to leave the owner's property.
>
> Any person enticing a slave to run away and any slave attempting to leave the province receives the death penalty as punishment.
>
> Any slave absconding or successfully evading capture for twenty days is to be publicly whipped for the first offense, branded with the letter R on the right cheek for the second offense, and lose one ear if absent thirty days for the third offense; and for the fourth offense, a male slave is to be castrated, a female slave is to be whipped, branded on the left cheek with the letter R, and lose her left ear.

Owners refusing to abide by the slave code or inflict specified punishment are to be fined and forfeit ownership of their slave(s).

The slave owner is obliged to pay the sum of four pounds for all
fugitives returned to the owner dead or alive by the commander of
any patrol company.

Slave houses are to be searched every fortnight for weapons and
stolen goods. For theft, the owner must punish the slave by whippings,
and for each additional theft, the punishment escalates—loss of one
ear, branding and nose slitting, and for the fourth offense, death.

No owner shall be punished if a slave dies under punishment; intentional killing of a slave shall cost the owner a fifty-pound fine.

No slave shall be allowed to work for pay; to plant corn, peas, or
rice; to keep hogs, cattle, or horses; to own or operate a boat; to buy or
sell; or to wear clothes finer than ordinary "Negro cloth."

In 1740 the following modifications were added to the code:

No slave shall be taught to write, work on Sunday, or work more than
fifteen hours per day in summer and fourteen hours in winter.

Willful killing of a slave exacts a fine of 700 pounds, and "passion"
killing, 350 pounds.

The fine for concealing runaway slaves is one thousand dollars and
a prison sentence of up to one year.

A fine of one hundred dollars and six months in prison is imposed
for employing any Black or slave as a clerk, anyone selling or giving
alcoholic beverages to slave, and for teaching a slave to read and write;
and death is the penalty for circulating incendiary literature.

Manumissions are forbidden except by deed, and after 1820, only
by permission of the legislature.[59]

All the English colonies of North America denied due process of law to
enslaved persons. Indeed, none of the traditional guarantees of English law
pertained to slaves, including denial of the writ of habeas corpus among the
southern slaveholding states.[60] Slaves were typically denied access to regular
courts, and blacks in general did not enjoy the benefits of jury trial, confron-
tation of witnesses, or counsel. Frequently in summary adjudications, no
court records were kept, which allowed for the use of conclusive presumptions, judgments based on insufficient evidence, and harsh punishment that
included whipping, maiming, castration, decapitation, dismemberment; or

execution through hanging and the burning of an enslaved person to death. In Virginia, Maryland, Mississippi, Missouri, Alabama, North Carolina, and Tennessee, slaves were barred from testifying against whites. Moreover, none of these restrictive slave laws were ever disallowed or overruled by the British Parliament, as was sometimes the case when a colony attempted to prevent the importation of slaves into its territory.

D. Continuities and Discontinuities after the Break from England: Slavery, Choice of Law, and the Need for Comity

While both the British Parliament and monarchy remained quiescent on the question of slavery's legality in the colonies, Lord Mansfield, Chief Justice of King's Bench, the highest common law court in England, declared slavery to be contrary to the common law of England in the celebrated case of *Somerset v. Stewart*.[61] The case involved an application for a writ of habeas corpus by James Somerset, a black man alleged to be the runaway slave of Charles Stewart. The writ was aimed at preventing Stewart from confining Somerset aboard a cargo ship on which he would later be transported to Jamaica for sale. Once his attempts to persuade the parties to moot the case failed, the Chief Justice eventually rendered an opinion that as reported included the following statements:

> [T]he only question before us is, whether the cause on the return [to the writ] is sufficient? If it is, the negro must be remanded; if it is not, he must be discharged. Accordingly, the return states, that the slave departed and refused to serve; whereupon he was kept, to be sold abroad. So high an act of dominion must be recognized by the law of the country where it is used. The power of a master over his slave has been extremely different, in different countries. The state of slavery is of such a nature, that it is incapable of being introduced on any reasons, moral or political; but only positive law, which preserves its force long after the reasons, occasion, and time itself from whence it was created, is erased from memory: It's so odious, that nothing can be suffered to support it but positive law. Whatever inconveniences, therefore, may follow from a decision, I cannot say this case is allowed or approved by the law of England; and therefore the black must be discharged.[62]

William Wiecek has examined the ways in which Lord Mansfield's *Somerset* opinion epitomizes both the features and problems of the judge-made law of slavery.[63] In comparison to the clear and specific statutes regulating the minutiae of behavior of blacks and whites under slave law, Professor Wiecek finds judge-made slave law to be indeterminate, ambiguous, equivocal, and in the end, uncertain. *Somerset* illustrates these defects. Lord Mansfield purported to address two narrow points of English law: whether a slave owner could forcibly seize a slave and remove him from the kingdom against the slave's will, and whether a slave could avail himself of the writ of habeas corpus (where a court orders that a prisoner is brought forth for a review of his detention) to prevent his seizure and removal. Nevertheless, in Wiecek's assessment, "*Somerset* burst the confines of Lord Mansfield's judgment."[64] The decision, in both its *ratio decidendi* (meaning the legal principle upon which a specific case is decided) and its rhetoric, fed the burgeoning appetite for anti-slavery law reform in England and in its American colonies., If any doubt remained, *Somerset* confirmed at the end of the eighteenth century that the relation between commercially and politically interdependent jurisdictions that alternately permit and prohibit slavery must lead eventually to a circumstance where slavery must either be accommodated and accepted everywhere or repudiated altogether.

The choice of law questions posed by *Somerset* ominously raised not only the legitimacy of slavery anywhere, whether in England or her colonies, but also the possibility that for commercial reasons alone the colonial tail could end up wagging the metropolitan dog.[65] Wealthy colonial merchants frequently sought to spend time to domicile in the mother country, and of course, they brought select members of their household slaves with them from the colonies. At the time of Lord Mansfield's *Somerset* decision, there were between fourteen and fifteen thousand slaves residing in the British Isles.[66] The fear among British slave owners generated by the protean possibilities of *Somerset* included the fear that the high court might set all these slaves free within the scope of a single judicial pronouncement. Lord Mansfield acknowledged this fear when he declared in apparent frustration of the parties' unwillingness to settle: "If the parties will have judgment, *fiat justitia, ruat coelum*"[67] (meaning let justice be done, though heaven falls).

Heaven did not fall as a result of *Somerset*. Having been decided on the eve of the successful American war of independence, however, it set a critical jurisprudential framework for future judicial decisions among the soon-to-be-established American states over questions of comity and choice of law in determining the status of enslaved persons brought voluntarily from a slave state to a non-slaveholding state, as opposed to those who might have escaped against their masters' will. Since chattel slavery, consistently with *Somerset*, was deemed by American courts to be contrary to both common law and natural right, its toleration in non-slaveholding states and territories was treated as a matter of comity shown toward the foreign positive law or municipal enactments of slave state jurisdictions.[68]

As Diane Klein has shown, the conception of comity in non-slaveholding state courts leading up to the civil war could, in some instances, be less tolerant than even their postbellum views.[69] This was due in part to the fact that the grant of enforcement of extraterritorial laws by a forum state had always been viewed as subject to an exception based on the public policy of the forum state. Traditionally, comity implied a relation of toleration and enlightened self-interest among separate sovereigns for the official acts of sister states, rather than the recognition of a legal obligation.[70] Thus, it was always possible that some official act or institution of a foreign jurisdiction might be held to violate the public policy of a forum state in which the act was sought to be enforced or the institution was sought to be recognized as legally binding. As Klein explains:

> From the beginning, states reserved to themselves the power to decline enforcement of truly repugnant out-of-state agreements, reminding the world at large that the enforcing court exercised its power in support of the out-of-state or "foreign" contract as a matter of comity only, of something like self-interested and pragmatic friendliness between two states, and not out of any felt or real sense of constitutional or other legal obligation.[71]

Somerset's choice of law legacy, to the common law jurisdictions of America on the issue of the legal effect of voluntary movement of enslaved persons from jurisdictions that did permit human bondage into those that did not, lasted up until the Supreme Court's disastrous *Dred Scott* decision, which in turn set the states divided by the issue of slavery on a path to civil war and the eventual, formal abolition of slavery.[72]

III. TYPOLOGY OF WRONGFUL ENSLAVEMENT SUITS PRIOR TO ABOLITION

Prior to the abolition of slavery, state slave law statutes and judicial decisions established the parameters of how wrongful enslavement claims might be brought, the elements of successful claims, and the extent of restitution, if any, required to be paid by purported masters found guilty of wrongfully enslaving a free person. Unsurprisingly, state slave laws made the prize of freedom exceedingly difficult to obtain through adoption of trial procedures that favored the continuance of slavery on racial grounds, limitation of the causes of action that could form the basis of a wrongful enslavement claim, and minimization of the monetary awards that successful plaintiffs could expect in restitution for their wrongful enslavement.

While acknowledging the legitimacy of perpetual racial slavery under municipal law, lawmakers in both the North and the South recognized that a person could become wrongfully enslaved in a number of ways: through the kidnapping of free blacks, through manumissions in a master's will that were not subsequently carried out by the executor of the master's estate, through the conversion of a term of service into perpetual service for persons ineligible by law for slavery—typically by means of fraudulent sales to unsuspecting buyers—or through breach of promise to set an enslaved person free upon payment of a sum certain upon attaining a specified age. Proof of a free maternal ancestor or proof that one's ancestors were not black but Indian was deemed sufficient to render a person ineligible for enslavement. After the decision in *Somerset*, voluntary travel to and residence in a free territory or jurisdiction was sometimes also sufficient to render an enslaved person free in the eyes of the law.[73]

Following the decision in *Somerset*, moreover, a division could be made between northern courts on the one hand, which generally permitted advocates of the wrongfully enslaved to bring habeas corpus claims, and southern courts and legislatures on the other hand—with the exceptions of Louisiana and Texas—which denied enslaved petitioners access to the common law writs of habeas corpus and *de homine replegiando* (meaning to release someone believed to be illegally held against his will). Southerners deemed the common law writs to be a threat to the right of property in an enslaved person. In *Daniel v. Guy*, the Supreme Court of Arkansas explained why the state legislature denied slaves, as persons belonging to the Negro race were presumed to be, the benefit of habeas corpus. Writing for the court, Chief Justice English explained: "The reason for denying slaves the benefit of *habeas corpus*, is manifest. They are property as well as persons, and if they could be discharged from bondage by a judge in vacation or term, the owner might be deprived of property without due course of law, there being no provision for trial by jury, etc., on the hearing of the writ of *habeas corpus*."[74]

Southern courts also frowned upon granting a writ of *de homine replegi-ando* to enslaved petitioners, even though, as a form of the writ of *replevin*, which permits a property owner to recover wrongfully detained property, jury trials for claims asserted under this writ were allowed. The additional feature of both writs that southern courts and legislatures found trouble-some included the possibility that the alleged slave might be set free pend-ing the outcome of the case to the prejudice of the alleged master's inter-est in the enslaved person's labor. In the Freedom Suit Act of 1795, Virginia abolished access to both of these common law writs for enslaved persons who were not in possession of documents of freedom.[75] Maryland, however, while it denied habeas corpus, granted that courts had jurisdiction to per-mit writs *de homine replegiando* to enslaved persons.[76]

In contrast to the North, southern states mandated that manumission suits be filed as common law tort actions. Enslavement was *prima facie tor-tious* since the common law defense of moderate correction was rejected in the case of slaves in favor of a higher degree of physical dominion.[77] The enslaved petitioners in an action at law would either allege assault and bat-tery or false imprisonment—using the archaic form of *trespass vi et armis* (meaning someone illegally used violence and caused injury to another). Moreover, the successful plaintiff in an intentional tort suit normally would be entitled to receive compensation, where the measure of recovery would be the amount necessary to restore the plaintiff to the status quo ante, and possibly even punitive damages for wanton misconduct. However, the courts in Virginia, Maryland, and Louisiana either denied successful claim-ants in wrongful enslavement cases any compensatory damages or only permitted the payment of nominal damages.[78]

Alternatively, advocates for enslaved persons in Southern courts could waive the tort and claim *indebitatus assumpsit* (meaning someone assumes the obligation of another) in an action at equity. This type of suit would be considered an action in restitution for the value of services rendered, as if there had been a labor contract between the enslaved person and his owner. In such an action, the defendant would be permitted to offset the plaintiff's recovery by the value of goods, services, or money already furnished to the plaintiff while enslaved.[79]

South Carolina and Georgia adopted statutes giving the guardian of wrongful enslavement claimants the right to bring an action of trespass in the nature of ravishment of ward.[80] The disadvantage for the wrongfully enslaved plaintiff under this form of action was that the plaintiff remained enslaved and at the mercy of his purported master *pendente lite* (meaning

awaiting the outcome of the trial). By contrast, Missouri adopted an inge-
nious procedure to mitigate the seeming unfairness of requiring a wrongfully enslaved plaintiff to remain with his purported master until the outcome of the case could be determined: the court would order the enslaved
person be hired out to a third party during the pendency of his suit for
freedom.[81] If the plaintiffs were successful in proving wrongful enslavement,
they would be entitled to the fund created by their employment. If plaintiffs
were unsuccessful, the fund created by their employment would be turned
over to the defendant. In *Gordon v. Duncan* the court asserted that, in cases
such as these, "nothing for indignity" would be paid to the wrongfully enslaved plaintiff, unless the litigant could show a wanton violation of liberty,
thus implying that a purported master was entitled to a presumption of
good faith.[82]

The requirement of securing a *guardian ad litem* (court-appointed
guardian in cases where infants or minors were parties) willing to sue on
behalf of persons who claimed to be wrongfully enslaved was based on the
precept that slaves as property could neither sue nor be sued under the
civil law.[83] In South Carolina and Georgia the requirement of a *prochain
ami* (meaning close friend or relative), willing to take on the enslaved person's cause in protracted and expensive legal battles, was established by
statute. Tennessee established this requirement as a matter of common
law.[84] These procedural hurdles, coupled with common restrictions on the
ability of slaves to offer testimony except against other slaves, effectively
limited the substantive right of enslaved persons to sue for freedom. In
many southern jurisdictions, even free blacks could not offer testimony
against any white person.

In modern terms, the requirement of securing a legal guardian—which
in effect amounted to the need for enslaved blacks to win the sympathies of
free whites—functioned as a rule of racial standing. Standing refers to the
constitutionally based requirement that plaintiffs allege a personal injury,
fairly traceable to the defendant's allegedly unlawful conduct, and likely to
be redressed by the requested relief.[85] As chattel property slaves had no right
to sue on their own behalf, and thus had no standing to complain of personal injuries done to them by persons presumed in law to be tortfeasors
(meaning a person who commits a tort). To say that a slave had no standing
was another way of characterizing the rule that the "next friend" of the slave
would act as guardian since the slave was incompetent. But a deeper point
should be observed in connection to this point of law, *viz.* that when the
slave's injury was fresh, and the tortfeasor was under the jurisdiction of the

courts, restitution was often refused to the wrongfully enslaved based on a kind of immunity based on race, characterized as good faith.

The Doctrine of the Master's Good Faith

In addition to denying what amounts to legal standing to persons claiming to have been wrongfully enslaved, the doctrine of the master's good faith and the presumption in favor of enslavement for those of servile color offered a kind of immunity to purported owners of slaves from the normal requirement of paying restitution as tortfeasors. Andrew Kull's research reveals that while there were some cases where a formerly enslaved person was permitted to recover restitution, he also finds that "in jurisdictions where slavery was currently recognized [the South]—as opposed to those in which slavery had previously been abolished [the North]—American courts followed a uniform, anomalous rule."[86] One Kentucky court coined the term "conventional exemption" to denominate the rule.[87] The rule was that successful claimants in wrongful enslavement suits would not be permitted to recover the value of their services while wrongfully enslaved if the defendant had acted in "good faith," that is, believed that the enslaved person was really his slave. Kentucky later codified the rule by statute, making liable only the master who acted in "bad faith."[88]

Courts in Louisiana, Virginia, and Maryland also denied successful freedom claimants the right to damage judgments in connection with a finding of wrongful enslavement. Andrew Fede traces the Virginia rule to the leading case of *Pleasants v. Pleasants*.[89] As Fede points out, "this no damages rule gave a dual benefit to the slaveholder defendants; they did not need to pay damages in tort, as if the form of action were a writ of *habeas corpus*, and they did not have to comply with the pretrial procedures in a *habeas corpus* proceeding, as if the action really were a tort action in trespass."[90]

And although Georgia and South Carolina did permit wrongfully enslaved persons to recover damages, they also required the plaintiff's next friend to seek damages in the freedom suit, rather than first establishing freedom and then seeking restitution from the tortfeasor defendant afterwards. If the next friend of the wrongfully enslaved person failed to join the damage action in the proceeding to establish freedom, the claim for damages could be denied based on the statute of limitations.[91] Only the courts in Tennessee permitted serial litigation, first on the issue of freedom, and next on the issue of damages.[92]

When nineteenth-century courts refused, on the ground of the master's good faith, to award restitution to plaintiffs of African descent who had been adjudicated to be wrongfully enslaved, the courts thereby refused to do ordinary justice that would have been done had the plaintiffs been white.[93] Moreover, they did so at a time when none of the procedural obstacles currently advanced against reparations were extant: no problem of standing for the plaintiff (other than post hoc discriminatory guardianship rules that demeaned the personhood of the enslaved), no problem of locating a culpable defendant, no problem of complex calculations of benefit or need for tracing distant or dissipated assets, and no problem of statutory time limits.

On the question of the applicability of time limits to slavery-era damage claims, however, in 1869, not more than four years after the end of the Civil War and passage of the Thirteenth Amendment abolishing slavery in the United States, the Supreme Court of Georgia sought to demarcate a temporal boundary that continues until the present day. In *Green v. Anderson*,[94] the court was asked to resolve a dispute between an heir, John Anderson, and the executor of the will, Moses Green. The testator of the will had been the master and owner of John and his mother, Louisa, prior to the war when John was still a minor. He bequeathed freedom to them both in his will and provided that a small amount of his estate be dedicated to their support. Rather than fulfill these terms, Moses Green denied Louisa her pension and denied John his freedom and the funds intended for his education and support, until the Civil War settled the question of John Anderson's freedom. Anderson then sued Green to enforce the terms of his former master's will with respect to his mother's pension and his own trust. Chief Justice Joseph E. Brown, writing for the court, held that the bequest was legally made under the laws of Georgia, both at the time of its creation and as of the date of the ensuing litigation, and that John Anderson had standing to enforce the trust created under his master's will as to his own bequest.

Nevertheless, the court found it necessary to disavow in part the suggestion of John Anderson's counsel that as a formerly enslaved person, John had the right to sue in Georgia state courts for any legacy given to him while being used as a slave. The court agreed that he could enforce the terms of his master's will that were in his favor, but that was a separate matter from seeking any tort damages for wrongful enslavement, or for wages during the period when he was kept as a slave. The court, therefore, expressed its holding precisely thus: "We hold that a freedman of legal age, may commence proceedings to enforce, in the Courts of this State, any existing legal or equitable right, created in his favor while he was a slave, that did not then contravene the policy or violate the laws of the State."[95]

The meaning of "then" in the court's holding is the temporal boundary referred to above. It refers to the time when slavery was legal, and slaves had no rights in their labor, and no rights in their persons that could be enforced against their masters or any white person. The court was quite conscious of how its procedural ruling was meant to affect substantive rights by interpreting the freedom and legacy of the freedman for him: "By his transition from slavery to freedom, no such right of the owner [to recover damages for injuries received during slavery] transferred to him." Thus, in the court's opinion, the statute of limitations, which "forever barred and foreclosed" such suits unless already instituted, was a mere jurisprudential afterthought.

IV. CONCLUSION

The law created a double standard based on the claimant's perceived racial appearance while confirming the master's unique power—within a system of regulations—to protect slavery as an institution, to grant or deny privileges to the enslaved, to manumit or to continue to enslave, to inflict cruel and excessive punishments or to be lenient, and to take the slave's life, limbs, sex, possessions, or kin with or without "reason" or consent.

With so much put at stake by the law between the status of free or enslaved, and consequently between black or white, the notion that in addition to a grant of freedom, damages ought to be paid to those found by courts to have been wrongfully enslaved, does indeed seem to be a solecism (or mistake). Why indeed should the legal double standard end with the presumptions of freedom and enslavement, and not extend as well to the damages to be paid to someone previously, if erroneously, held in slavery? The general contempt heaped on the heads of the enslaved was certainly broad enough to encompass a denial of damages to wrongfully enslaved petitioners. Continuation of the doctrine that no restitution is owed to those enslaved, or their descendants, suggests that less has changed in the contemporary understanding of the wrongfulness of slavery than might be supposed based on abolition alone.

NOTES

1. *Green v. Anderson*, 38 Georgia 655 (1869).

2. See Ariela J. Gross, "When is the Time of Slavery? The History of Slavery in Contemporary Legal and Political Argument," 96 *California Law Review* 283 (2008): 311.

3. 36 Tennessee 397, 4 Sneed 397 (1857). See also *State v. Mann*, 13 North Carolina 263, 2 Dev. 263 (1829) (hirer of slave permitted to batter slave as would the owner).

4. 60 U.S. (19 How.) 393 (1857).

5. See Christopher Eisgruber, "The Story of Dred Scott v. Sandford: Originalism's Forgotten Past," in Michael C. Dorf, ed., *Constitutional Law Stories*, 2nd ed. (New York: Foundation Press, 2009), 157–61.

6. See infra, note 71 and accompanying text discussing distinction between "freedom suits" and "manumission."

7. Cf. *Gordon v. Duncan*, 3 Missouri 385, 387 (1834) (successful plaintiff in freedom suit entitled to fund created by hiring out his labor services *pendente lite*). See also Andrew Kull, "Restitution in Favor of Former Slaves," *Boston University Law Review* 1277 (2004): 84, n. 19.

8. *Gordon v. Duncan*, 387.

9. 60 U.S. (19 How.) 393.

10. John L. T. Sneed, ed., *Tennessee Reports: Reports of Cases Argued and Determined in the Supreme Court of Tennessee*, vol. 36 (St. Louis: G.I. Jones, 1878), 398.

11. See Andrew Fede, *People Without Rights: An Interpretation of the Fundamentals of the Law of Slavery in the U.S. South* (New York: Garland, 1992).

12. Andrew Fede, *Roadblocks to Freedom: Slavery and Manumission in the United States South* (New Orleans: Quid Pro Books, 2011), iv. More pointedly, Alan Watson writes, "Procedure for slaves' crimes was more summary, penalties were more severe when the offender was a slave, and there were crimes that in effect could only be committed by slaves." Alan Watson, *Slave Law in the Americas* (Athens: University of Georgia Press, 1989), 72.

13. See Thomas R. R. Cobb, *An Inquiry Into the Law of Negro Slavery in the United States of America* (New York: T. & J. W. Johnson, 1858; Reprint, 1968), 248.

14. See Benjamin Joseph Klebaner, *American Manumission Laws and the Responsibility for Supporting Slaves*, Virginia Magazine of History and Biography 63, no. 4 (October 1955): 443–53.

15. *Pleasants v. Pleasants*, 6 Virginia 319, 2 Call 319 (1799).

16. See A. Leon Higginbotham Jr. and Greer C. Bosworth, "Rather Than the Free: Free Blacks in Colonial and Antebellum Virginia," 26 *Harvard Civil Rights-Civil Liberties Law Review* 17 (Winter 1991).

17. See, e.g., *Hudgins v. Wrights*, 11 Virginia (1 Hen. & M.) 134 (Virginia 1806).

18. See Mark Graber, *Dred Scott and the Problem of Constitutional Evil* (Cambridge: Cambridge University Press, 2006).

19. *In re African-American Slave Descendants Litigation*, 471 F. 3d 754 (7th Cir. 2006).

20. A representative sample of useful historical literature would include: Taunya Lovell Banks, "Dangerous Woman: Elizabeth Key's Freedom Suit—Subjecthood and Racialized Identity in Seventeenth Century Colonial Virginia," 41 *Akron Law Review* 799 (2008); Eric Gardner, "'You have no business to whip me': The Freedom Suits of Polly Wash and Lucy Ann Delaney," 41 *African American Review* 33, no. 1 (2007); Andrew Kull, "Restitution in Favor of Former Slaves," 84 *Boston University Law Review* 1277 (2004); Paul Finkelman, "The Centrality of the Peculiar Institution in American Legal

Development," 68 *Chicago-Kent Law Review* 1009 (1993); Angela Onwuachi-Willig, "The Story of Hudgins v. Wrights," in Rachel F. Moran and Devon W. Carbado, ed., *Race Law Stories* (New York: Foundation Press, 2008), 147; Fede, *Roadblocks to Freedom.*

21. See Gross, "When Is the Time of Slavery?"

22. See Robert Westley, "The Accursed Share: Genealogy, Temporality, and the Problem of Value in Black Reparations Discourse," 92 *Representations* 81 (Fall 2005): 106.

23. See Stephen Best and Saidiya Hartman, "Fugitive Justice," 92 *Representations* 1 (Fall 2005).

24. Gross, 287–303.

25. Ibid.

26. 375 F. Supp. 2d, 780.

27. Ibid.

28. Watson, *Slave Law in the Americas.*

29. 26 Virginia (5 Rand.) 678 (1827).

30. Ibid.

31. Ibid., 680.

32. Ibid., 681.

33. Ibid., 688–89.

34. See Fede, at 8 (observing that Jedediah Purdy has coined the terms "the anomaly model" and "the conciliatory model" to describe the difference between those who believe that slavery was fundamentally different from other forms of human relationships and those who believe that slavery lay along a spectrum analogous to other legal bonds), citing *The Meaning of Property: Freedom, Community, and the Legal Imagination* (New Haven: Yale University Press, 2010). Fede himself argues in favor of the anomaly model.

35. Except where indicated, the historical details included in subsections II (B) and (C) are based on the account given in Charles M. Christian, *Black Saga: The African American Experience, A Chronology* (Jackson, TN: Basic Civitas Books, 1995).

36. See Edmund S. Morgan, *American Slavery, American Freedom: The Ordeal of Colonial Virginia* (New York: W. W. Norton, 1975), 297–307, *passim.* Morgan notes that "probably the first known Negroes to arrive [in Virginia], in 1619, were slaves," and further explaining the grounds for believing that the Dutch would be the vendors of slaves to English colonies in the West Indies and on the mainland.

37. See James Deetz, *Flowerdew Hundred: The Archaeology of a Virginia Plantation 1619-1864* (Charlottesville: University of Virginia Press, 1993).

38. See Winthrop Jordan, *White Over Black: American Attitudes Toward the Negro, 1550-1812* (Chapel Hill: University of North Carolina Press, 1968), 67; Max Farrand, ed., *The Laws and Liberties of Massachusetts* (Cambridge: Harvard University Press, 1929), 4. But cf. id. at 74–75 arguing that Maryland passed a statute in 1639 that exempted (presumably Negro) slaves from the rights, liberties, immunities, and privileges of the English.

39. Jordan, *White Over Black*, 81. Jordan cites William Waller Hening, ed., *The Statutes at Large Being a Collection of All the Laws of Virginia*, 13 vols. (1809-23; Reprint, Kalamazoo: University of Michigan, 2009) I, 539, II, 26.

40. Jordan, *White Over Black*, 78–80 (proposing that the "negro" in question may not have been female).

41. Ibid., 75.

42. Ibid., 78.

43. Ibid., 69–70.

44. Ibid., 70–71.

45. See Banks, "Dangerous Woman."

46. John Hope Franklin and Alfred A. Moss Jr., *From Slavery to Freedom: A History of Negro Americans*, 6th ed. (New York: Alfred A. Knopf, 1988), 32.

47. On the economic value of slaves over indentured servants, see also Morgan, *American Slavery*, 299–308. Morgan claimed that "the point at which it became more advantageous for Virginians to buy slaves was probably reached by 1660."

48. See Jordan, *White Over Black*, 80–82. Jordan describes the symbiosis between anti-black prejudice and slavery in Maryland and Virginia that dynamically "join[ed] hands to hustle the Negro down the road to complete degradation." Jordan suggests that this interactive growth, rather than the borrowing of the enslavement practices of other societies, explains the nature of African slavery on these mainland English colonies.

49. Ibid., 79.

50. Ibid., 81.

51. Ibid., 82.

52. Ibid., 85.

53. Ibid., 92.

54. See Morgan, *American Slavery*, 299.

55. See A. Leon Higginbotham, *In the Matter of Color: Race and the American Legal Process: The Colonial Period* (New York: Oxford University Press, 1978), 100–149; Edgar J. McManus, *A History of Negro Slavery in New York* (New York: Syracuse University Press, 1966), 79–99.

56. See Jordan, *White Over Black*, 82.

57. Ibid., 94.

58. For the influence of Barbados on the development of South Carolina slave law, see Jordan, *White Over Black*, 84–85. See also Watson, *Slave Law in the Americas*, 68–76.

59. Fede, supra note 12, at 97–98.

60. Texas and Louisiana are the exceptions. See Fede, *Roadblocks to Freedom*, 153.

61. Lofft 1, 98 Eng. Rep. 499 (K.B. 1772).

62. Lofft at 19, 98 Eng. Rep. at 510.

63. William M. Wiecek, "Somerset: Lord Mansfield and the Legitimacy of Slavery in the Anglo-American World," 42 *University of Chicago Law Review* 86, no. 1 (Autumn 1974): 87.

64. Ibid., 108.

65. England was economically dependent on her colonies for trade, and many of England's colonists were dependent on slave labor for economic survival, if not upward mobility.

66. See Wiecek, supra note 61, 95.

67. *Somerset v. Stewart*, 98 Eng. Rep. (1772), 509.

68. See Diane J. Klein, "Paying Eliza: Comity, Contracts, and Critical Race Theory—19th Century Choice of Law Doctrine and the Validation of Antebellum Contracts for the Purchase and Sale of Human Beings," 20 *National Black Law Journal* 1 (2007).

69. Ibid., 12–15, citing *Hone v. Ammons* 14 Illinois 29 (1852) (refusing to uphold the terms of a contract for sale of an enslaved person on public policy grounds) and *Rodney v. Illinois Central* 19 Illinois 42 (1857) (refusing to uphold claims for civil damages in the case of a runaway enslaved person on public policy grounds). Klein, "Paying Eliza," 16–17, cites *Roundtree v. Baker* 52 Illinois 241 (1869) (upholding the terms of a contract for sale of an enslaved person after passage of the Thirteenth Amendment abolishing slavery).

70. Klein, "Paying Eliza," 4–5. Explains the development of comity in relation to contract principles, its application to the antebellum American interstate context, and its traditional public policy exception.

71. Ibid.

72. On the facts, Dred Scott was voluntarily taken by his purported master from the state of Missouri, where human bondage was legal, into territories that prohibited slavery. Both the state Supreme Court of Missouri and Justice Taney for the majority in the federal case rejected the common law rule that the voluntary removal of Scott to a territory that prohibited slavery voided his enslavement.

73. Litigation based on travel to or residence in a free jurisdiction is properly characterized as a "freedom suit," since it was most often contrary to the will of the master. By contrast, manumission suits are conceptually distinct even if the ultimate issue to be decided was the freedom of the litigants. Manumission expressed the will of the master.

74. See *Daniel v. Guy*, 19 Arkansas 121, 132, 1857 WL 545 (1857) (under state statute all persons permitted to file writs of habeas corpus except a "negro or mulatto held as a slave"). *Accord Clark v. Gautier*, 8 Florida 360 (1859); *Weddington v. Sloan*, 54 Kentucky (15 B. Mon.) 147 (1854); *Field v. Walker*, 17 Alabama 80 (1849); *Thornton v. DeMoss*, 13 Mississippi 609 (1846); *Ex. parte Renney v. Mayfield*, 5 Tennessee (4 Hay.) 165 (1817).

75. See *Nicholas v. Burruss*, 31 Virginia (4 Leigh) 289, 298, 1833 WL 2087 (1833).

76. See *Johnson v. Medtart*, 4 H. & J. 24, 1815 WL 274 (Maryland 1815).

77. See *James v. Carper*, 36 Tennessee 397, 4 Sneed 397 (1857) and *State v. Mann*, 13 North Carolina 263, 2 Dev. 263 (1829).

78. For the law in Maryland and Virginia, see Andrew Kull, "Restitution in Favor of Former Slaves," 84 *Boston University Law Review* 1277, no. 19 (2004), 1282–86, citing *Pleasants v. Pleasants*, 6 Virginia (2 Call) 319, 356 (1800), *Peter v. Hargrave*, 46 Virginia (5 Gratt 12) 12 (1848), *Queen v. Ashton*, 3 H. & McH. 439 (1796), *State v. Van Lear*, 5 Maryland 91 (1853), *Franklin v. Waters*, 8 Gill 322, 328 (Maryland 1849), and *Jason v. Henderson*, 7 Maryland 430, 441–42 (1855); and for the law in Louisiana, see Judith Kelleher Schafer, *Slavery, the Civil Law, and the Supreme Court of Louisiana* (Baton Rouge: Louisiana State University Press, 1994), 245, citing *Delphine v. Guillet*, No. 4249, 11 Louisiana Ann. 424 (1856) and article 177 of the Civil Code of 1825.

79. See Kull, "Restitution in Favor of Former Slaves."

80. For the South Carolina statute, see transcription from David J. McCord, ed., *The Statutes at Large of South Carolina*, vol. 7 (1840): 397–98. For the Georgia statute, see William M. Wiecek, "The Statutory Law of Slavery and Race in the Thirteen Mainland Colonies of British America," *William and Mary Quarterly* 34.2 (1977): 258, 265. See also *Knight v. Hardeman*, 17 Georgia 253, 256–57, 1855 WL 1818 (1855) (for the 1770, 1835, and 1837 acts); Steven M. Wise, "The Entitlement of Chimpanzees to the Common Law Writs of *Habeas Corpus* and *De Homine Replegiando*," 37 *Golden Gate University Law Review* (2006): 219.

81. See *Gordon v. Duncan*, 3 Missouri, 385 (1834). See also *Daniel v. Roper*, 24 Arkansas 131, 134 (1863).

82. *Gordon v. Duncan*, 386.

83. See Catherine Bodine's Will, 34 Kentucky (4 Dana) 476, 1836 WL 2089 (1836).

84. See Fede, *Roadblocks to Freedom*, 140–41. Fede cites *Doran v. Brazelton*, 32 Tennessee (2 Swan) 149, 1852 WL 1834 (1852).

85. See *Cato v. U.S.* 70 F.3d 1103, 1109 (9th Cir. 1995).

86. See Kull, "Restitution in Favor of Former Slaves." See also *Hickham v. Hickham*, 46 Missouri App. 496 (Ct. App. 1891); *Handy v. Clark*, 9 Delaware (4 Houst.) 16 (1869); *Kinney v. Cook*, 4 Illinois (3 Scam.) 231 (1841).

87. *Aleck v. Tevis*, 34 Kentucky (4 Dana) 242, 250 (1836).

88. See Act of February 12, 1840, ch. 282, §2, 1839 Kentucky Acts 173.

89. 6 Virginia (2 Hen. & M.) 193, 1808 WL 578 (1808). See Fede, *Roadblocks to Freedom*, 350–51.

90. *Pleasants v. Pleasants*, 6 Virginia (2 Hen. & M.) 193.

91. See *Daniel v. Roper*, 24 Arkansas 131, 1863 WL 440 (1863).

92. See *Woodfolk v. Sweeper*, 21 Tennessee (2 Hum.) 88 (1840); *Matilda v. Crenshaw*, 12 Tennessee (4 Yerg.) 249 (1833).

93. See *Aleck v. Tevis*, 34 Kentucky (4 Dana) 242, 248-49 (1836).

94. 38 Georgia 655 (1869).

95. Ibid., 662.

3

EMANCIPATION FROM WHITENESS
Witnessing Disability and Jubilee

DAVID R. ROEDIGER

IN CONCLUDING HIS PIONEERING STUDY OF SLAVERY, THE HISTORIAN
George Rawick reflected not only on the span of U.S. history but also on Reconstruction. He argued that "the pressure of blacks for equality" after the
Civil War consistently "intensified" class conflicts in the country.[1] Rawick's
observations are intriguing, but they leave us with questions as to why this
should be the case. The twentieth-century African American novelist James
Baldwin, writing in the wake of the modern civil rights movement, made
a similar observation. Baldwin trusted no automatic spread of impulses toward freedom across the color line. Long after the high points of civil rights
struggles, he still felt the need to invite the "white man [to] become a part of
that suffering and dancing country he now watches wistfully."[2] Such a move
seemed to Baldwin to be a precursor for changes in the outcomes of struggles for justice and in the inner lives of whites, whom Baldwin regarded as
being both in misery and denial.

During the period under consideration in this essay, a profound deepen-
ing of the stakes in social struggles among whites apparently did happen.
Historians and African Americans viewed the rebuilding of the South after the Civil War differently. What scholars came to refer to as the Reconstruction Period, African Americans called the time of Jubilee. Not only
did slaves win their freedom in the Civil War, white workers also built an
unprecedented national labor movement around the visionary demand of
an eight-hour working day. Women meanwhile mounted the first serious
national campaign for suffrage and undertook an unprecedented public
discussion of domestic violence in their homes. These staggering developments were so beholden to the slave's self-emancipation that the latter was
what Karl Marx referred to in an address to U.S. workers at the time as the

"moral impetus . . . to your class movement" and of other movements as well.[3]

The emancipation of slaves inspired working-class whites to imagine their freedom. They to some extent joined the mass of suffering humanity. They could no longer take for granted the ideological connections of whiteness with independence and with the ability that had been hard-wired into antebellum U.S. nationalism. This essay illustrates that emancipation not only freed enslaved African Americans after the war, it provided an "emancipation from whiteness."[4] Furthermore, it argues that the terrible costs of the war simultaneously included disillusionment and despair. Both intensified the short-lived and necessarily contradictory efforts by whites to imagine and to pursue new freedoms for themselves.

The first section of this essay grounds its contributions to studying the Civil War and its aftermath in disability studies, and especially in the scholarship of the historian Douglas Baynton. Baynton's work provides a guide to how various forms of oppression connect, and to the specific role of ability and disability in shaping post–Civil War discourses regarding equality. The second section offers a brief history of the glorious coming of emancipation as an alternative to the bleak realities of wartime destruction. The self-active seeking of freedom by slaves and nominally free blacks saturated U.S. culture during and just after the war. Such motion made possible a brief emancipation from whiteness by the end of the war.

WHITENESS, ABILITY, CARNAGE

Douglas Baynton is a historian of whiteness and disability. His essay on disability and inequality critiques whiteness in a way that parallels Cheryl Harris in her treatment of whiteness as property. His arguments reinforce the conclusions reached by Harris regarding the assumptions of whites about their entitlement to power. They argue that white privilege was the natural order of things and that even whites with meager resources shared a belief in their superiority over blacks. Baynton begins his investigation with presumptions about victims of white male power. He shows that in order to fight for equal rights, African Americans, women, and immigrants challenged arguments of their disability. To secure civil rights, African Americans disputed that they lacked intelligence and reason. They rejected claims of their likely disability once emancipated and enfranchised. Women also challenged the assertion of female irrationality, hysteria, and weakness. They rejected claims that civil rights made them "monstrous."[5]

White men did not make defensive arguments. Indeed, the nation's republican experiment predicated itself on the independence not only of the new nation, but also of its white male citizens. Increasingly, the enfranchised came to include unpropertied white men, so that race and gender grounded civil rights explicitly. Consequently, "whiteness as property" was enough to enable full political citizenship for white males even in the absence of ownership of wealth. White men constituted the vigorous—those able to productively "husband" the land, justifying settler colonial dispossession of Indians; able to own and supposedly control their own labor; able to own property; able to rule households; able to "master" slaves, and able to vote. Such ideology elided differences of class among whites, as many scholars have noted. Baynton's insights underline that it further omitted the presence of what is now called disability among all sectors of the population, including white men.[6]

Any cursory readings of antebellum literature at its grandest or most popular state would belie the notion that disability followed racial lines with white men being the universally able. Herman Melville's greatest works, from "Bartleby," to *Benito Cereno*, to *Moby Dick*, to *The Confidence Man*, all decisively turn on white disability, and the best-selling urban *noir* writings of George Lippard and others are peopled by characters embodying and causing disabilities. However the lawyer-narrator of Melville's "Bartleby," who presided over an office in which every adult employee suffered from work-related disabilities, alternately processed the title character's work-related mental illness as utterly idiosyncratic or as a condition of "humanity." Generally, disability was certainly present but could not lead to questioning the masculinity or ability of white men. The self-satisfied narrator never had to consider what disability meant within a nation fabricated on the ideology of white male independence and ability. To mount such a challenge required going over the top in terms of both plot and symbolism, as did Edgar Allan Poe's arresting 1839 short story "The Man That Was Used Up." In it, an African American servant daily reassembles the limbless white military hero referred to in the title from prostheses.[7]

Powerful discourses typically mitigated and effaced tensions between white male disability and independence. Mary Klages's *Woeful Afflictions: Disability and Sentimentality in Victorian America* shows that reformers could selectively call on a substantial moral philosophy tradition making empathy rather than rationality and productivity the keys to social citizenship. They could shift the debate in the antebellum years from whether those with limited hearing, sight, and/or mobility were "normal" to whether they were "normalizable." But in doing so they often stressed economic independence, training disabled workers in the very crafts that industrialization was elbowing aside. When more feelings-based solutions were attempted—emphasizing that the disabled had capacities to feel and that the desirability of feeling for them was central to "True Womanhood" and "True Manhood"—the danger was that normalizing seemed a mostly domestic matter, divorced from public realms and republican rights. As Klages writes, "In rejecting disability as a sign of inhuman difference . . . reformers had to embrace disability as a sign of weakness, suffering, and pathos."[8] This set of significations sat uneasily alongside constitutional presumptions of ability and independence among white men.

Thus, no solution to the problem of where to place the population of not fully normalizable white males existed when the Civil War swelled their ranks to unprecedented proportions. In the North alone, almost 282,000 soldiers survived their injuries. With victims of what would now be called post-traumatic stress disorder added in, and given that about three-fifths of the 364,000 killed in the war died of disease and other non-combat causes (often after living with illness for a time), disability surpassed death as a consequence of combat for the over two million soldiers and sailors serving the Union. Overwhelmingly young or middle-aged, white, and formerly "able," these disabled veterans were intimately associated with the heroism of republican patriotic sacrifice. But that sacrifice often left them unable to provide for families. The Confederacy suffered even more wounding of soldiers proportionally, reaching perhaps 15 percent of all participants, leaving the South with about 137,000 survivors of injuries. The historian Lisa Long puts the total number of casualties not resulting in death at half a million, totaling losses on both sides. Sixty thousand amputations resulted from the Civil War; three-quarters of amputees survived. While the dead could be memorialized in a way consigning the "republic of suffering" to the past, the disabled presented greater challenges. As Susan-Mary Grant, the leading historian of the war and disability, has written, a pattern of "scholarly and public preference for the sacrificial dead over the living veteran" quickly took hold and continues to shape the Civil War memories we preserve. She argues that Southern disabled veterans were "lost boys," at sea and invisible in a society premised on "white masculine selfhood that stressed individual agency and independence." Much the same could be said of the North's forgotten wounded.[9]

During the Civil War and after, care for the wounded overwhelmingly fell to women. The healing labor of women was on display alongside the wholesale disabling of tens of thousands of mostly white men. They showed incredible courage in the face of danger in war zones and were witnesses of horrific injuries and human suffering. This situation ultimately interrupted connections between white manhood and fitness for citizenship. Though displays of feminine heroism were often strikingly public, they were more often intimate. Perhaps the most telling representation of the new realities of gender and disability was Winslow Homer's "The Empty Sleeve" engraving that appeared in *Harper's Weekly* on August 26, 1865. In it, a man and woman inhabited the semi-public space of a plush carriage moving along the beach. Her face was earnest, able, and as somber as that of her passenger, whose disability gives the sketch its title. She drove the carriage. "The Empty Sleeve at Newport; Or, Why Edna Ackland Learned to Drive," the short fiction accompanying the image, is far more upbeat in its love-conquers-all ending but reflected the ideological work necessary to make optimism possible. Captain Harry Ash, the amputee in the story, had returned from war and was ordered to seek the healing sea breezes at Newport to recover. He recognized Edna Ackland, driving on the beach, a black male servant sitting behind her. Ash had hoped Ackland would be waiting for him after the war, but his disability compounded their class differences in ways that made this seem impossible. She was of the "Uppertendom" and he distinctly was not. Now the war had left him with "his left sleeve pinned empty to his breast, and his whole frame as feeble as that of any child." Feeling she could not love a broken man "shut off from manly sports for life . . . an invalid to be nursed and tended," Ash wished for his own death and chiseled the carefree image of her driving the locus of his rage. "I grieve" at seeing "a woman unwomanly," Ash told her bitterly in reflecting on her physical prowess. It was only when Edna confessed her love by revealing that she had learned to drive in anticipation of his needs as a disabled veteran, did Ash again consider the possibility of them being together. He asked at once for her forgiveness, compassion, and love, to which she gave him unconditionally. As a couple, the relationship helped Ash restore his manhood and Edna her femininity. In the very strained closing lines, he is said to guide her driving, "so that in reality, she is only his left hand, and he, the husband, drives."[10]

Military policy necessarily addressed the vexed issue of disability. Both the armies formed an "Invalid Corps," attempting to make use of the wounded and diseased in lighter duty and to facilitate the return of the disabled to combat. The Union's efforts in this regard enrolled 60,000 troops,

1. Winslow Homer. *Our Watering Places—The Empty Sleeve at Newport. Harpers Weekly* (August 26, 1865).

far outdistancing the numbers in the entire army before the war. The name of the forces eventually changed to the Veterans Reserve Corps; however, Cripples Brigade, Cripple Brigade, and Infidel Corps were also heard—the last tugging at broad social anxieties connecting disability and alleged dissolute habits.[11]

The war effort likewise raised the issue of disability in an awareness of the extent to which prospective enlistees and draftees were declared unfit for service. The popular war song "The Invalid Corps" actually focused on all those judged unable to serve. Its lyrics suggested the ways in which war exacerbated the distance between able masculine social citizenship and disability:

> *Some had "cork legs" and some "one eye"*
> *With backs deformed and crooked.*
> *I'll bet you'd laugh'd till you had cried*
> *To see how "cute" they looked.*

In another example of musical identification of Invalid Corpsmen with being unfit to serve from the start, rather than hurt in battle, a surgeon dismissed a recruit with:

Your lungs are much affected,
And likewise both your eyes are cock'd
And otherwise defected.

Slurs implied that the invalids were fit but unwilling to serve in the war; therefore, the Corps set up "asylums for shirkers and cowards." As one officer observed, wounded men often begged to be sent back to combat rather than to stay in conditions more conducive to recovery. They wanted to avoid wearing the sky blue Invalid Corps uniform that troops saw as degrading and to more generally avoid paying "the price of being called invalid." One injured soldier reckoned "purgatory" preferable to Invalid Corps service.[12]

The sustained and consequential policy response of the federal government to wartime disability recapitulated the problem of squaring white images of manly independence with the ravages of war. The massive Civil War pension program, begun in 1862, inaugurated important aspects of the modern welfare state, as historian and political scientist Theda Skocpol has shown. In doing so, the program originally targeted for aid the disabled (and families of those killed in battle), awarding benefits to those maimed or made chronically ill in the service of the Union. Only later, after 1890, did it more approximate an across-the-board benefit for surviving Union veterans as a group. Historians of disability and race Larry Logue and Peter Blanck point out that the claiming of a military pension was a risky way for veterans to "reaffirm their manly devotion" to the nation. Such pensions honored those who, as the *New York Times* phrased it, "sacrificed health [and] competence" to the nation's cause.[13]

The pension program grew to be massive, eventually serving about three-quarters of a million military veterans and families at one moment in the 1890s and many more than that overall. From 1880 until 1910, about a fourth of total government revenues went to such pension payments and in some years the figure approached 50 percent. Wisconsin's Robert M. La Follette estimated in his autobiography that as much as a third of his time in Congress, between 1885 and 1891, went to running down inquiries regarding military pensions. The preservation of records necessitated by the pension program so strained the architecture of one depository, the historic Ford's Theatre where Lincoln was slain, that two floors collapsed in 1893, killing twenty-two people.

Pensions were a white entitlement but with important complications. Because whites served more frequently in the Union ranks without the period of exclusion suffered by African Americans; because their service was better documented than blacks; because their dependents and spouses were more readily identifiable than those of black men; because they had more access to political power to influence public policy than African American veterans, they were favored by the pension boards over black applicants, even when physicians recommended awarding the pension to the latter group. Hence, the majority white race also appeared on pension rolls more frequently than blacks. The greatest freedom fighter associated with the Civil War military, the ex-slave and Underground Railroad activist Harriet Tubman, led many hundreds of slaves to freedom during the war. But Tubman fought for her pension for several decades, and when she finally began drawing it, it was because she was a widow. Slaves emancipated during the war who became soldiers fared most poorly in the pension bureaucracy. However, black disabled veterans did join Northern whites in drawing federal pensions; Confederate veterans, on the other hand, suffered belated and relatively meager state pensions. Such a pattern interrupted any firm connections between being a deserving citizen and being white. The pension system served as a model for late-nineteenth-century African American claims for reparations for their enslavement. Furthermore, the discriminatory manner in which pensions were awarded to them further energized their demand for reparations.[14]

According to the most thorough history of race and disability in the Civil War, to collect a pension applicants had "to make public presentation of potentially stigmatizing disabilities." Heroism and neediness made the disabled veteran an apt symbol of republican sacrifice, but not of republican manhood. The pension process screened out those with "vicious habits," which helped certify the pensioners seen as deserving, avowedly dependent recipients. Bearing what many participants in a penmanship contest for disabled veterans thought of as "honorable scars," applicants occasionally had to admit to being "a permanent cripple for life," as one contestant in the same competition lamented. In 1860 revisions of pension law recognized as categories those needing "constant personal aid and attention" and those "incapacitated for performing any manual labor." Beneficiaries thus certifiably lacked both independence and capacity for free labor, the cornerstones defining white republican manhood.[15]

Disability was at once to be celebrated for its connection to heroism and hidden for its connection to weakness. The featuring of the disabled in memorial celebrations of the war and the record of some politicians emphasizing their war-related disabilities in political campaigns join the dignified images of amputees produced by artists to show that wounds could sometimes be borne as honorable. Frances Clarke, a disability scholar, forcefully makes the point, showing that the northern disabled veterans at times personified a lost limb as itself a heroic soldier "sacrificed to maintain the integrity of home and nation." They mourned its loss and moved on, sometimes certain that they would be whole in heaven, and often did not conceal injury with prosthetic devices. But the refusal of prosthetic devices could also be read as reflecting a desire to be apart from the benevolent societies making the provision of limbs a key to rehabilitating and debilitating charity.

During and just after the war, participation rates of Union veterans in the pension program remained relatively low. The bureaucracy busied itself producing guidelines for compensating disabilities (one arm lost at the shoulder yielded $18 a month, but if lost at the elbow, a sixth less). Yet in 1865, less than 2 percent of Civil War veterans in "civil life" had enrolled as pensioners. Even regarding 1875 Skocpol observes that only one survivor in sixteen was on the rolls; twice that proportion of Union soldiers had suffered wounds and would have had a good case for pensions, but many refrained from making claims. Such abstention is perhaps unsurprising in light of the attitudes reflected in the words of United States Sanitary Commission head Henry Whitney Bellows, who branded the injured veteran as potentially not only "physically but morally disabled." When participation rates grew, the pension program became associated with charges of wholesale fraud, again disrupting connections of the state to the deserving veteran.[16]

Gender and race persistently reflected the complex connections of war-caused disability with being fit for citizenship but eligible for pensions. Disability connected injured veterans to women at the level of policy. For a time during the war, Confederate authorities granted draft exemptions ensuring that if a plantation were owned by a *"femme sole"* (meaning an unmarried woman), or an "unsound" man, an overseer might be provided.

Union policies specifically indicating a preference for employing "able-bodied" African American men as contraband and later as troops also connected gender, race, and ability. After the war Union pensions went to widows and to disabled men. The freed slave and disabled veteran, simultaneously heroic and suspect, appeared in tandem again and again. The veteran in the penmanship contest who bemoaned having to identify as a "cripple" added that to do so was to lose "our place in society," inspiring him to think that he "might as well be black." The pairing sometimes told a story of discrimination, as in the singling out late in the war of black and "invalid" troops as the only ones ineligible for reenlistment bonuses, a brutality

2. Thomas Nast. Pardon and Franchise. *Harpers Weekly* (August 5, 1865).

that the officer of one official report branded as based on "inequality and injustice."

There were promising glimmers of common interests, as in the exalted places the Invalid Corps and African Americans were accorded in early postwar patriotic celebrations. Their roles were especially dramatic in early commemorations of Memorial Day—an African American–initiated, and for a time racially diverse, site of memory of an emancipatory war as opposed to the vehicle for the celebration of white reconciliation across sectional lines that the day later became. Nonetheless, the sense that each group was under scrutiny regarding their fitness for rights made interracial mobilization around disability issues difficult to broach. The decision to move many white Invalid Corps officers into positions of power in the Freedman's Bureau suggests the ways that connections could coexist with assumptions about hierarchy. The best-documented example is Colonel Charles F. Johnson, whose career spans both organizations and demonstrates tremendous political growth from deep wartime racism to a steady commitment to defending the lives and interests of free African Americans. Fred Pelka, who gathered Johnson's letters for publication, meticulously charts these dynamics and their "limits," showing the transformations possible around issues of disability and race before Johnson's death in 1867. Over time, as Grant shows, retreating from Reconstruction also entailed turning away from such potential transformation, and from both the disabled veteran and African Americans.[17]

The figure of the black veteran amputee used by Thomas Nast in an 1865 *Harper's Weekly* cartoon arguing for African American voting rights and painted with such dignity by Thomas Waterman Wood, especially challenged the separation of the rights of disabled veterans from those of freed people. Nast in particular paired his portrait of the black amputee without franchise with a drawing of "Pardon," featuring prominent forgiven Confederates.[18]

Ubiquitous encounters with unthinkable suffering demonstrated how fragile and ordinary white male ability was. Just before the Civil War, white supremacist and New York writer Dr. John H. Van Evrie asserted that whites "naturally" surpassed blacks in intellect. He considered the possibility that there were "idiotic, insane or otherwise incapable" whites, but he claimed they were exceptions to the rule. Military combat not only put capability of black men on display, it swelled the ranks of disabled whites dramatically. Moreover, the fratricidal carnage proved a poor setting in which to exalt the rationality of white male citizenship. In the moment when the dependency of increasing numbers of white men became apparent, women showed unimagined capacities for independence.

Women's nursing of the wartime wounded was perhaps the most dramatic example of how disability mattered in reshaping other axes of inequality. But more generally, women's contributions to patriotism in the North and to treason in the South often highlighted both their own abilities to carry on household economic activities independently and their attempt to rebuild male bodies and spirits in the wake of sudden male disability. LeeAnn Whites has written that the Southern soldier "had to recognize, if only unconsciously, the extent to which his manhood and independence was . . . built upon the foundations of women's service and love."[19] To add that such was still more pointedly true for the disabled veteran is to appreciate Baynton's points regarding the pervasiveness of disability as a category in its own right and as one helping constitute other categories of inequality. White men's claims to a unique fitness, even the ability for independence, faced challenges not only from disability in their own ranks, but also from changing relations with African Americans and white women. The most dramatic change was undoubtedly the seemingly impossible self-emancipation of four million slaves.

WITNESSING JUBILEE

The presence of those desiring freedom provoked divided responses among white troops. But as the war became bloodier and more uncertain, many wished that the danger could be shared and hardship alleviated through the use of ex-slaves as laborers. The reasoning could be eminently practical. As Charles Graham Halpine indicated in the popular 1862 song, "Sambo's Right to Be Kilt"

> *Some tell me 'tis a burnin' shame*
> *To make the naygers fight,*
> *And that the trade of bein' kilt*
> *Belongs but to the white.*
> *But as for me, upon my soul!*
> *So lib'ral are we here,*
> *I'll let Sambo be shot instead of myself*
> *On ev'ry day in the year.*[20]

Other soldiers reflected on the need for making service-work available to women who fled from slavery. As Leslie Schwalm's account of emancipation in the upper Midwest shows, formerly enslaved women made decisive contributions to the war effort by "cooking, sewing, washing, caring for horses, and nursing the sick and wounded." However, many whites vacillated on the question of accepting their presence and using their services early in the war. In July 1862, for example, an Iowa soldier stationed in Mississippi connected his own miseries regarding lack of good food to the refusal to allow slaves to cross Union lines to lend a hand. Dismissed from the army, the soldier later complained the army threatened to court-martial troops caught employing an escaped slave as a cook.[21]

Reactions to contrabands, as those runaway slaves sheltered behind Union army lines were called, were never predictable but often transformative. In the spring of 1862, Commodore John Rodgers Goldsborough, the commander of an encampment of contrabands at Fernandina Island, Florida, waited nearly three weeks to be able to mail a letter to his wife. The letter grew and grew, reaching about fifty pages of often vivid description of the scene. Goldsborough reported that he threatened African Americans on the island with return to slavery if they did not obey his orders. He fretted that the recalcitrance of the men in particular would undermine plans to make the island self-sufficient. As Goldsborough learned more about the conditions these people had endured under slavery, he began to understand them better. "Their tales of cruelty" by masters, he wrote, "are too awful to relate and their manner of escape in several instances is truly wonderful." He witnessed couples separated by masters joyously reuniting on the island and saw the importance many parents gave to the education of their children. Indeed, he found that "grown-up Negroes" were equally "eager to go to school and learn" after a day's work. Women perceived to be "more industrious" than men made "excellent washers and ironers," Goldsborough surmised. Deep into the letter, he predicted worriedly that large numbers of African Americans would eventually migrate to the North in search of a better life. However, when the Confederate soldiers tried to capture and re-enslave or even murder African Americans on Union–held St. Simon's Island, he described the resulting raid as "diabolical."[22]

William Ball of the 5th-Wisconsin Battery offered an especially comprehensive view of the reasons that Union troops saw benefits in embracing aid from escaped slaves in a series of letters from early in the war. "No wonder," he wrote, "soldiers become abolitionists as they go south if they were not before." For Ball the war brought a series of object lessons in the cruelty of masters, including violence to slaves whom he saw as phenotypically white. Ball reported that fleeing slaves often brought horses and mules with them, as well as knowledge of Confederate troop movements. He found those who came, men and women, to be "very useful as cooks . . . or hostlers." He praised their intelligence, heroism, and bearing. According to Ball, "They bear the privations of camp life cheerfully; living with the hope that at the close of the war," they would "find a home where the crack of the cruel driver's lash, or the bay of fierce bloodhound is not heard." He thought as early as May 1862 that contrabands were "virtually free" and hoped they would remain so.[23]

Flight to freedom and the Confederate brutality it occasioned made many white soldiers turn to supporting abolitionism and to the idea that social relations could change more broadly. Such soldiers frequently saw the work of contrabands as critical and noted how passionately African Americans labored for the Union cause. Connecting the zeal of runaway slaves to serve the Union cause as laborers and their apparent strong desire for freedom, many whites began to believe that African American workers were superior to northern white workers in military employment. As a superintendent of contraband labor reported, "the lowest estimate is . . . that one negro is worth three soldiers." Two slaves presenting themselves to a Union officer in Baton Rouge in the summer of 1862 found little sympathy. Returned to their master, they then showed up again, wounds gaping from beatings and each wearing a "horrid three-pronged iron collar." On re-entering Union lines, they finally found sanctuary. Troops cheered their commander who defied Union policy by refusing to return the runaways, knowing that doing so could lead to his arrest and court-martial. Although we generally think that runaway slaves as fugitives encountered Union officers upon entering an army camp, they frequently met enlisted men the moment they crossed the line. The resulting direct-action abolitionism—receiving a so-called fugitive slave on human terms—meant that familiarity with the need for manpower and later the witness of the valor of black troops were not the only factors conditioning the often favorable opinions of white troops toward enlisting African American troops. Indeed, one recent account has held that General John C. Frémont's efforts to free enslaved blacks in Missouri early in the war stemmed in part from his imitating the direct actions of white troops who first refused to return runaway slaves. Another scholar notes that later in the war rank-and-file white troops occasionally encouraged the immediate enlistment of runaway slaves, without the direct intervention of their commanding officer.[24]

Conversely, there are countless stories of African Americans still enslaved in the South using their knowledge of the landscape to hide and provide provisions for Union troops who were dodging Confederate soldiers. Not only did these African Americans help Union troops elude capture, they directed them to the Underground Railroad that had taken many of their family and friends to freedom up North. These Union troops, among whom were prisoners of war, had the harrowing experience of being chased by bloodhounds, just as runaway slaves had done. Representations of their daring escapes frequently appear in familiar tropes in the narratives of African Americans who had fled slavery. Frederick Douglass grounded postwar appeals for civil rights partly on the involvement of heroic men and women who had risked their lives assisting fleeing Union troops. As he told an assembly of Republicans in 1879, "We were your friends in the south when you had no other friends there. The soldier boys knew we were their friends when they were escaping from Andersonville, Libby, and Castle Thunder. They didn't like to see white men at that time." Instead, he continued, "Uncle Tom, and Uncle Jim, and Caesar . . . would feed them when hungry, show them the way when lost, and shelter them when they were without" homes.[25]

White soldiers frequently remembered how enslaved African Americans aided them. At times, these soldiers would return the benevolence by assisting runaway slaves seeking to recover property they had left behind. In early in 1862, before President Abraham Lincoln announced the Emancipation Proclamation, and even before the Union started enlisting African Americans into the armed forces, white enlisted men recompensed some of the people who had helped them recover belongings they had left behind. Their gesture, however, did not please some of their commanding offers. For example, General William Tecumseh Sherman vehemently protested when he discovered that his troops were seeking justice by assisting contraband slaves. Sherman insisted, "The Clothing & effects of the negro are the property of the master & mistress." In sum, many white soldiers confronted the real choice that Huck Finn had faced in fiction: to return an enslaved person to slavery or abet his or her liberation. Even though many white soldiers were sympathetic to the plight of runaway slaves early in the war, they acquiesced to their commanders and sent the slaves back to the plantations they had risked their lives to escape. A desire to be done with the war by winning it convinced many rank-and-file Union troops to support the end of slavery and, unevenly of course, to support black enlistment. Such assessments prompted many of these soldiers to celebrate passage of the Emancipation Proclamation and the Thirteenth Amendment.[26]

Moreover, the positive impression made by the contrabands and black soldiers was not restricted to their desire for freedom or their valor in battle. Colonel Thomas Wentworth Higginson left a glimpse into the culture of African Americans. They wrote vibrant poetry and music, he indicated, referencing the black troops who served under him; their poetry illustrated a fluency in the English language, and the music was rhythmic. Higginson transcribed the song "I Know Moonrise," praising lyrics for containing the "flower of poetry" and words that celebrated the "dark soil" of the land. Lingering over a single line, "I'll lie in de grave and stretch out my arms," prompted him to exclaim that "Never . . . since man first lived and suffered, was his infinite longing for peace uttered more plaintively."[27]

In recounting how free African Americans helped transform the white mind about their race, the Civil War, and emancipation itself, it is imperative also to note how art provides a useful paradigm to evaluate black culture. During the war the radical Pennsylvania Republican William Kelley predicted that future poets would single out the "NEGRO SOLDIER" as the figure about whom Americans would "sing in the highest strains." Many artists almost immediately began to make their fascination with black soldiers known to readers. The wartime market of "patriotic envelopes" produced commercially as both memorabilia and for sale yielded an astounding

3. *Southern Currency.* Civil War envelope, ca. 1863.

15,000 varieties of design for envelopes manufactured by nearly 300 companies. As one would expect, the images reflected support for the Union as
the country that liberated the slaves. These envelopes portrayed remark-
able images of slaves as contraband. Indeed, some of the drawings included
stereotypes, and even made a mockery of African Americans. The artists
seemingly believed it was hilarious to make fun by using the word "contraband," as a way to compare black refugees with the minstrel music commonly performed during the century.

But they also, from the earliest months of the war, made the drama of
the slave fleeing to freedom central to the imagery of the war, capturing
in it a sense of possibility for the Union and vulnerability of the Confederacy. A single drawing could combine the parody of black speech with an
awareness that the flight to freedom continued long traditions of escaping
slaves using the North Star as their guide to freedom. The illustrations also
showed how the black flight from bondage drained the South of the very
"currency" upon which the Confederacy depended on.[28] Another envelope
image, probably from 1861, illustrated the flight an enslaved woman to freedom; the artist labeled the piece "Secession." As Steven R. Boyd, the leading
student of these envelopes observed, "two years before the Emancipation
Proclamation [the images] raised the specter of the abolition of slavery . . . a
freedom secured in part by African Americans' willingness to take an active
role in their own liberation."[29]

The popular artwork of Henry Louis Stephens and Winslow Homer
similarly show how artists began to back away from using racist caricature

4. Untitled, 1863.

in their work. Late in the war, artists began producing dignified images of African Americans, and made them integral to the drama of the age. Stephens would contribute significantly to a small but compelling body of art on disability after the war in which he explored wartime surgery, amputation, and the crisis in the nation itself.[30] Few caricaturists, North or South, drew more vicious anti-black stereotypes than did Stephens early in the war. His 1860 *Vanity Fair* drawing, "Substance and Shadow," positions white supremacist politician Stephen A. Douglas midair, posed in a minstrel dance. Douglas, popularly called the "Little Giant," simultaneously looks babyish and dissipated in the illustration. The African American shadow behind him, also drawn to racial stereotypes, utterly overwhelms the politician. The May 1862 Stephens sketch "The New Frankenstein" features an image of a hulking black figure seemingly ready to toss Jefferson Davis off of a cliff. Like other Stephens drawings, "The New Frankenstein" portrayed African Americans as monsters, complete with horns, as opposed to being sentient beings. In "The Monotonous Minstrel," Stephens portrays Horace Greeley's abolitionist tune as being so boring and repetitive that even Lincoln ignores it. The drawing also represents the slave population

No. 6

BLOW FOR BLOW.

5. James Fuller Queen with
Henry Louis Stephens.
Blow for Blow, ca. 1863.

along with black abolitionists as monkeys who dance to Greeley's tired and monstrous acts. *Vanity Fair* cartoons traded on anti-abolitionist and racist stereotypes, especially those connecting slaves to monkeys and apes, and appealed to images of monstrosity that raised specters of disability menacing republican freedom.[31]

The struggle of African Americans for freedom changed things up to a point, although none of the *Vanity Fair* drawings anticipated the quiet human dignity of an untitled Stephens watercolor that commemorated the Emancipation Proclamation. Stephens depicts an African American apparently learning about being actually free for the first time, reading the document by firelight, much as President Lincoln had legendarily done in his youth. Neither caricatured nor fearsome, the old man appears dignified and cerebral, elegantly dressed in red, white, and blue colors; he seems enlightened and ready for citizenship. As one recent account posits: "The Emancipation Proclamation compelled Stephens to reconsider his previously virulently anti-abolitionist propaganda." Even *Vanity Fair* greeted the Emancipation Proclamation with a favorable cartoon that described a promising new door opening up for African Americans.[32]

CAMPAIGN SKETCHES.

OUR JOLLY COOK.

6. Winslow Homer.
Our Jolly Cook, 1863.

Stephens also collaborated with James Fuller Queen, a Philadelphia lithographer, in a series of twelve chromolithographs depicting the evolution of its black subject from a slave to a Union soldier. The key image, "Blow for Blow," shows the hero fighting back against a whipping by the master, an assertion of desire for freedom directly echoing Frederick Douglass's account of the turning point in his life, and acting quite independently of help from the North.[33]

The composed and dignified (about-to-be) emancipated female slave emerged gloriously in Winslow Homer's small painting from the end of the Civil War, *Near Andersonville.* The work aptly captures the extent to which Frederick Douglass prophetically asserted that slaves would not only fight for emancipation, they would also play a vital role in the defeat of the South. The evolution of Homer's thinking when portraying African Americans during the war is striking. While traveling with the Army of the Potomac, he sketched the contributions of some of the contrabands early in the war, producing the especially arresting watercolor *Study of a Negro Teamster* (1862). Historian Peter Wood, an expert on Homer, calls the *Negro Teamster* illustration "condescending [in its] outlook so prevalent among

7. Winslow Homer.
Near Andersonville,
1865–86.

Northern whites especially early in the war."[34] Surely the Homer portrayal of blacks in the drawing *Our Jolly Cook*, from 1863, once again shows African Americans in a demeaning way.

The depiction of African Americans in *Near Andersonville* could hardly be more different than the foregoing works. If Homer's *The Empty Sleeve* is arguably the finest portrayal of disability in art produced in the Civil War, *Near Andersonville* is surely the finest painting illustrating the drama of emancipation. *Our Jolly Cook* and *Near Andersonville*, produced at almost the same time, invite comparison.

The subject of a fascinating recent short book by Wood, *Near Andersonville* re-narrates the Civil War in a way that was made possible when memories of the conflict were fresh. The title refers to the infamous Georgia prison where Union soldiers captured by the Confederacy were imprisoned. The tiny image in the upper left of the painting barely shows the captured troops, presumably being taken to Andersonville. Though open for only the last fourteen months of the war, Andersonville accounted for approximately one-twentieth of all deaths of Northern troops during the war. This in-the-corner drama—martial and white—is minimized, marginalized, and almost smudged. Meanwhile, a slave woman is made the center of attention and light, with a composed countenance reflecting her contemplation of opportunities the war presented for her as a black and modern actor in history. Her African head wrap, Wood observes, also gestures towards the "liberty cap" so present in the iconography of revolutionary art at the time. Her shirt, he adds, suggested the "Garibaldi blouse" that was a fashion rage in the 1860s, modeling itself after the wardrobe of Italian revolutionary Giuseppe Garibaldi. The latter himself figured in making the Civil War a revolution, joining in international pressure for emancipation in 1862 by offering to send forces to support the United States if the Union pledged to liberate the slaves.[35] Long a part of the revolutionary transatlantic world, African Americans in *Near Andersonville* reflect on the meaning of freedom.

The woman in the painting appears to be calm, neither perspiring nor dirty, apparently not engaged in the drudgery of slave life, even during daylight. This made her one of the numberless participants who joined in the general strike of the slaves without leaving the plantations. Her quiet repose contested the authority of mistresses and the depleted ranks of overseers on increasingly unmanageable plantations. She stands then as a fitting illustration of Du Bois's observation that the general strike not only reflected "the desire to stop work" but also was conducted "on a wide basis against the conditions of work." The challenges that slaves presented, as Armstead Robinson and Thavolia Glymph suggest, deepened gender and class tensions that ultimately spelled disaster for the Confederacy. The subject slave "moved silently," as Du Bois puts it, "listening, hoping, hesitating," but fervently moving forward to transform hearts and minds at a time when such change seemed nearly impossible. Her glory, and the tragedies produced by the war, affected, among much else, such powerful counternarratives to the standard placing of able white men at the center of the nation that a brief, important emancipation from whiteness could occur.[36]

NOTES

1. George P. Rawick, *From Sundown to Sunup: The Making of the Black Community* (Westport, CT: Greenwood, 1972), 159.

2. James Baldwin, *The Fire Next Time* (1963; New York: Vintage, 1993), 96.

3. For Marx, see International Workingmen's Association, "Address to the National Labor Union" (May 12, 1866), found at www.marxists.org/archive/marx/iwma/documents/1869/us-labor.htm.

4. David R. Roediger, *The Wages of Whiteness: Race and the Making of the American Working Class* (London and New York: Verso, 1991), 173.

5. Douglas Baynton, "Disability and the Justification of Inequality in American History," in Paul K. Longmore and Lauri Umansky, ed., *The New Disability History: American Perspectives* (New York: New York University Press, 2001), 35, 37, 39–40, 33–57. Cf. Cheryl Harris, "Whiteness as Property," *Harvard Law Review* 106, no. 7 (1993): 1709–91; Cheryl Harris, "Finding Sojourner's Truth: Race, Gender, and the Institution of Property," *Cardozo Law Review* 18, no. 2 (1996): 309–409.

6. Baynton, "Disability and the Justification of Inequality in American History," 35, 37, 39–40, 33–57. For a superb study of US slavery and disability, see Jenifer L. Barclay, "Cripples All! Or, the Mark of Slavery: Disability and Race in Antebellum America, 1820-1860" (PhD diss., Michigan State University, 2011). For a discussion of race, slavery, and disability, see Dea H. Boster, *African American Slavery and Disability: Bodies, Property, and Power in the Antebellum South, 1800-1860* (New York: Routledge, 2013), 17–33, 121–24.

7. Herman Melville, "Bartleby the Scrivener" (1853; New York: Melville House, 2010); George Lippard, *The Quaker City, Or, The Monks of Monk-Hall*, 2 vols. (Philadelphia: by the author, 1847). See also Cynthia Hall, "'Colossal Vices' and 'Terrible Deformities' in George Lippard's Gothic Nightmare," in Ruth Beinstock Anolik, ed., *Demons of the Body and Mind: Essays on Disability in Gothic Literature* (Jefferson, NC: McFarland, 2010). For Poe, see http://xroads.virginia.edu/~hyper/POE/used_up.html; and the discussion in Susan-Mary Grant, "Reconstructing the National Body: Masculinity, Disability, and Race in the American Civil War," *Proceedings of the British Academy* 154 (2008): 285–86.

8. Mary Klages, *Woeful Afflictions: Disability and Sentimentality in Victorian America* (Philadelphia: University of Pennsylvania Press, 1999), 21, 17–20, 34–43.

9. Table 2-23, "Principal Wars in which the US Participated: US Military Personnel Serving and Casualties," prepared by Washington Headquarters Services, Directorate for Information Operations and Reports, US Department of Defense Records, as reprinted by United States Civil War Center at http://web.archive.org/web/20070711050249/http://www.cwc.lsu.edu/other/stats/warcost.htm; Grant, "Reconstructing the National Body," 281 ("preference"), 289–90; Lisa Long, *Rehabilitating Bodies: Health, History, and the American Civil War* (Philadelphia: University of Pennsylvania Press, 2004), 67; Grant, "The Lost Boys: Citizen-Soldiers, Disabled Veterans, and Confederate Nationalism in the Age of People's War," *Journal of the Civil War Era* 2 (June 2012): 233 ("selfhood"), 234–59; Drew Gilpin Faust, *This Republic of Suffering: Death and the American Civil War* (New York: Vintage, 2008).

10. Unsigned, "The Empty Sleeve at Newport; Or, Why Edna Ackland Learned to Drive," *Harper's Weekly* (August 26, 1865), 534. See also Jalynn Olsen Padilla, "Army of 'Cripples': Northern Civil War Amputees, Disability, and Manhood in Victorian America" (PhD diss., University of Delaware, 2007), 165–66 and *passim*.

11. Charles F. Johnson and Fred Pelka, *The Civil War Letters of Colonel Charles F. Johnson, Invalid Corps* (Amherst: University of Massachusetts Press, 2004), 14 ("shirkers," "defected," and "begged"), 133 ("Infidel"), 1–39.

12. "The Invalid Corps," reprinted at the Civil War Zone, www.civilwarzone.com/ TheInvalidCorps.html ("cork"). Pelka's excellent introduction to *The Civil War Letters of Colonel Charles F. Johnson* compellingly connects anxiety and disability. For "purgatory" see "Henry C. Gilbert to Hattie Gilbert" (November 22, 1863), in Henry C. Gilbert Letters at Clements Library at University of Michigan; for "Cripple Brigade," see "Thomas D. Willis to Brother Seth" (February 2, 1864), in Thomas D. Willis Letters at Clements Library at University of Michigan.

13. Theda Skocpol, *Protecting Soldiers and Mothers: The Political Origins of Social Policy in the United States* (Cambridge: Harvard University Press, 1992), 102–51; Larry M. Logue and Peter Blanck, *Race, Ethnicity, and Disability: Veterans and Benefits in Post-Civil War America* (Cambridge, GB: Cambridge University Press, 2010), 3.

14. Faust, *This Republic of Suffering*, 255–56; Catherine Clinton, *Harriet Tubman: The Road to Freedom* (New York: Little, Brown, 2004), 193–205; Skocpol, *Protecting Soldiers and Mothers*, 113–14, 121–22, 139–40; Logue and Blanck, *Race, Ethnicity, and Disability*, 57, 41–82; Mary Frances Berry, *My Face Is Black It Is True: Callie House and the Ex-Slave Reparations Movement* (New York: Vintage, 2006), xiv, 34–35, 48; Jim Downs, *Sick from Freedom: African-American Illness and Suffering during the Civil War and Reconstruction* (New York: Oxford University Press, 2012), 146–61.

15. Logue and Blanck, *Race, Ethnicity, and Disability*, 3 ("stigmatizing" and "permanent cripple"), 19 ("constant" and "manual"), 32 ("vicious habits"), 1–40; George Fredrickson, *The Inner Civil War: Northern Intellectuals and the Crisis of the Union* (1965; Urbana: University of Illinois Press, 1993), 79–112.

16. Frances Clarke, "'Honorable Scars': Northern Amputees and the Meaning of Civil War Injuries," in Paul Cimbala and Randall Miller, ed., *Union Soldiers and the Home Front: Wartime Experiences, Postwar Adjustments* (New York: Fordham University Press, 2002), 389–90 ("integrity"), 393, 361–94; Padilla, "Army of 'Cripples,'" 149–54; Grant, "Reconstructing the National Body," 302 (Bellows), 296–317; Laurann Figg and Jane Farrell-Beck, "Amputation in the Civil War: Physical and Social Dimensions," *Journal of the History of Medicine and Allied Sciences* 48 (October 1993): 468; Skocpol, *Protecting Soldiers and Mothers*, 106–9, 143–46, 275–76.

17. Thavolia Glymph, *Out of the House of Bondage: The Transformation of the Plantation Household* (Cambridge: Cambridge University Press, 2008), 121 ("unsound"); Logue and Blanck, *Race, Ethnicity, and Disability*, 3 ("our place" and "might as well"); Johnson and Pelka, *The Civil War Letters of Colonel Charles F. Johnson*, 33 ("limits"), 31–37, 300–301, 304–17; David W. Blight, "The First Decoration Day," at www.davidwblight.com/ memorial.htm; David W. Blight, *Race and Reunion: The Civil War in American Memory* (Cambridge: Harvard University Press, 2001), 64–90; Downs, *Sick from Freedom*, 126.

18. Grant, "Reconstructing the National Body," 307–8, reproduces the Wood paintings. Nast's "Pardon and Franchise" appeared in *Harper's Weekly* (August 5, 1865), 488–89.

19. Fredrickson, *The Inner Civil War*, 79, 98; LeeAnn Whites, *Gender Matters: Civil War, Reconstruction, and the Making of the New South* (New York: Palgrave, 2005), 21; see also Whites, *The Civil War as a Crisis in Gender: Augusta, Georgia, 1860-1890* (Athens: University of Georgia Press, 1995), 48, 112–14, 137–48, 200–201, 223; Laura Edwards,

Gendered Strife and Confusion: The Political Culture of Reconstruction (Urbana: University of Illinois Press, 1997), 107, 113–14. Van Evrie as quoted in Baynton, "Disability and the Justification of Inequality in American History," 38. See also Susan-Mary Grant, "To Bind Up the Nation's Wounds: Women and the American Civil War," in Susan Kleinberg, Eileen Boris, and Vicky Ruiz, ed., *The Practice of U.S. Women's History: Narratives, Intersections, and Dialogues* (New Brunswick: Rutgers University Press, 2007), 106–25.

20. Irwin Silber, ed., *Songs of the Civil War* (New York: Columbia University Press, 1960), 308–9, 328–30. For careful recent work on the wartime migration of slaves to freedom, see Yael A. Sternhell, *Routes of War: The World of Movement in the Confederate South* (Cambridge: Harvard University Press, 2012), 95–107.

21. Leslie A. Schwalm, *Emancipation's Diaspora: Race and Reconstruction in the Upper Midwest* (Chapel Hill: University of North Carolina Press, 2009), 60, 280 n.43.

22. "Commodore John Rodgers Goldsborough to Mary Pennington Goldsborough" (April 21–May 8, 1862), Hargrett Rare Books and Manuscript Library, University of Georgia. Thanks to Bao Bui for research assistance on this citation. On the rebels' desire to recapture slaves from the island, see also W. E. B. Du Bois, *Black Reconstruction in America, 1860-1880* (1935; New York: Free Press, 1998), 61. On public executions of those fleeing slavery, see Sternhell, *Routes of War*, 127.

23. Ball's letters are in the US Army Military History Institute in Carlisle, Pennsylvania. For the quotes, see "Ball to his brother Quigley" (March 28, 1862); "Ball to his brother D. Smith" (March 29, 1862); "Ball to his brother Quig" (June 10, 1862); see also "Ball to his brother Quig" (May 30, 1862); "Ball to his sister Lib" (August 13, 1862); "Ball to his brother Smith" (September 8, 1862). Also reporting particular horror at treatment of a white and blue-eyed slave, a master's son, was "George W. Landrum, US Signal Corps, to his sister Amanda" (April 15, 1862), in George W. Landrum letters, VFM 4704, Ohio Historical Society, Columbus.

24. Ira Berlin et al., ed., *Freedom: A Documentary History of Emancipation, 1861-1867*; Series I, Volume III, *The Wartime Genesis of Free Labor: The Lower South* (Cambridge: Cambridge University Press, 1990), 20; Schwalm, *Emancipation's Diaspora*, 58; Donald Martin Jacobs, "A History of the Boston Negro from the Revolution to the Civil War" (PhD diss., Boston University, 1968), 362–70; Chandra Manning, *What This Cruel War Was Over: Soldiers, Slavery, and the Civil War* (New York: Vintage, 2008), esp. 13, 44–51, 76–78, 94–96, 189–204; for reservations about the patterns of egalitarianism that Manning carefully lays out, see Gary Gallagher, *The Union War* (Cambridge: Harvard University Press, 2011), 79–82. On rank-and-file German Americans' increasing sympathy with slaves' suffering in wartime Missouri, see Alison Clark Efford, *German Immigrants, Race, and Citizenship in the Civil War Era* (New York: Cambridge University Press, 2013), 93–94; see also Rebecca J. Scott, *Degrees of Freedom: Louisiana and Cuba after Slavery* (Cambridge: Harvard University Press, 2005), 35.

25. Evan Kutzler, "Crossing Tracks in the Confederate South: The Underground Railroad, Race, and Union Prisoners of War" (unpublished paper, University of South Carolina, Department of History, 2013); John C. Inscoe, "'Moving through Deserter Country': Fugitive Accounts of the Inner Civil War in Southern Appalachia," in Kenneth W.

Noe and Shannon H. Wilson, ed., *The Civil War in Appalachia* (Knoxville: University of Tennessee Press, 1997), 158–86; William B. Hesseltine, "The Underground Railroad from Confederate Prisons to East Tennessee," *East Tennessee Historical Society's Publications* 2 (1930): 60, 66. The Douglass quotation is from Frederick Douglass, "Alonzo B. Cornell and the Republican Party: An Address Delivered in Utica, New York, on 30 October 1879," in *The Frederick Douglass Papers, Series One: Speeches, Debates, and Interviews, Volume 4: 1864-80*, ed. John W. Blassingame and John R. McKivigan (New Haven: Yale University Press, 1977), 541, 533–42. In the same volume see also Frederick Douglass, "We are Here and Want the Ballot Box: An Address Delivered in Philadelphia, Pennsylvania, on 4 September 1866," 127, 132–33. Thanks to Evan Kutzler for material in this paragraph.

26. Glymph, *Out of the House of Bondage*, 207 (on Sherman); for Frémont, see Mark A. Lause, *Race and Radicalism in the Union Army* (Urbana: University of Illinois Press, 2009), 51.

27. Thomas Wentworth Higginson, *Army Life in a Black Regiment* (Boston: Houghton, Mifflin, 1900), 283–84.

28. The image is found in the digital American Memory collection of the Library of Congress, in the section reproducing "Civil War Treasures from the New York Historical Society" at http://memory.loc.gov/ndlpcoop/nhnycw/aj/aj01/aj01048v.jpg. In the same digital collection, for minstrel-inflected racist imagery see especially "Bress de Lor, We Am Contraband" and "Music by the Contra-Band." For further images showing the importance of the threat posed to masters by the flight of contrabands and the purposeful nature of their actions, see "Slave Escaping at Fort Monroe" and "Contraband of War; or Volunteer Sappers and Miners."

29. "Contraband Barricade" is at the American Memory digital collection at http://memory.loc.gov/ndlpcoop/nhnycw/aj/aj01/aj01029v.jpg. See also Steven R. Boyd, *Patriotic Envelopes of the Civil War: The Iconography of Union and Confederate Covers* (Baton Rouge: Louisiana State University Press, 2010), 3, 72 (Figure 4:31), 69–77; Schwalm, *Emancipation's Diaspora*, 87–89.

30. Wood, *Black Scare*, 45 (for Kelley); Sarah Burns, *Painting the Dark Side: Art and the Gothic Imagination in Nineteenth-Century America* (Berkeley: University of California Press, 2004), 141, 144, 195–96.

31. Burns, *Painting the Dark Side*, 114–16, 142–46, with several *Vanity Fair* illustrations reproduced therein. In vol. 5 of that magazine, see especially 129 (March 15, 1862); 139 (March 22, 1862); 286 (June 14, 1862, invoking the North Star as a symbol of flight to emancipation); in vol. 6, see 11 (July 6, 1862); 60 (August 2, 1862); 102 (August 30, 1862); 119 (September 6, 1862); 123 (September 13, 1862); 204 (October 25, 1862).

32. See the Library of Congress press release "Mazie Harris to Discuss Civil War Era Chromolithographs by Henry Louis Stephens at Library of Congress" (November 17, 2008), at www.loc.gov/today/pr/2008/08-216.html; "The New Place," *Vanity Fair* 6 (December 27, 1862), 307.

33. For Douglass, see his *Narrative of the Life of Frederick Douglass* (Boston: Anti-Slavery Office, 1845), 60–74. The lithograph and description are housed in the digital collections of the Library Company of Philadelphia at http://lcpdams.librarycompany .org:8881/R?RN=102006422.

34. Peter H. Wood and Karen C. C. Dalton, *Winslow Homer's Images of Blacks: The Civil War and Reconstruction Years* (Austin: University of Texas Press, 1988), 34, 33–37, including the illustrations discussed. Homer also illustrated disability caused by the war; see Burns, *Painting the Dark Side*, 196, and the discussion of "The Empty Sleeve" earlier in this essay.

35. Peter H. Wood, *Near Andersonville: Winslow Homer's Civil War* (Cambridge: Harvard University Press, 2010), esp. 58, 59, 74–77; Don H. Doyle, "Bully for Garibaldi," *New York Times* (September 26, 2011).

36. Du Bois, *Black Reconstruction in America*, 67; Wood, *Near Andersonville*, 59 (quoting Du Bois); Armstead L. Robinson, *Bitter Fruits of Bondage: The Demise of Slavery and the Collapse of the Confederacy, 1861-1865* (Charlottesville: University of Virginia Press, 2005), esp. 134, 181, 283; Glymph, *Out of the House of Bondage*, esp. 68–71. Change in popular cartoon images of blacks was significant but far more uneven; see Nickels, *Civil War Humor*, 115–50.

4

WHITENESS IN THE TWENTY-FIRST CENTURY
The Decline of One-Drop Reasoning in Jurisprudence after 1980

ERICA COOPER

BEFORE 1900, STATE COURTS AND LEGISLATURES HAD BEEN STRUG-
gling to define the identity of mixed-race Americans for more than two
hundred years.[1] They frequently used multiple and competing classifications, including "colored or mixed race" for individuals who were neither
completely white nor black. Upon the emancipation of African Americans
in 1865, several southern states passed laws to codify the one-drop rule
by designating people with any degree of African ancestry whatsoever as
black.[2] The one-drop rule immediately had social and legal implications
for mixed-race individuals. Under community standards it had been established that appearance and knowledge of a person's racial past were de
facto criteria in determining blackness.[3] However, as pervasive as these
customs had become, Americans did not always agree on locating a person's racial identity. With the codification of the one-drop rule, it is ironic
that state legislatures and courts did not always agree on who was actually
white. While approximately ten southern states adopted the one-drop rule,
roughly four applied "blood" fractions to determine racial identity. Florida
allowed mixed-race marriages beyond the fourth generation; Kentucky allowed youths with less than one-sixteenth black "blood" to attend public
schools with white children; and Missouri allowed mixed-race Americans
to marry if they had less than one-eighth African ancestry.[4] Hence, a white
racial identity has never been ironclad in American culture or under its
laws. Nevertheless, to possess a white identity was a significant value in the
twentieth century, and mixed-race people who believed in their whiteness
contested allegations of their black racial identity. Judges were called upon
to settle these controversies.

Scholars have not appreciated the way these judges have used rhetorical analysis when construing racial identity.[5] This essay investigates the way judges used rhetoric in racial identity cases in legal discourses. During the early twentieth century, people who believed they were white sued their states to confirm their white racial identity. Lawyers and judges in Louisiana initially applied a broad construction of the one-drop rule in racial identity cases. From 1900 to 1930 these lawyers and judges seem to have ignored the one-drop rule in all cases that did not involve school-aged children attempting to attend a segregated school. By 1940 petitioners faced formidable cadres of conservative lawyers and judges who began to gradually apply a strict construction of the one-drop rule, which meant that any African ancestry whatsoever would confirm the racial identity of the petitioner.

The highly publicized Susie Phipps case, decided in 1982 and 1985, will illustrate how the courts enforced the historic one-drop rule. However, in the years following the Susie Phipps case, the *de jure* one-drop rule began to wane in state courts. This discussion shows how the legal significance of the one-drop rule changed over time and how courts came to reject the one-drop rule completely by the turn of the twenty-first century, even though the theory continues to be recognized in American culture. This essay will examine the transformation of the one-drop rule as well as analyze how whiteness was redefined by the turn of the century.[6]

A CRITICAL THEORY DEFINED

I will use the "ideograph" to analyze the rhetoric of the legal community of lawyers and judges. Michael Calvin McGee, a renowned American communication scholar and social critic, coined the term in 1980 to analyze the relationship between language and ideologies. McGee explains that an ideograph is a form of "language characterized by slogans while promoting a specific ideology."[7] In other words, ideographs serve as the vocabulary or linguistic units that are the basis of an ideology and are the building blocks of ideological, political discourses. Moreover, many scholars contend that an ideograph can expose the interests and motives of any hidden political agenda held by the majority.[8] Using the ideograph, this chapter will reveal how the one-drop doctrine served as a tool to legitimize a rigid color line that was rooted in racism. Phillip Wander, a leading scholar who has created another critical rhetorical theory, states that the "linguistic basis of an ideograph reveals the ideological commitments of the discursive com-munity."[9] Wander further explains that an ideograph "is transcendent; it is as much an influence on the belief and behavior of the elite as well as the rest of society."[10] Understanding what is meant by an ideograph is useful in my analysis of lawyers and judges and their interpretation of the one-drop rule, which they frequently used as an ideograph.

McGee makes it abundantly clear that it is "inherently persuasive" when people in power deploy political rhetoric or, for the purpose of my analysis, the creation of legislation or jurisprudence. As he explains it, the way we use language can "dictate discussion and control public belief and behavior."[11] Hence, readers should not minimize the language used by people in power, including judges and legislators. These legislative rhetoricians can mold standards, establish linguistic boundaries, and forge an ideological system that rewards or punishes people who live under their authority. They can also control human behavior and shape public conduct.[12] Thus, terms like the "one-drop rule" are unique because such terms can be used strategically to achieve political, social, or economic goals.

According to McGee, the meaning of an ideograph may expand or con-tract as its linguistic relationships to other terms respond to situational or contextual changes.[13] In certain situations, people are forced to use a par-ticular term as it becomes a more dominant feature in their discourses. The context in which words are used will determine their ideographic signifi-cance. In this chapter, I illustrate how the one-drop rule emerges as an ideo-graph. I also trace its rise to power, operating as the dominant ideograph in jurisprudence in matters involving racial identity during the early part of the twentieth century. As the dominant ideograph during this time period, the one-drop rule contributed to a system where any person accused of having any African lineage, no matter how remote, was legally identified as black, even if he or she looked white. This analysis will also highlight the decline of its ideographic significance during the end of the twentieth century and into the twenty-first century.

THE SOCIO-LEGAL CONTEXT

Scholars have described the ways in which Jim Crow legislation influenced social, legal, and political discourses after the Civil War. After 1877 most southern states imposed political, economic, and social restrictions on

African Americans, including those who looked white.[14] On the surface, some of the laws initially appeared to be race-neutral. For example, the Louisiana Constitution did not mention race and did not establish any criteria for classifying mixed-race people. Nevertheless, Jim Crow statutes appeared with devastating consequences. These policies enforced a rigid color line that affected mixed-race people who looked nearly white. The national government went along with these state laws, and the Supreme Court formally endorsed racial segregation in *Plessy v. Ferguson* in 1896, by way of an ideograph, which colloquially became known as separate but equal.[15]

American society made many more uses of *Plessy v. Ferguson* than the Supreme Court justices might have intended. While the Supreme Court did not define racial identity, the flexible standard used for race gave way to the rigid one-drop rule. Due to a lack of clear or reliable criteria that had been previously used to evaluate racial identity, debates about whiteness remained troubling. In response to the ambiguities of appearance and the white-male fear that black men would engage in sexual intercourse with white women, the state legislature began to enact new versions of these statutes in 1894. Lawmakers revoked an 1870 statute that had allowed mixed-race marriages. The new law made it a crime for blacks and whites to share the same bed, a statute which lawmakers affirmed in 1908. The Louisiana law specifically established "That concubinage between a person of the Caucasian or white race and a person of the *negro or black race* is hereby made a felony."[16] Living together was considered proof of violating the law regulating interracial sex. Though the legislature intended to outlaw close and intimate associations between blacks and whites, these statutes were complicated by two facts. First, the state had been tolerant of interracial relationships for a long time, and the new policy would be difficult to enforce in communities that had mingled to the extent that it was difficult to figure out who was white or black. Second, the legislature had intentionally left what it meant by "a person of color" vague. Hence, the interpretation of this racial classification fell to state courts.[17] That is, did a person of color include a "colored" person, a black person or a "negro," who should also be subject to "one-drop" restrictions?

The Louisiana had passed the Railway Accommodations Act (1890) to separate the races in intrastate travel. The law made it obligatory that conductors aboard the train be able to identify blacks and whites, which was not always easy in New Orleans where white-looking Creoles were in large numbers. The parents of Edith and Belle Lee fit into this category, and had self-identified as white people. Railroad authorities called their whiteness into question when they challenged the racial identity of the children. The parents put the children on a train owned by the New Orleans Great Northern Railroad Company. They had purchased first-class tickets for the girls to be seated in the coach set aside for whites. Edith and Belle did not initially face a problem because the conductor believed them to be white. Evidently, a passenger aboard the train knew the girls, complaining that they were African Americans. Even though the teenagers were only eight miles from their destination when he acquired the information, the conductor felt duty-bound to remove the girls under the accommodations act. The conductor may have been liable under state law and charged with a misdemeanor had he failed to enforce the accommodations law upon notice that the passengers were black.

The parents believed their girls were white and sued the company for the way the conductor had treated the girls. During the deposition it was discovered that their father was white and their mother was said to be of mixed blood, but the degree of admixture was not ascertained at the trial. District court judge Thomas M. Burns ruled against the plaintiff under a strict interpretation of the law. The term "colored," Burns concluded, included individuals with "an appreciable admixture of negro blood." On appeal, the state Supreme Court considered the controversy within the context of the separate coach law. Justice John R. Land wrote the opinion for the Supreme Court, employing one-drop reasoning by pointing out that any person with an "appreciable mixture of negro blood belongs to the colored race."[18] Furthermore, he continued, "the burden of proof was on the plaintiff to establish that his children belonged to the white race." The court, therefore, ruled in favor of the defendant because the plaintiff did not satisfy the burden of proof for his claim to white privilege. While it would seem that the court had ended the controversy concerning the one-drop rule, the judges were not unanimous.

That same year, the state Supreme Court reviewed *State v. Treadway*, which was brought under a state ban on interracial marriages. Octave Treadway was uncontested as a white man, but Josephine Lightell Treadway, his wife, had been accused of being an octoroon, notwithstanding that she had always self-identified as white. The Treadways were charged with violating the 1908 law that prohibited intimate relations between blacks and whites. Frank D. Chretien, the trial judge, faced the question of determining whether Josephine was a person of color or whether she was white. The state took the position that any trace of African blood, no matter how slight, made a person black. The defense argued that any remote African ancestry she might have had was so slight that she should be classified as white. Moreover, the defense asserted that since whites were the superior race the defendant's white "blood" should have canceled out any inferior black "blood" she might have had. Judge Chretien emphasized that under community standards a colored person was someone with any trace of African ancestry whatsoever. However, he ruled that under state law an octoroon was not a person of color, and therefore was not black.[19] Chretien obviously rejected the one-drop rule under the theory that someone who was one-eighth black could no longer be classified as African American.

On appeal to the state Supreme Court, the majority evaluated the intent of the legislature in enacting the 1908 statute. Writing for the majority, Justice Oliver O. Provosty explained that the question before the court was "whether an octoroon is 'a person of the negro or black race' within the meaning of the statute." The prosecutor contended that under community standards the term colored and "negro" were synonymous. Furthermore, he conceded, that while a "negro was necessarily a person of color, a person of color was not necessarily a negro."[20] Louisiana law did not provide for a strict definition of a "negro"; hence, the court could not say that a person of the defendant's background was in that racial class and subject to the restriction thereof. The court affirmed the district court with a vote of 3–2. This decision reveals that the court was not pleased with the way the legislature had crafted the 1908 law; hence, the judges seemingly urged lawmakers to provide clearer standards for racial identity. The court found the separate car act to be clearer than the interracial marriages law. However, the court did not want to apply the accommodations law to intimate relationships.

The state Supreme Court noted that the weakness in the law was one of definition. It could not say under the current state law that a colored person was automatically considered black. The court decision aroused public opinion because it clearly diverged from community norms, where the standard for racial identity had evolved to include colored as a synonym for black. The *Daily Times* in Baton Rouge rightly predicted that legislation for separation of the races would be revised in light of recent court opinions. The newspaper suggested that nearly white people would need to be considered colored, to bring state laws in line with community norms. Within a month, the legislature answered with a new code, which placed "colored" and "negro" in the same racial class. The 1908 law targeted "negroes" only, as if "colored" persons could be considered white; the new law did away with that loophole, which led to mixed-race people being classified as white.[21]

The Louisiana legislature seemingly abandoned the permeable racial classification system that had been accepted in the state for more than two hundred years. Mixed-race people who had been classified as "white" on the basis of their physical appearance and association with other whites would now find themselves on the other side of the color line, and tensions over application of the law would continue in Louisiana. The state Supreme Court would establish the tone that would allow a nearly white person to provide evidence of his or her whiteness as sufficient proof of their racial status. In our system of justice, the court seemed to have said, a person is innocent until proven guilty. Until the evidence proved otherwise, a party who seemed to have had a reasonable claim to white privilege was deemed to be white.

Consequently, when the Louisiana Supreme Court reviewed *Duvigneaud v. Loquet*, it was clear that the color line was subject to controversy. Adelard Duvigneaud had married Anne Marie in 1853, and they had one son, Raoul. Upon the death of his first wife, he remarried and had other children. Upon Duvigneaud's death, children from the second marriage contested Raoul's claim of inheritance by arguing that his mother was white and their father was a man of color, which rendered Raoul's claim invalid under state law. Louisiana, they alleged, made it illegal for a mixed-race individual to marry a white. If the state endorsed this interpretation of the law, Raoul would be considered a bastard child, and their father's estate would go to the descendants from the second marriage, which was valid under state law. The plaintiffs conceded that Duvigneaud was the son of a white man, but maintained that his mother was a "colored woman." They based their proof on the testimony of witnesses who claimed that their mother had told them about the racial status of Raoul's grandmother. The court, however, considered their testimony to be hearsay, contradictory, and unreliable. The court rejected the one-drop arguments of the plaintiffs, instead finding the marriage license of Duvigneaud and his first wife, the Catholic priest who performed the marriage, and the consent of the groom's white parents to the marriage to be compelling evidence that his bride was also white.[22] The court also used Raoul's physical appearance and his reputation in the community to conclude that he too was white.

Though Duvigneaud's children from his second marriage had failed to disinherit their brother on grounds that their father's first marriage was not legal under state law, their assault on the marriage was a useful tool of other plaintiffs seeking to legally end a marriage. Annulment cases, therefore, provided the courts another opportunity to evaluate the meaning of the one-drop rule. Courts all across the country faced this problem at one time or another. State courts did not always give white males the relief they were seeking, frequently choosing to protect the women whom they had accepted in marriage. In 1916 Henry Robert Neuberger asked a Louisiana court to give him an annulment in his marriage to Mary Delia Gueldner, claiming that he did not know of her quality of invisible blackness. The Supreme Court, however, looked to compelling evidence that supported the whiteness of the defendant. Justice Oliver Provosty, writing for the majority, explained that Gueldner had always been accepted as white in the community. Her father was undeniably white and her mother had always passed as white. Gueldner had also attended schools alongside whites without controversy about her racial identity. The court saw her on the witness stand and listened to people talk about her, with all concluding that she was white. The court did not find persuasive the plaintiff's claim that he had recently discovered that she was of African ancestry. The Supreme Court, therefore, affirmed the trial judge in holding that the marriage was valid under state law.[23]

The Louisiana court was following a national trend of protecting married women whose husbands tried to divorce them under the claim of invisible blackness. In New York, for example, Leonard Kip Rhinelander, bowing to pressure from his wealthy father who threatened to disinherit him for marrying a woman of color, tried to void his marriage to Alice Beatrice Jones only five weeks after their nuptials. In his defense, Rhinelander claimed that he was not aware of Alice's trait of invisible blackness, and he asked the court to enforce the one-drop rule to end the marriage. The scandal attracted attention from all across the country, with the majority of people undoubtedly believing that a "colored woman" would automatically lose in a dispute involving a rich white man from high society. Rhinelander, however, lost the case because the jury was not persuaded that his bride had deceived him about her background. On appeal, the state appellate court reached the same conclusion.[24]

Although Louisiana courts early rejected one-drop reasoning in estate and divorce cases, judges endorsed it in public school cases. Typically, these cases involved children who had been accepted under community standards as "white" but were later accused of being a racial passer. Schoolmasters expelled these children to uphold segregation of the races. Louisiana courts would eventually adopt terms as "passing as white" to justify the denial of white skin privilege. Passing as white is just one example of how the one-drop rule was used rhetorically to cultivate the social definition of race.

The term established a white racial identity as well as providing that "colored" people were also black and thereby excludable from privilege.

The situation began to change in Louisiana during the 1920s when state courts began to review public school cases. The Louisiana Supreme Court, like state supreme courts elsewhere, viewed public education cases differently from those that took away rights from a party. In *Van Camp v. Ohio*, for example, the Ohio Supreme Court anticipated the 1896 ruling of the United States Supreme Court in *Plessy v. Ferguson* when it looked for educational accommodations available to "colored" children as it barred them from the Ohio public schools. By separating the races, the court found that it was not depriving the civic right to an education from African American children who had the opportunity to get an education in segregated schools. Likewise, the Louisiana Supreme Court used the same criterion in two school cases that came before it in 1918.

The Oberly family had been sending their child to the white public school Calcasieu Parish for roughly seven years. Evidently due to a rumor passing around the school that their child had a quality of invisible blackness, the schoolmaster expelled her from the institution. Her parents sued the school district, but a local court refused to order the parish to readmit her. Despite its record of expanded whiteness to include parties who looked white, the Oberlys' appeal to the state Supreme Court was met with a surprising opinion on January 3, 1918. In *Oberly v. Calcasieu Parish School Board*, Justice Provosty, writing for the majority, dismissed the case, claiming that the court did not have jurisdiction. The case did not meet the court's financial standard for review, he wrote, nor did it fall into the classes of cases that would warrant a review by the court.[25] While the court dodged the issue by refusing to review the dispute, public education cases would not go away, as parents contested how school directors classified their children as black.

Henry Billiot and his wife filed a complaint against Terrebonne Parish in the Ohio district court claiming that the school district had wrongly classified their children as black. Their three children, ages eight, ten, and twelve, had been attending the parish school without any problems. Apparently, a rumor circulated that the children were actually black, and not white. The schoolmaster thereupon removed the children from the school without consulting their parents, and they sued the district, seeking their readmission. After Judge William E. Howell heard the case and ruled against them, the Billiots appealed the case to the Supreme Court. The defense attorney maintained the argument that the schoolmaster dismissed the children because they were "of the colored race." Here again the courts avoided the issue, with Justice C. William O'Neill denying jurisdiction in the case. The majority claimed that the financial amount involved in the suit did not meet the court's standards for hearing the case. As O'Neil put it, "Our conclusion is that we have not jurisdiction of the suit, and that it should be transferred to the court of appeal."[26] The court also said the claim of slander did not have anything to do with this case.

While the Louisiana Supreme Court clearly endorsed the one-drop rule in the foregoing cases, its opinions were nuanced under the claim of a lack of jurisdiction. In *Sunseri v. Cassagne*, the court worked carefully but ultimately enforced the one-drop rule. *Sunseri* is significant because it is the first Louisiana Supreme Court case that used ancestry to establish a black racial identity. Cyril P. Sunseri had married Verna Cassagne fully believing she was white, as he was. After they had consummated the marriage Sunseri learned that people were saying that his wife was actually colored. When Cassagne refused to grant him a divorce, he filed a petition for an annulment. Cassagne clearly had the phenotype of a white individual, and told the court that she had lived as white her entire life. She provided evidence that showed she was born in the white wing of a maternity ward in the hospital. She attended a white church and had been baptized as a white. Cassagne had performed whiteness by attending school with whites and did not face any opposition. She also enjoyed white privilege in various accommodations, including railroad cars and hotel rooms, without controversy. Cassagne claimed that her friends and associates were all white, and thus under community standards she had been regarded as completely white. Sunseri presented birth records as evidence to show that Cassagne had black relatives, including an aunt. On the basis of this evidence the trial judge granted the annulment.[27]

Cassagne appealed the case to the state Supreme Court. Judges on the high court sympathized with the appellant because they did not want to deny her the material rights of a wife. The court initially ignored the birth certificates obtained from the Recorder of Births and Marriages for the Parish of New Orleans "that defendant is a member of the colored race." These records had been the basis for the trial judge's opinion that Verna was colored. The court found it persuasive that her immediate friends and associates were all white, which they believed confirmed her identity as a Caucasian. Nevertheless, the Supreme Court held that the certificates were compelling, and if admitted into evidence they would shape the ruling of the court. Instead of relying on them, the court remanded the case for further review, thereby sidestepping the major issue in the case.[28]

However, the lower court reached the same conclusion it had decided earlier, and the case was again appealed to the Supreme Court. The court took the position that Cassagne was white until it was proven otherwise. It left it to her to provide evidence to counter the documentary evidence furnished by the plaintiff. The court also accepted evidence that traced Cassagne's ancestry back to 1808, where it found convincing evidence of her distant African lineage. The Supreme Court finally handed down a ruling in the case, concluding that Cassagne fit the description of a colored person under state law because she had one-drop of African "blood."[29]

It is clear that by mid-century the Louisiana Supreme Court firmly supported the "traceable amount rule" for documenting blackness. However, in *Villa v. Lacoste*, the district court and the Supreme Court rejected the plaintiff's request to annul his marriage to Josephine Lacoste on the grounds that she was secretly a Negro.[30] According to Brattain, Villa's attorneys attempted to use one-drop reasoning to define Filipino as "persons of color" or "Negroes."[31] As Justice E. Howard McCaleb explained:

> The recordation of two of the persons involved in this suit as colored has been explained to my satisfaction and there is nothing in the evidence to indicate that there was ever any Negro blood in the family of either the plaintiff or the defendant. The only color involved at all is that of the Filipino. While the plaintiff had made out a prima facie case by introducing the records, the defendant has explained those records with reasonable certainty.[32]

Despite the fact that Filipinos describe themselves as "colored," as far as Louisiana's courts were concerned, these nonwhite, non-African groups were legally accepted as white people under the law. This case further demonstrates how the one-drop term cultivated a rigid color line whenever African ancestry was present.

During the 1950s, Louisiana adopted new laws and policies that were used to uphold the one-drop rule. According to Brattain, between 1950 and the mid-1960s Louisiana's legislature passed 133 additional segregation statutes—more than any other southern state.[33] Throughout the decade, Louisiana's state officials became more concerned with documents that contained a person's legal racial status. By 1955, children were required to provide a birth certificate or another form of official documentation as proof of their race to register for public school. In 1958 any person who wanted to obtain a marriage license was required to provide legal documentation that revealed one's racial identity. Brattain explains how the New Orleans Board of Health compiled a "race list" of "Negro" surnames as a way of keeping track of the racial classification of its citizens.

To enforce one-drop reasoning, state courts adopted the "beyond a reasonable doubt" criterion whenever individuals attempted to contest a "colored" racial designation on official documents such as birth certificates.[34] The burden was placed upon the person who attempted to claim an absence of Negro ancestry. One example of the difficulties associated with "beyond a reasonable doubt" standard occurs in *Dupas v. New Orleans*.[35] The plaintiff contested the surname as it appeared on his birth certificate as well as the racial classification as "colored." By adopting the beyond a reasonable doubt standard, the state court concluded that Dupas failed to provide enough evidence to demonstrate that he did not possess any Negro ancestry. The court denied his legal right to claim "whiteness."

After 1950 other mixed-race individuals found themselves on a different side of the color line when attempting to claim white privilege. In *Schlumbrecht v. Louisiana State Board of Health*, the plaintiff's parents contested a birth certificate that identified her as "colored." Upon review of the evidence, it was discovered that a third party had informed the State Board of Health that Gwendolyn Schlumbrecht had "traceable amounts of Negro ancestry."[36] In the end, the court concluded that she possessed "one two-hundred and fifty-sixth Negro blood (1/256)."[37] She was classified as "colored" due to the racial status of an ancestor nine generations prior to her birth. Although the Court of Appeals reversed the trial court's decision, the plaintiff's lawyer, Robert Redmann, still stated his trepidation that the traceable amount law stood to affect every single white person in the state of Louisiana. Under the existing "traceable amount" doctrine, a girl who was 99 percent white had been recognized as "black" under the eyes of the law. Immediately after this case was decided, state legislators and other state actors were concerned that "whiteness" had been too rigidly defined by the one-drop doctrine. In late 1970, the legislature passed a new state law: "In signifying race, a person having one-thirty second or less of Negro blood shall not be deemed, described or designated by any public official in the state of Louisiana as 'colored,' a 'mulatto,' a 'black,' a 'negro,' a 'griffe,' an 'Afro-American,' a 'quadroon,' a 'mestizo,' a 'colored person' or a 'person of color.'"[38] Supporters concluded that this new law was designed to ensure that some white people remained on the "white" side of the color line.[39]

In sum, Louisiana's state laws adopted at the start of the twentieth century involuntarily placed mixed-race and white people on the "black" side of the color line with the assistance of the one-drop rule. Even after a less restrictive state statute was adopted, mixed-race and white individuals were unable to successfully claim a white identity. Due to the fact that previous racial classification standards, such as appearance or reputation, had allowed some individuals with African ancestry to be lawfully identified as white, it was impossible to provide enough evidence to satisfy the reasonable doubt standard once the traceable amount rule was endorsed. According to Virginia R. Dominguez, the implications of Louisiana's jurisprudence negatively influenced Creole identity and attitudes toward race during the 1970s and 1980s.[40] Instead of occupying an intermediate status between Negro and white, many Creoles attempted to self-identify as "white."[41] Those who successfully claimed to be "white" were constantly concerned about the vulnerability of their white status.[42] As a result, many Creoles, regardless of the degree of intermixture, chose to hide their genealogies for fear of being placed on the "wrong" side of the color line.[43] By 1970, mixed-raced persons and many whites had been redefined as "colored" or "black."

AN IDEOGRAPHIC ANALYSIS OF THE SUSIE PHIPPS CASE

Prior to 1977, Susie Elizabeth Rita Guillory Phipps had never questioned her racial identity. Phipps had always known that she was white. Her confidence was shaken when she applied for a passport for a trip to South America. To complete the passport application, Phipps was required to submit a copy of her birth certificate. Unfortunately, she did not have access to it and had never seen it before. Phipps, therefore, applied for a copy from the Department of Health and Human Services Vital Statistics office. Once she obtained the copy, Phipps discovered that she and her parents were listed as "colored." In several interviews, Phipps stated that she was shocked because she believed that her parents, Simea Fretty and Dominique Guillory, were white. According to Art Harris of the *Washington Post*, Phipps was so certain that her parents were "white" that she buried them as such. Phipps also stated: "Nothing is bad about being black if you're black, but I'm white. I was never black. I was raised white."[44]

Phipps refused to accept her birth certificate and began to contact other relatives to inquire about the racial classification that was listed on their birth certificates. Several of her siblings also discovered that birth certificates issued between 1919 and 1941 listed their parents and themselves as "colored."[45] Hence, Phipps and her siblings attempted to correct the problem by speaking with employees at the Department of Health and Human Services, requesting new birth certificates that indicated that they were "white." After the department refused to comply, Susie Phipps filed a petition, a writ of *Mandamus*, to obtain a court order to have their individual designations and that of their parents corrected, that is, changed to "white" on each birth certificate. In addition, her attorneys, Brian Begue and Earl Maxwell, questioned the constitutionality of racial classification law. They argued that the law was based on the traceable amount rule (or one-drop reasoning) and that its premises primarily targeted white people. This sentiment was further supported by other journalists who concluded that "under this law, any traceable amount of black heritage was enough to warrant a designation of black."[46] Gregory Jaynes, a reporter for the *New York Times*, observed: "the 1970 law is the only one in the country that gives any equation for determining a person's race. Elsewhere in the nation, race is simply a matter of what the parents tell the authorities to record on the birth certificate, with no questions asked."[47] Despite the rigid racial hierarchy that was created by this law, Phipps's attorneys also argued that without an official statement about the DNA genetic makeup for each ancestor, it was impossible to determine how much Negro blood a person possessed.

The judgments from the district court and the Court of Appeals are significant because they demonstrate how Louisiana's state courts were able to deny "whiteness" to mixed-race and white people in the early 1980s. The one-drop rule emerged as the dominant ideograph or ultimate term of the ideology, controlling the meanings of other ideographs that also exist within the discourse. As the dominant ideograph, the one-drop rule limited the plaintiff's ability to claim whiteness while revealing the racist political agenda of the state courts. The presence of this ideograph controlled the uses or meanings of other ideographs such as "white" and "colored" that were also present in this racialized discourse. According to Justice Frederick Ellis, the term "colored" "is generally accepted to apply to a person with Negro blood or with some admixture of Negro blood, although it has been applied to a person of some other race than white. This is true of the dictionary definitions of the word as well as in the jurisprudence." In the district court's response to Phipps, the meanings of ideographs such as "colored," "white," "black," and "purity" were controlled by the linguistic or ideographic relationship that formed between the "one-drop" ideograph and another ideograph, the "1/32 blood fraction." Once "white" had been redefined as "a state of racial purity" rather than as connected to physical attributes, the court responded by imposing the "no room for doubt" criterion to enforce this standard. This made it impossible for any person claiming whiteness to achieve this goal due to the permeable racial classification system that had existed for hundreds of years in Louisiana.[48]

In Ellis's statement the meaning of the phrase, "The term colored is generally accepted to apply to a person with Negro blood," is ambiguous and can be interpreted in several ways. For example, "colored" could refer to a person of 50 percent Negro blood. Likewise, it could be used to describe a person with any amount of African blood no matter how indistinguishable, as in the Schlumbrecht case. If the latter interpretation is used, the phrase reflects how the one-drop rule cultivated the meaning of "colored" in 1982.

There are two reasons why the last interpretation seems to characterize this court's response. The history of the racial classification system in Louisiana during the early part of the twentieth century and the 1970 law cultivated the social discourse of 1982. The prior uses or the vertical structure of the "colored" ideograph had been molded by the presence of the one-drop ideograph since the 1920s. The one-drop rule established the meaning of "colored" in all social, legal, and political discussions in Louisiana and elsewhere for more than fifty years. Any dictionary's account of the meaning of "colored" in 1982, as cited by Justice Frederick Ellis, would have reflected this social history. In essence, Ellis's observations illustrate how one-drop arguments continued to be used as the primary method of denying claims to "whiteness."[49]

Although one-drop arguments had been endorsed by Louisiana's state courts even before the 1970 law was adopted, they continued to shape legal discussions about racial identity in Louisiana during and immediately after the statute was adopted in 1970. Based on the evidence provided by the state of Louisiana in this dispute, colored "is generally accepted to apply to a person with ANY Negro blood." This interpretation highlights the continued dominance of the one-drop term during the early 1980s in Louisiana.

The interconnectedness of the ideographs "colored" and the "one-drop rule" also influences the meanings of other ideographs that are present within this discourse of race. "White" is defined as not possessing any African ancestry. Although the definition of "white" is not explicitly mentioned in this phrase, its meaning is implied as a result of the presence of the dominant ideographs and the subsequent linguistic or ideographic relationships that serve as the foundation for this discourse of race. The linguistic relationship between "colored" and the "one-drop rule" supports an opposing ideographic relationship between "white" and "purity." The dominance of the one-drop ideograph defined "colored" as a state of "impurity" based on any presence of Negro blood, and "white" as a state of "racial purity" marked by an absence of Negro blood.

In comparison to the first phrase, a second phrase "*or with some admixture of Negro blood*" is also significant. Although it is not clearly defined, "colored" is not determined on the basis of a definite "amount" or "fraction" of Negro blood. Since the phrase implies that "colored" was based on any mixture of Negro and "other" ancestry, it is reasonable to conclude that its use during this case was determined by the 1970 blood-fraction (trace amount) statute. While the 1/32 law had been adopted only eleven years prior to the *Phipps* case, other blood fraction laws had existed for more than two hundred years in other states.[50] In an effort to objectively define racial identity, blood fraction laws were introduced into this discourse about racial identity.[51] Since blood fraction statutes were the only non-one-drop criteria that legislatively occupied a more significant role within this discussion, these laws enforced one-drop reasoning once the fractions of ancestry became smaller and smaller.

The 1982 definition of "colored" is significant for several reasons. First, it illustrates the pervasiveness within this discourse of the one-drop ideograph, which continued to control the uses of several ideographs such as "colored," "mixed race," and "white." Second, the presence of the one-drop rule influenced the creation, development, and enforcement of blood fraction laws. The state could have adopted a different blood fraction formula such, as ¼ or ½, to determine a white identity. However, it chose to select a fraction that requires an individual to possess less than 3 percent ancestry instead of 25 or 30 percent. In response to Phipps's claims, the state provided genetic evidence to determine how much Negro blood Phipps's parents possessed. The district court concluded that her father, Dominique Guillory, had 4.25/32 or 13.215 percent Negro blood.[52] In comparison, her mother, Simea Fretty, had 6.75/32 or 21.09375 percent Negro blood. Based on these percentages, the state concluded that Phipps had 5.5/32 or 17.875 percent Negro blood. However, Phipps needed to possess less than 3 percent Negro blood to overcome a "colored" racial designation according to the statute. Third, this definition reveals that the two dominant ideographs, "one-drop rule" and "blood-fraction rule," worked together to control the meanings of "white," "mixed race," and "colored" and to negate the significance of other ideographs such as "physical appearance" and "association" that previously had been used to determine racial identity.[53]

In addition to defining "colored," Ellis provides a definition of "white" where the dominance of the one-drop ideograph is clear. According to Ellis, white is defined:

> in Webster's Third New International Dictionary as "belonging to a racial group or subdivision of a racial group characterized by reduced skin pigmentation, typically represented by the European Caucasoids, and usu. Specif. distinguished from person belonging to groups marked by black, brown, yellow, or red skin coloration," or being of white ancestry either wholly unmixed with Negro blood or having an admixture of Negro blood less than that specified in various statutes of some states of the U.S.[54]

This definition is similar and yet distinct from the one offered for "colored."

There are several implications associated with Ellis's definition. Physical appearance reappears as an ideograph within the discourse on racial identity. Ellis's full statement indicates that it no longer can serve as the dominant ideograph. It is not the sole basis for determining race. Instead, it is used only to reinforce the racial hierarchy that is established by the one-drop rule where whiteness is a state of racial purity. Physical appearance is just additional evidence to illustrate racially pure and impure groups. Ancestry emerges as another dominant ideograph because it serves as the ultimate determinant of whether someone is black or white even if there are ambiguities associated with physical appearance. Ellis's passage offers evidence of how physical appearance operates as a less important ideograph that is secondary to the one-drop rule in determining whiteness.

Justice Ellis's observations further reflect this ideological standpoint rooted in racism within the following passages:

> In this case, it is entirely clear that the relators have the appearance of "white" people. They have fair skins and, in some cases, blue eyes and blond hair. It is also entirely clear that they are of mixed white and Negro blood. With respect to the five Guillory siblings, it is equally apparent that they were considered in their community as colored; that they sat on the colored side of the aisle in church; that they attended a colored school; and that many of their close relatives consider themselves as colored.[55]

It is argued that, because of the inexact meaning of Negro, mulatto, quadroon, colored, gens de coleur and other similar terms used in these records, it is impossible to conclude exactly the degree of Negro blood in the relators' veins. I agree that it is not possible from the evidence to establish the exact degree of Negro blood in the relators' veins. Scientific evidence in the record is to the effect that, although it is probable that an individual inherits equally the genes of his ancestors, it is impossible for the grandchild of a person to inherit no genes whatsoever from that person, so that the grandchild of three white persons and a Negro could have no Negro genes whatsoever.[56]

The audience can conclude that whiteness is exclusive. Phipps faced this reality as a "mixed-race" identity was imposed upon her despite her "white" physical appearance.[57] Once the district court heard all of the evidence presented, it held that Phipps and all but two disputants failed to prove that they were "white." The challenges regarding the legality of Louisiana's racial classification scheme rooted in one-drop reasoning were also overruled. After careful analysis, it is clear how this blood fraction law was wielded against mixed-race and white people in their attempts to claim whiteness in Louisiana.

Similar to the jurisprudence created by the district court, the Court of Appeals' decision in 1985 is influenced by the one-drop rule. Unhappy with the district court's verdict, Phipps appeared before the Court of Appeals, Fourth Circuit in 1985. Her attorney, Begue, continued to argue that Phipps should be identified as "white." Despite Begue's attempts, the Court of Appeals supported the district court's judgment. It concluded that Phipps had not provided enough evidence to prove that beyond a reasonable doubt that she possessed less than three percent African ancestry.

The Court of Appeals came to the same conclusion as the district court notwithstanding their use of a different rhetorical strategy. As Justice Charles R. Ward stated:

Finally, we conclude that the now infamous "one-thirty second" statute, *La*. R.S. 42:267 which was repealed in 1983, is not relevant to this case. All evidence indicates that the disputed racial designations were not made by a public official but by the attending midwife or by the parents themselves, unaware of and unaided by the criteria of 42:267.[58]

If, in 1985, the meaning of "colored" was not based on the law that existed prior to 1983, what factors determined its meaning? Instead of exploring the contemporary uses of colored and white in 1985, the court explored the vertical structure of these terms to identify how they were defined at the time in which birth certificates were issued to the plaintiff's parents. Ward responds to this question in the subsequent passage:

> As to the six appellants who presently have birth certificates, we find that they failed to prove by a preponderance of the evidence that their parents' racial designations are incorrect. Expert testimony indicated that the very concept of the racial classification of individuals, as opposed to that of a group, is scientifically insupportable. Individual racial designations are purely social and cultural perceptions, and the evidence conclusively proves those subjective perceptions were correctly recorded at the time appellants' birth certificates were issued. There is no proof in the record that Simea or Dominique Guillory preferred to be designated as white. They might well have been proud to be described as colored. Indeed, we have no evidence that during their lifetimes they objected to the racial designations in dispute in this case. Accordingly, we hold that the defendant state officers have no legal duty to alter the birth certificates.[59]

Ward's response is particularly unique because it fails to mention the one-drop rule explicitly. His interpretation of the meaning of "colored" is subject to the way in which it was defined between 1919 and 1941. As demonstrated in the previous section, the one-drop ideograph influenced Louisiana's jurisprudence and legislation during the time in question. Cases such as *Cassagne, Sunseri,* and *Lacoste* confirm the state's commitment to endorse the one-drop rule during the first part of the twentieth century. Since the state was able to trace the Guillory family's judicial history back to the 1700s, it would have been impossible to prove that each family member lacked any African ancestry due to the common practice of miscegenation that existed in Louisiana prior to the dawn of the twentieth century.[60] As a result, Guillory and Fretty were legally classified as colored, and this classification was lawfully imposed upon their children. Ultimately, the previous restricted uses of "colored" grounded in one-drop reasoning served as the basis for its use in 1985.

In comparison to Ward's discourse, Justice Joan Bernard Armstrong's dissenting opinion also supports the conclusion that whiteness is defined by examining its prior uses or vertical structure. According to Armstrong:

Although the majority is correct in pointing out that the plaintiffs themselves have not been specifically classified by the State, i.e., their birth certificates do not indicate the race of the child, I am compelled to point out that the society in which plaintiffs grew up, and perhaps to a lesser extent our present society, classify one according to ancestral designations, "you are what your parents are." Since plaintiffs' parents were designated as "colored", plaintiffs will continue to be regarded as members of the black race by some segments of our society no matter what they proclaim themselves to be. Given this past and present reality I must disagree with the majority holding that the constitutionality of LSA-R.S. 42:267 is irrelevent [*sic*].

The most significant part of this passage is the statement "the society in which plaintiffs grew up, and perhaps to a lesser extent our present society, classify one according to ancestral designations, 'you are what your parents are.'" If racial classification was contingent upon the race of one's parents, the standards that determined the race of one's parents must be used to establish the race of the offspring. By tracing the history of race during the early part of the twentieth century, the one-drop rule solely determined the plaintiff's racial identity. Previous terms such as "association" or "physical appearance" disappeared or became less relevant within this discourse.

POST–CIVIL RIGHTS JURISPRUDENCE

Although the lower court and the Court of Appeals endorsed one-drop reasoning in the Phipps case in 1982 and 1985, it is debatable whether its dominance prevailed in other cases after 1980. In cases where the boundary of the color line was in question, several state and federal courts reintroduced ideographs into this discourse that had been excluded after the one-drop rule had become the dominant ideograph. By the end of the twentieth century, the presence of former and new ideographs challenged the significance of the one-drop rule. The 1980s, 1990s, and the start of the twenty-first century were also characterized by a new phenomenon. Instead of attempting to claim "whiteness," some individuals argued that this legal racial classification had been wrongfully imposed upon them.

In a case where an individual rejected a racial classification as "white," the Supreme Court of Minnesota refused to acknowledge the existence of a set of racial categories. In *Greene v. Minnesota Department of Human Services* (2008), the plaintiff insisted that he was Native American and not "white."[61] To resolve this dispute, the court never provided any criteria to establish a color line. Instead, the court claimed that identity was a political classification rather than one based on race.

In contrast to Minnesota, some courts, including the Massachusetts Supreme Court, utilized physical appearance and the rule of association to define whiteness. In 1977 brothers Philip and Paul Malone were accused of racial fraud when they stated on a job application that they were black. Using the "eyeball test," or relying upon physical attributes, their boss drew the conclusion that the brothers were in fact "white." Once they were fired, the plaintiffs filed a suit before the Massachusetts district court and the Court of Appeals.[62] Using the same one-drop arguments that were previously endorsed by virtually all state and federal courts for the majority of the twentieth century, the brothers provided a photograph of their maternal great-grandmother who they claimed was "black." They argued that despite their physical appearance, their black ancestor justified their placement on the "black" side of the color line.[63] The brothers also provided evidence to support the rule of association to demonstrate their involvement within the black community such as their NAACP membership.

The hearing officer appointed by the fire department utilized fixed criteria to determine their racial identity. His standard included: "(i) Visual observation of physical features; (ii) documentary evidence establishing black ancestry, such as birth certificates; and (iii) evidence that the Malone's or their families held themselves out to be black and are considered black in the community."[64] Based on the physical appearance test, the hearing officer argued that the brothers were visibly white. In addition, the district court justice declared that for the past three generations there was not one individual who had been identified as anything other than "white." This is significant because none of their ancestors had been identified as "colored" during the eras in which the one-drop rule clearly determined who was white.[65] In addition, the Supreme Court of Massachusetts ignored evidence of the Malones' involvement in the black community, declaring it insufficient proof to support the self-identification or group acceptance criteria. Therefore, *Malone* represents a challenge to the prior ideological perspectives about racial identity in the United States. Although one-drop arguments were used by attorneys, the Supreme Court of Massachusetts endorsed other ideographs. In the case of the Malone brothers, "physical appearance" was the vehicle for determining that the Malone brothers were white.

Like the Malone brothers, Mary Christine Walker, in 1988, was also accused of racial fraud for attempting to "pass as black." Her employer requested a copy of her birth certificate after Walker identified herself as "black" on a job application.[66] In response, Walker filed a suit requesting that "the US District Court in Colorado order the Department of Vital Statistics to issue a new birth certificate to her."[67] Walker explained that her parents were interracial and that they had written "white" on her birth certificate believing that she would have more opportunities if people believed that she was white. Walker also explained how her darker siblings were called "Niggers" when they were younger. Unlike the Malone brothers, Walker collected evidence from high-ranking officials in the black community and black radio stations to support her claim of being "black." She did not rely on the one-drop rule to reject her racial classification. Walker succeeded in challenging her racial classification as white by using another ideograph, "reputation," to serve as the foundation of her argument. Unlike the Supreme Court in Massachusetts, in 1989 the US District Court in Colorado endorsed the rule of association, self-identification, and the group acceptance standards to determine that Mary Walker was not white. Ultimately the court ordered the Department of Vital Statistics in Kansas to issue Walker a new birth certificate with the corrected racial classification as "black."

Similar to the Malone and Walker cases, in *Perkins v. Lake County Department of Utilities*, another US District Court was asked to determine the boundaries of "whiteness." The plaintiff denied that he was "white" despite the fact that he had been previously identified as such. Using the group identification standard, the lower court observed that the plaintiff did not live in an Indian community nor had he participated in any cultural events. It also used the physical appearance test and a new ideograph—the self-identification test—to rule that the plaintiff was "white."[68] Upon appeal, the US District Court explored the plaintiff's pedigree and discovered that his parents and grandparents were classified as either "white" or "mulatto" during the late nineteenth and early twentieth centuries. Despite the presence of African ancestry, this court rejected one-drop arguments that the plaintiff was "black." Instead, the federal court relied upon testimonies from witnesses who stated that they believed the plaintiff was Native American and not white on the basis of his physical appearance. In addition to physical attributes, the court also accepted the plaintiff's testimony that he has always self-identified as a Native American. In essence, the appellate court's discourse in *Perkins* further demonstrates an ideological shift. One-drop reasoning was ignored while former and new terms established the boundaries of whiteness in the twenty-first century.

In the *Walker*, *Perkins*, and *Malone* cases, the one-drop rule failed to remain the dominant ideograph. In all three cases, the ideograph was present but no court endorsed it. The presence of new and old ideographs such as physical appearance, association, and self-identification forced its removal from the legal discourse. While the Malone brothers were unsuccessful in proposing one-drop arguments to support their claim of blackness, Walker and Perkins opted to discard one-drop arguments and were successful in challenging a "white" racial classification. In essence, this discursive shift reveals the meanings of "white" and "colored" were determined by other ideographs and new ideographic relationships during the late 1980s and 1990s.

In addition to addressing legal challenges to a white racial classification, courts at the end of the twentieth century and at the start of the twenty-first century responded to other issues involving racial identity. In *Houston v. Metro Transit Authority* in 1997, US District Court Judge Lynne N. Hughes acknowledged that multiple standards such as blood fraction laws and the one-drop rule had been previously used to define racial groups. However, Hughes stated that the only standards the federal government acknowledges are the rule of association and group association. In *Smulls v. Roper*, the petitioner challenged the removal of the lone black person from a jury. The trial court refused to comment on the racial composition of the jury pool. In comparison to *Greene*, the trial court judge also stated that any legal or legislative criteria to distinguish between racial groups failed to exist. US Appellate Court Justice William Corrigan confessed, "I don't know what constitutes black. Years ago they used to say one-drop of black blood constitutes black. Can anyone enlighten me on what black is?" Despite Bye's professed confusion regarding racial identity, the prosecution never challenged the defense attorney's assessment of the racial identity of the juror in question. Based on the evidence presented, the one-drop rule was a nonfactor in this case. Instead, physical appearance was used as the basis of determining the racial identity of the jury.

Although there is clear evidence that the state and federal courts failed to enforce one-drop arguments in instances where individuals attempted to challenge a white racial classification after 1980, there is evidence that some courts other than Louisiana's state and federal courts endorsed one-drop arguments in special situations. In the *Gristede vs. Unkechauge Nation*

(2009), one-drop arguments were upheld. The US District Court for Eastern New York was asked to determine whether the defendants were immune from a lawsuit on the basis of their sovereign status as an Indian tribe.[69] To avoid the suit, the defendants needed to demonstrate that they were of the same race or the descendants of the original Unkechauge tribe. The court reviewed historical documentation regarding the Unkechauge tribe, including all of the contact that it had with Europeans and African Americans. An ethno-historian testified that the interactions with these non-Indian groups had terminated the "purity" of the tribe. With the assistance of the one-drop rule, he concluded that the descendants were not of the same race as the original members of the tribe. In an unusual chain of events, the plaintiffs argued that the presence of African ancestry was sufficient evidence to demonstrate that the defendants were "mulattoes" and not Indians or white. In contrast, the tribal chief also used the one-drop blood quantum, to argue that anyone with a drop of Unkechauge blood is a member of the tribe. Since the defendants met the one-drop quantum, they should be recognized as members of a sovereign tribe. In the end, the appellate court endorsed one-drop arguments regarding Indian, rather than African, ancestry and supported the self-identification standard to reject whiteness as well as an avoidance of placement on the black side of the color line. As in the *Malone, Walker*, and *Perkins* cases, the meaning of "white" in 2009 was modified. Several plaintiffs were able to show how one-drop arguments adversely affected missed race people.

CONCLUSION

This chapter adopts an interdisciplinary approach to examining the boundaries of "whiteness" in jurisprudence after 1980. An analysis of the historical development of racial identity in Louisiana during the first part of the twentieth century is used to illustrate how the color line in the United States was rigidly defined by the one-drop ideograph. The one-drop rule restricted who had a right to lawfully claim "whiteness." Little scholarship has been allocated to addressing the significance of the one-drop rule in legal discourse at the end of the twentieth century and into the twenty-first century. This discussion serves as a foundation for examining the role of one-drop ideograph in legal discussions about racial identity during this period. Based on the research presented, this chapter reveals that toward the end of the twentieth century several courts became more reluctant to adopt one-drop arguments when determining whiteness. By examining the linguistic choices of judges and attorneys, the waning significance of this ideograph is visible. This chapter suggests that state and federal courts are committed to supporting a more permeable color line, one where mixed-race individuals have more autonomy over their placement on the color line.

McGee's ideographic theory was used to highlight the rise and fall of the one one-drop term in contemporary jurisprudence. He argues that the dominant terms (ideographs) within a political discourse reflect the most influential ideological perspectives at a given time. Using McGee's critical theory, this chapter explored how mixed-race and white people were involuntarily placed on the black side of the color line throughout the first part of the twentieth century.

Louisiana's legislative and judicial history during the first part of the twentieth century reveals how the one-drop rule contributed to the emergence of a rigid color line that affected millions of people who had been socially accepted as mixed race or white. In 1982 and 1985, Susie Phipps attempted to prove that she was white. Continuing to serve as the dominant ideograph in Louisiana's jurisprudence during the late twentieth century, the "one-drop rule" narrowly defined whiteness as a state of racial purity free from the presence of any African ancestry. Using scientific evidence, the state established that the plaintiff and her parents were racially mixed. Therefore, Phipps was denied the ability to claim whiteness.

Although the Phipps case reveals the codification of whiteness via the one-drop term during the 1980s in Louisiana, this relationship is not characteristic of all of the jurisprudence during this period. In contrast to the first part of the twentieth century, more individuals rejected "whiteness" in the latter. In *Malone, Walker,* and *Perkins,* the plaintiffs legally challenged a "white" racial classification, and, instead of continuing to enforce one-drop arguments, the courts endorsed other standards to determine whiteness. As the one-drop rule lost relevance, whiteness was more loosely defined.

In addition to Phipps, there is one case in which the courts supported one-drop arguments to establish the color line after 1980. Despite the presence of one-drop reasoning, *Gristede* represents a potentially significant ideological shift in jurisprudence on racial identity. The court failed to place a person on the colored or black side of the color line despite the presence of African ancestry. In addition, the manner in which the one-drop rule is used in the twenty-first century is in stark contrast to prior uses. The one-drop doctrine developed a new horizontal structure, one where it was used to determine alternative racial delineations rather than African ancestry. In sum, since 1980 state and federal courts have redefined whiteness; this definition contributes to a less rigid color line as compared to the past due in part to the declining significance of the one-drop ideograph.

NOTES

1. Erica Cooper, "One Speck of *Imperfection:* Invisible Blackness and the One-Drop Rule: An Interdisciplinary Approach to Examining Plessy v. Ferguson and Jane Doe v. State of Louisiana," (PhD diss., Indiana University, 2008), ProQuest Dissertations and Theses (AAT 3315914); Frank W. Sweet, *Legal History of the Color Line: The Rise and Triumph of the One Drop Rule* (Palm Coast: Backintyme, 2005).

2. F. James Davis, *Who Is Black? One Nation's Definition* (University Park: Penn State University Press, 2010); Sweet, *Legal History of the Color Line*.

3. Cooper, "One Speck," chapters 3–4; Sweet, *Legal History of the Color Line*.

4. Pauli Murray, ed., *States' Laws on Race and Color* (Athens: University of Georgia Press, 1997), 77, 164, 254.

5. Francis Mootz, *Rhetorical Knowledge in Legal Practice and Critical Legal Theory* (Tuscaloosa: University of Alabama Press, 2006); Linda Greene, "Race in the Twenty-first Century: Equality Through the Law?" in Kimberly Crenshaw, Neil Gotanda, Gary Peller, and Kendall Thomas, ed., *Critical Race Theory: The Key Writings that Formed the Movement* (New York: New Press, 1995), 449–65; Janice Schuetz, *Communicating the Law: Lessons from Landmark Legal Cases* (Long Grove: Waveland, 2007); Diana Williams, "Justice, Color Blindness and the Octoroon in Homer Plessy's Louisiana" at http://citation.allacademic.com/meta/p_mla_apa_research_citation/1/1/6/5/8/p116586_index.html; James Boyd Williams, *Hercules' Bow: Essays on the Rhetoric and Poetics of the Law* (Madison: University of Wisconsin Press, 1989); Ariela J. Gross, "Litigating Whiteness: Trials of Racial Determination in the Nineteenth Century South," 108.1 *Yale Law Review* (1998): 109–88; Celeste Michelle Condit and John Lucaites, *Crafting Equality: America's Anglo-African Word* (Chicago: University of Chicago Press, 1993); David Ball, *Theater Tips and Strategies for Jury Trials* (South Bend: National Institute for Trial Advocacy, 1994).

6. *Philip Malone and Paul Malone v. Civil Service Commission and the Department of Personnel Administration* (1995) 646 N.E.2d 150, 38 Mass. App. Ct. 147; Peggy Peterman, "After Growing up Hiding Her Race, A Former Teacher Fights to Claim Her Ancestry in a World of Black and White," *St. Petersburg Times*, September 15, 1989, 1D; *Arthur Perkins v. Lake County Department of Utilities, et. al* (1994) 860 F. Suppl. 1262; *Houston Contractors Association v. Metropolitan Transit Authority of Harris County* (1997) 993 F. Supp. 545; *Gristede Foods Inc. v. Unkechauge Nation* (2009) 660 F. Supp. 2d 442; *Herbert Smulls v. Don Roper* (2006) 467 F.3d 1108; *Buddie Greene vs. Commissioner of the Minnesota Department of Human Services and Aitkin County Health and Human Services* 755 N.W.2d 713.

7. Michael Calvin McGee, "The Ideograph: A Link between Rhetoric and Ideology," 6 *Quarterly Journal of Speech* (1980): 6.

8. Kenneth Burke, A *Grammar of Motives* (New York: Prentice Hall, 1935), 43–46; Richard Weaver, *The Ethics of Rhetoric* (Chicago: Gateway, 1953), 211–32; Rosalind Coward and John Ellis, *Language and Materialism* (London: Routledge, 1977), 61–152; Earnest Cassier, *Language and Myth*, trans. Susanne K. Langer (1946; New York: Dover, 1953), 62–83.

9. Philip Wander, "The Ideological Turn in Modern Criticism," *Readings in Rhetorical Criticism*, ed. Carol Burgchard, 2nd ed. (State College, PA: Strata, 2000), 107.

10. Ibid.

11. McGee, "The Ideograph," 5.

12. Ibid., 6.

13. Ibid., 10.

14. Albert Blaustein and Robert Zangrado, eds., *Civil Rights and African Americans* (Evanston, IL: Northwestern University Press, 1991), 311.

15. *Plessy v Ferguson* 163 U.S. 537 (1896).

16. La. Acts 1908, No 87; Maurice J. Naquin Jr., "Criminal Law—Miscegenation—Definition of 'Cohabitation,'" 19.3 *Louisiana Law Review* (April 1959): 703–4.

17. Alecia P. Long, *The Great Southern Babylon: Sex, Race, and Respectability in New Orleans* (Baton Rouge: Louisiana State University Press, 2005), 209–10; *State of Louisiana v. Treadway* (1910), Sup court of Louisiana, Docket no 18149 (52 So. 510, Supreme Court of Louisiana (1910).

18. *Laws of Louisiana*, vol. 111 (1890), 152; *Lee v. New Orleans Great Northern RR* (1910) 125 La. 236; *Southern Reporter* (So., So. 2d), vol. 2, 182; Sweet, *Legal History of the Color Line*, 408; *Second Decennial Edition of the American Digest: A Complete Digest*, vol. 4, (St. Paul, MN: West Publishing, 1916), 266; District of Columbia Court of Appeals, *Reports of Cases Adjudged in the Court of Appeals of the District*, vol. 36 (Rochester, NY: Lawyers Cooperative Publishing), 57.

19. Ibid.; Charles B. Hersch, *Subversive Sounds: Race and the Birth of Jazz in New Orleans* (Chicago: University of Chicago Press, 2007), 100.

20. Ibid.; Lilia Moritz Schwarcz, "Not Black, not White: Just the Opposite; Culture, Race and National Identity in Brazil" (working paper), at file:///C:/Users/sm714/Downloads/Schwarcz47.pdf; Ruth Colker, *Hybrid: Bisexuals, Multiracials, and Other Misfits Under American Law* (New York: New York University Press, 1996), 125.

21. Naquin, "Criminal Law—Miscegenation—Definition of 'Cohabitation,'" 703–4.

22. *Duvigneaud v. Loquet et al.* (1912) 131 La. 568; *Southern Reporter*, vol. 59 (St. Paul, MN: West Publishing, 1913), 992–94.

23. *Neuberger v. Gueldner* (1916) 139 La. 758, *Southern Reporter*, vol. 72, 220; *Neuberger v. Gueldner* (1916) 139 La. 758.

24. See Earl Lewis and Heidi Ardizzone, *Love on Trial: An American Scandal in Black and White* (New York: W.W. Norton, 2001); Angela Onwuachi-Willig, *According to Our Hearts: Rhinelander v. Rhinelander and the Law of the Multiracial Family* (New Haven: Yale University Press, 2013).

25. Sweet, *Legal History of the Color Line*, 421; Frank W. Sweet, "Triumph of the One Drop Rule: Essays on the Color Line" (May 1, 2005), at http://essays.backintyme.biz/item/16.

26. *Southern Reporter*, vol. 79, 79.

27. *Sunseri v. Cassagne*. Nos. 34572, 35504. Supreme Court of Louisiana. 31 October 1938 and 5 February 1940; Virginia R. Dominguez, *White by Definition: Social Classification in Creole Louisiana* (New Brunswick, NJ: Rutgers University Press, 1986).

28. *Robert Green v. City of New Orleans*, Court of Appeals of Louisiana, Orleans (1956); *State Ex Rel. Treadway v. Louisiana State Board of Health*, 61 So. 2d 735 (1952); 221 La. 1048 (1952).

29. *State Ex Rel. Lytell v. Louisiana State Board of Health*, 153 So. 2d 498 (La. Ct. App. 1963).

30. *Villa v. Lacoste et al.* (1948) 213 La. 654.

31. Michelle Brattain, "Miscegenation and Competing Definitions of Race in Twentieth Century Louisiana," 81.3 *Journal of Southern History* (2005): 653.

32. *Villa v. Lacoste et al.* (1948) 213 La., 654.

33. Michelle Brattain, "Miscegenation and Competing Definitions of Race in Twentieth-Century Louisiana," in Jacqueline Jones, ed., *Best American History Essays* (New York: Palgrave, 2007), 199–234.

34. Ibid.

35. *State of Louisiana ex rel. Ralph Dupas v. City of New Orleans*, No. 44118, Supreme Court of Louisiana, 12 December 1960.

36. *Gwendolyn Ann Schlumbrecht v. Louisiana State Board of Health*, No. 3520, Court of Appeals of Louisiana, Fourth Circuit, 2 February 1970.

37. Gregory Jaynes, "Suit on Race Recalls Lines Drawn Under Slavery," *New York Times* (September 30, 1982), 30.

38. *Jane Doe v. State* (1985) 479 So. 2d 369.

39. Jaynes, "Suit on Race," 16.

40. Dominguez, *White by Definition*, 36–40.

41. Ibid.

42. Ibid., 36.

43. Ibid.; Art Harris, "Louisiana Court Sees No Shades of Gray in Woman's Request," *Washington Post* (May 21, 1983).

44. Ibid.

45. *Doe v. Louisiana*.

46. "Woman Seeks Change in Racial Designation," *New York Times* (November 23, 1984).

47. Jaynes, "Suit on Race."

48. *Doe v. Louisiana*.

49. Sweet, *Legal History of the Color Line*; Davis, *One Drop Rule*.

50. Jayne O. Ifekwunigwe, "Let Blackness and Whiteness Wash Through: Competing Discourses on Bi-racialization and the Compulsion of Genealogical Erasures," *Scattered Belongings: Cultural Paradoxes of Race, Nation, and Gender* (London and New York:

Routledge, 1999), 170–93; Jane Purcell Guild, "Who is a Negro?" 67.6 *Journal of Negro Education* (1964): 83–85; Sweet, *Legal History of the Color Line*, chapters 7, 9; 117–32, 153–80; Frank W. Sweet, "Timeline of B/W 'racial' determination in the United States," 1 July 2007 at http://backintyme.com/essays/?p=34; Peggy Pascoe, "Miscegenation Law, Court Cases, and Ideologies of "Race," 83.1 *Journal of American History* (1996): 44–69; Cheryl Harris, "Whiteness as Property," in Kimberle Crenshaw, Neil Gotanda, Gary Peller, and Kendall Thomas, ed., *Critical Race Theory: The Key Writings that Formed the Movement* (New York: New York University Press, 1995), 276–91; Bela August Walter, "The Crime Against Color: The Case Against Race-Based Suspect Descriptions," 103.3 *Columbia Law Review* (2003): 662–88; Ian Haney Lopez, "White by Law," in Richard Delgado, ed., *Critical Race Theory: The Cutting Edge* (Philadelphia: Temple University Press, 1995), 551–63.

51. Sweet, *Legal History of the Color Line*.

52. *Doe v. Louisiana.*

53. Ibid.

54. Ibid.

55. *Jane Doe et al. v. State of Louisiana, Department of Health and Human Services, Office of Vital Statistics and Registrar of Vital Statistics*, consolidated with *Susie Smith et al. vs. State of Louisiana, Department of Health and Human Services, Office of Vital Statistics and Registrar of Vital Statistics* (1982) Civil District Court for the Parish of Orleans State of Louisiana Division D Docket No. 78-9513, 81-4201.

56. Ibid.

57. Caroline Rand Herron, Michael Wright, and Carlyle Douglass, "The Nation in Summary: Louisiana Drops Racial Fractions," *New York Times* (June 26, 1983); "Slave Descendant Fights Race Listing," *New York Times* (September 15, 1982).

58. *Jane Doe v. State of Louisiana* (1985) 479 So. 2d 369.

59. Ibid.

60. Ira Berlin, *Slaves Without Masters: The Free Negro in the Antebellum South* (New York: Pantheon, 1975), 77; Gwendolyn Hall, *Africans in Colonial Louisiana: The Development of Afro-Creole Culture in the Eighteenth Century* (Baton Rouge: Louisiana State University Press, 1992), 29–32.

61. 755 N.W.2d 713.

62. 38 Mass. App. Ct. 147.

63. Ibid.

64. Ibid.

65. Ibid.

66. "Black Gains Right to Shed White Label," *New York Times* (September 1, 1984); "The Color of Bureaucracy," *Washington Times* (September 7, 1989).

67. Peterman, "After Growing Up Hiding Her Race," 1D.

68. 860 F. Supp. 1262.

69. 660 F. Supp. 2d.

5

CHARLES W. CHESNUTT, WHITENESS, AND THE PROBLEM OF CITIZENSHIP

DONALD M. SHAFFER

IN 1889 CHARLES W. CHESNUTT ASKED A PROVOCATIVE QUESTION in the essay "What is a White Man?"[1] By this single interrogative, Chesnutt boldly challenged the reified racial discourse taking place at the time. While Congress had ended slavery, established citizenship by virtue of being born in the United States, and assured citizens of equal protection of the laws, due process of law, and certain privileges and immunities, African Americans lost ground as southern whites regained control of state governments and passed laws providing for racial segregation. Moreover, in 1896 the US Supreme Court decided *Plessy v. Ferguson*, which upheld racial segregation under the guise of "separate but equal."[2] Chesnutt captured this problem, writing that race relations "ought to be . . . a matter of serious concern to Southern white people." He also accused southern whites of undermining "the Constitution and laws of the United States."[3]

Slightly more than a decade later, Chesnutt would explore the disjuncture between the democratic ideals of citizenship and the reality of American racial segregation. Both of his "color-line" novels portray mulatto characters whose ability to pass into white society challenges the limits of American social customs and racial norms.[4] Through his portrayal of the black mulatto in these novels, Chesnutt argues for an inclusive ideal of citizenship in contrast to the Jim Crow society being fashioned in the United States. In this paper, I will examine perhaps his most celebrated color-line novel, *The House Behind the Cedars*, as a literary and legalistic engagement with the problem of citizenship. Through a reading of Chesnutt's racial nonfiction, including several of his unpublished essays and speeches, I also want to show how the novel engages Chesnutt's perspective on race, particularly his unconventional (and at that time certainly radical) view of "whiteness" as social construction in the service of racial dominance.

Chesnutt developed his perspective on race in the essay "What is a White Man?"—a perspective that would continue to shape both his fiction and nonfiction writings.[5] While he ostensibly sets out to define "whiteness" in the essay, his primary focus is the liminal class of black folk then often referred to as "mulattoes." Describing the legal categories of race in the South, Chesnutt makes these observations:

> The colored people were divided, in most of the Southern States, into two classes, designated by law as Negroes and mulattoes respectively. The term Negro was used in its ethnological sense, and needed no definition; but the term "mulatto" was held by legislative enactment to embrace all persons of color not Negroes. The words "quadroon" and "mestizo" are employed in some of the law books, tho [sic] not defined; but the term "octoroon," as indicating a person having one-eight of Negro blood, is not used at all, so far as the writer has been able to observe.[6]

The "ethnological sense" in which the term Negro was used identified people of African descent with dark skin or dark features as simply black. On the other hand, people with African ancestry who were not black by appearance and could pass as white presumably required legal definitions to identify them. In the Jim Crow society of the late nineteenth century, this legal categorizing of racial identity was therefore both a means of insuring racial purity and upholding social conventions, with the goal of keeping blacks and whites separate. Knowing who had a legitimate claim to "whiteness" in contrast to those who could "pass for white" was paramount in the racial enterprise of racial segregation. For this reason, light-skinned Americans of African ancestry violated the legal mandate of racial separation and threatened the ideal of white racial purity. Racial purists intended to limit the access of light-skinned Americans to white privilege.

As the legal boundaries of Jim Crow society were drawn, whiteness as an exclusive ideological concept was simultaneously inscribed onto virtually every social institution in America. The legal codification of whiteness vis-à-vis *Plessy v. Ferguson* institutionalized racial difference, a high court decision that had profound social implications for black people then recently recognized as citizens of the country with voting rights just three decades removed from slavery. Scholars have mapped the ideological reformation of whiteness in what has been described as the nadir in the black experience after Reconstruction.[7] As Angelo Robinson argues, the reformation of whiteness in the post-Reconstruction South was part of the rigid drawing of the color line following the end of slavery and the beginning of racial segregation. Robinson writes:

> With the loss of the "citizen-versus-slave dialectic" legislated by the Emancipation Proclamation, white supremacy could no longer be based solely on citizenship status. During slavery whiteness was normalized and deemed invisible, whereas enslaved African Americans were "raced" as an inferior deviation from the white norm. After slavery, however, the laws forced whiteness to abandon its "unmarked and unnamed" feature and be remade to show its face for the first time.[8]

The instantiation of whiteness as social privilege within the legal and structural system of segregation was at the same time an undermining of black citizenship. Ironically, then, a society in pursuit of democratic coherence following the political polarization of the Civil War sought now to remake itself as a biracial, apartheid social system. Therefore, if blackness as a racial category had once signified racial inferiority in the context of American slavery, it now signified second-class citizenship in the context of racial segregation.

The figure of mulatto, or the passing figure, emerges in this sociopolitical context as an emblematic reminder of the contradictions inherent to American racial ideology. These biracial characters were both personal testament to the possibility of racial unity as well as ill-conceived products of social taboo and miscegenation. It was precisely for these reasons that the mulatto character in fiction—the "passing figure" whose racial ambiguity threatened the incoherent social order of segregation—became a potent symbol of social protest. As a foil to white racial purity, the "passing figure" expressed the idea of race as social construction thereby providing a means of countering notions of white supremacy. Chesnutt's interest in black mulattoes placed him within a popular and longstanding tradition of African American authors who strategically deployed the passing figure in their writing. Harriet Beecher Stowe in *Uncle Tom's Cabin*, William Wells Brown in *Clotel*, Francis E. W. Harper in *Iola Leroy*, and others have marshaled the sentimentality and moral potency of the "passing figure," often portraying him or her as the "tragic mulatto," despised by whites and misunderstood by blacks, or the "messianic negro," tacitly chosen by accident of birth to lead her people into the promised land. These were transcendent characters whose whiteness gained them access into the social mainstream while their blackness gained them authenticity as potential saviors for a race of people in need of social uplift. As individuals who could perform whiteness through passing, they also attested to the social fiction of race and to the arbitrariness of racial distinctions. The so-called one-drop rule, which defined "black blood" as a contagion and a source of racial impurity, was challenged by stories that depicted mulatto characters as the paragons of moral virtue and duty. William Dean Howells's novel *An Imperative Duty* and James Weldon Johnson's *The Autobiography of an Ex-Colored Man* would revise the trope in significant ways, portraying mulatto characters that ultimately reject their racial and moral commitments to live out their lives as white individuals. However, even in its revised form, "passing figures" are portrayed in these novels as victims of social forces beyond their control. The racial passer reluctantly disavowed any claim to an African lineage. In these stories the decision to pass as white simply became an act of survival.

The mulatto as a trope of the racial passer also carried with it the racial ideology of southern society. *Mulatto* is a derivative of the Spanish word *mulato*, which itself is derived from the word *mula*, meaning mule—the hybrid offspring of a horse and a donkey.[9] In the racial valence of the South, this meant that the mulatto, or person of mixed racial lineage, was often looked upon as a social anomaly or racial cipher, as a liminal person positioned betwixt and between racial categories. The association between mules and mulattoes in southern culture thereby stigmatized persons of mixed racial lineage as the ill-born products of miscegenation, a pejorative term describing sexual intercourse between whites and blacks.

As Joel Williamson observes, this association between mules and men rested on biological mythology. Analogous to the mule that possessed no mule antecedents and therefore could produce no mule descendants, the mulatto was defined in southern racial valence as someone without a legitimate past or a discernible future. Describing the South's fatalistic attitude toward mulattoes, Williamson writes: "[Southerners believed] as the mule dies, so too dies the mulatto. The association with mules also carried the implication that the hybrid could be continued only by an artificial contrivance, by an unnatural act of mating that ought not and does not have to be, which, in fact, if we but know the truth, must be made to be by straining against the winds and tides of nature."[10] Williamson's observations point to the inherent paradox of the black mulatto. The figure of the mulatto was simultaneously inside and outside of southern racial normativity, as the term signified at once an "unnatural act of mating" as well as an all-too-pervasive reality of southern society. It is precisely for this reason that Chesnutt and other authors often appropriated the subversive figure of the mulatto in their fiction.

In *The House Behind the Cedars*, Chesnutt marshals the figure of the mulatto as an epistemological foil to expose the legal incongruities of race in America. Indeed, racial distinctions were the fly in the ointment where the promise of free citizenship for blacks was concerned. Equally so, mulattoes represented the ideal of whiteness and racial purity. In the novel, the mulatto signifies a rhetorical point of departure in the reified discourse of race in America, a counter-hegemonic figure that collapses racial binaries, and, perhaps most importantly, a liminal figure who attempts to bridge the ideological divide between ascriptive Americanism and full citizenship for blacks. Indeed, what distinguishes the novel from other color-line novels is its critical commentary on the ideology of racial difference. In negating the essentialist specter of racial difference, Chesnutt's novel ironically affirms the black subjectivity of its mulatto characters. They ultimately appear to us as fleshed-out individuals despite (or perhaps because of) their struggle to avail themselves as complex human beings. This represents the seemingly contradictory aim behind Chesnutt's novel and, indeed, much of his other fiction—to eschew racial difference while simultaneously affirming the black self.[11]

Critical appraisals of Chesnutt's fiction have often focused on his use of "mixed-raced" characters. The work produced by luminaries like Warner Sollors and William Andrews provide insight into Chesnutt's use of the passing figure as a racial foil.[12] However, these accounts often fail to address the larger problem of citizenship implicit in Chesnutt's fiction and the emphasis he placed on this problem in much of his nonfiction. The tendency has been rather to read Chesnutt's construction of race in his novels as merely an attempt to establish the artificiality and arbitrariness of race. Arguing in the same vein, Keith Byerman describes *The House Behind the Cedars* as "a thought experiment . . . that track[s] the meaning of such arbitrariness."[13] Byerman is "interested in the performance of race in [the novel] rather than in the nature of its reality."[14] However, as my reading of the novel contends, the discourse of race, or more accurately the performance of whiteness, is part and parcel with "the nature of its reality." That is to say, Chesnutt locates race in general and whiteness in particular within specific material and symbolic practices that provide the social institutional foundations for race formation. Thus, Chesnutt emphasizes in his fiction and nonfiction the inscription of race in social custom and the law, and the extent to which its realities are immediately borne out within social institutions. As sociologist Eduardo Bonilla-Silva has argued, "ideologies are meaning in the service of power."[15] Race as ideology, then, gives meaning to social hierarchies that would otherwise appear constructed and arbitrary. Chesnutt highlights in the novel the arbitrariness of whiteness as a racial construct, to be sure; but he does so by exposing the social apparatus that provides the institutional basis for racial distinctions.

Chesnutt's marshaling of the tragic mulatto places him within a long-standing tradition of mixed-race heroines whose portrayal reveals the intersection of gender and race. Chesnutt's portrayal of Rena Walden (who is later renamed Rowena Warwick) reveals some of the ways in which race and gender (and to a lesser extent, class) are at play in the construction of a coherent self despite the incongruities of racial segregation in America. In her reading of the novel, Melissa Ryan suggests as a "provocative possibility" that Chesnutt's heroine was a "cross dressed" version of the author himself.[16] Indeed, in a letter to George Washington Cable, the progressive southern novelist, Chesnutt describes with excitement his novel in progress, with the eponymous title "Rena," before it later became *The House Behind the Cedars*.[17] It may be argued that his choice of a central black female perspective in the novel afforded Chesnutt an unconventional means of challenging racial meanings by revealing the ways in which race functioned within the context of law and within the context of social custom. Rena's love affair with a white suitor violates the social taboo of sexual relationships between blacks and whites. In this way, Chesnutt couches the terms of his consideration of racial categories and distinctions within a popular and familiar narrative framework, the sentimental novel of passing. However, Ryan makes the important distinction between Chesnutt's use of this popular melodramatic literary vehicle and the subversive quality of his work of fiction: "Beneath the surface text of the sentimental novel lies a framing of gender difference that penetrates more deeply into the problem of race that Chesnutt seeks to interrogate. John and Rena present two ways of thinking about identity and the assertion of whiteness: Rena is her body, while John is his name."[18]

However, while the "assertion of whiteness" reflects one of the immediate challenges for John and Rena, both of whom decided to pass as white, their decision to pass is motivated by the more general problem of social identity and citizenship in the novel. That is to say, Chesnutt's characters are motivated to assert whiteness because they wish to live as full citizens in a society incapable of accepting them as such were they to live openly as black people. Racial passing becomes the only means of establishing full citizen-ship for John and Rena, but this decision exacts an enormous psychological cost for both. Their assertion of whiteness also means a denial of self—or more precisely a denial of their origins (as symbolized by the surreptitious image of the "house behind the cedars") as well as a denial of their personal connections (as revealed in John and Rena's abandonment of their mother). For both characters, it is not merely a matter of asserting agency through whiteness or asserting personal identity through blackness; rather, the *kind* of agency or citizenship they gain as white people is fraught with the same contradictions inherent to a society that denies full citizenship to people based on racial difference.

Dean McWilliams argues that the portrayal of Rena Walden in the novel "casts doubt on [the] assertion of the mulatto's sovereign independence."[19] Rena's choices are conditioned by racial ideology; so, too, is her sense of belonging in a racist society threatened by her tenuous position in it. Mc-Williams suggests that Rena's self-identity is divided both racially and psychologically:

> In *The House Behind the Cedars*, emotional confusion occurs not only around Rena, but within her. She cannot escape this confusion be-cause not only does she live in a racist society, but that society also lives within her. She is not exempt from the contradictory pressures of her culture: they blind her, they frustrate her hopes, and finally they destroy her life.[20]

As McWilliams's comments suggest, we cannot simply read Chesnutt's fe-male protagonist as the offspring of sentimental fiction—the traditional tragic mulatta whose personal sacrifice stands as a testament to moral duty and racial commitment. Rather, Rena is the product of a racially hegemonic society in which black people were simultaneously within and without nor-mative structures of being. For this reason, Chesnutt's characters are per-haps best understood as both the subjects of their own personal racial fic-tion and the objects of a larger racial narrative that necessarily shapes and determines their self-identities.

Chesnutt rightly understood race as a social fiction, but he also under-stood it as material reality. Matthew Wilson situates Chesnutt in an intel-lectual tradition in which "environmental explanations of racial difference" provided a basis for understanding the social process of racial formation.[21] From this perspective, racial differences are shaped within particular historical and political contexts. Indeed, Chesnutt's view of race is shaped by what Wilson describes as an "environmentalist perspective," but I would add that the "logical extension" of this perspective is realized in Chesnutt's portrayal of characters that reject the standard definitions of race privileged by structures of power. From the standpoint of his fiction, race is something that is produced both within normative social structures and without in the minds of individuals. Thus, how his characters position themselves privately as individuals and publicly as citizens is always informed by racial ideology and the social structures in which race is reproduced. Chesnutt's use of the passing figure or mulatto/a reveals the inherent fissures within the social structures that reproduce race. As my reading of the novel will reveal, the (de)construction of whiteness vis-à-vis the figure of the mulatto/a exposes the inherent fiction of race as a means of delimiting the terms of citizenship. In other words, Chesnutt portrays John and Rena, both of whom pass for white in the novel, as good citizens in the context of normative social structures, even or especially because their very presence within these racially segregated spaces threaten the prevailing social order. To this extent, they strain the underlying logic of Jim Crow segregation, not merely because of their ability to perform whiteness but also because of the internal conflicts that shape their bifurcated self-identities.

The novel revolves around the lives of two black characters, both of whom are able to pass as white. At the outset of the novel, one is already passing when we find him lurking behind corners in the small town of Patesville, North Carolina, where much of the novel is set, although his motives, and indeed, his identity are not immediately clear to the reader. We eventually learn that his name is John Warwick, a pseudonym he has taken in place of his birth name, John Walden, in order to hide his racial past. While his birth name suggests the transcendent quality of his racial status as a black mulatto (perhaps an allusion to Thoreau's transcendent space of Walden Pond), his chosen name signifies his mastery of "whiteness" as performance. Upon learning of his identity, we are then made aware of his purpose. John has returned to his hometown in hopes of reuniting with his mother and sister. His main purpose for this reunion, however, is to convince his sister, Rena Walden, to leave Patesville and return with him to Clarence, South Carolina, where she too would share in his secret and pass as white. Because of the recent death of his wife, John appeals to his sister for help in raising his only child. His underlying motives, however, go to the liminal existence of the black mulatto figure. Thus, his appeal to his sister is also an attempt to mitigate the isolation forced upon him because of his secret.

Although John's story provides the narrative frame for the novel, a story we are given in greater detail through a flashback chapter, the novel centers on the perspective of Rena Walden. In fact, the original title for the novel was "Rena Walden." Importantly, as a black woman who is able to pass as white, Rena can realize the vaunted Victorian principle of "marrying well." Nevertheless, Chesnutt endeavored to portray her as an "everyday woman." In a letter written to George Washington Cable, Chesnutt explains the subtle revisions he makes to her character by shading her so that "she is not quite so superior a being, leaving her to depend for her interest more on the element of common humanity."[22] In telling her story, Chesnutt appropriates the thematic conventions of romance literature. After she follows her brother to South Carolina, Rena immediately finds herself in the midst of a burgeoning romance with a white man, George Tryon, a lawyer with professional ties to her brother. As a matter of course, Tryon proposes to Rena (after all, this is romance literature). The dilemma this creates for Rena derives from the tenuous nature of her relationship with Tryon. His love for her is conditioned by the presumption that she is who she claims to be—a white woman of legitimate (albeit meager) social standing. Rena's fear that he might discover her secret assumes two possibilities: the first is that he would simply rescind his marriage proposal and perhaps also "out" her brother. The other possibility, and the much greater penalty, is that he would completely renounce his love for her in the fateful moment when the scales have been removed from his eyes and he sees her for who she really is. When he does discover her secret because of a chance encounter, it is the look in Tryon face, one "pale as death, with starting eyes," that confirms her worst fear.

The opening of the novel attests to the overwhelming power of racial difference in shaping the lives of these characters. When Warwick tries to persuade his mother to allow Rena to leave the house behind the cedars and accompany him to South Carolina, he offers this explanation:

A mother's claim upon her child is a high and holy one. Of course she will have no chance here, where our story is known. The war has wrought great changes, has put the bottom rail on top, and all that—but it hasn't wiped *that* out. Nothing but death can remove that stain, if it does not follow us even beyond the grave. Here she must forever be—nobody. With me she might have got out into the world; with her beauty she might have made a good marriage; and, if I mistake not, she has sense as well as beauty.[23]

What Warwick simply refers to as "that stain," a common metaphor to describe the stigma attached to blackness, assumes a double meaning in the passage. Rena is black by ancestry although white by phenotype. She is "stained" because of her association with a race of people forced to reside at the bottom rungs of society. She is not, however, stained in the literal sense of possessing dark skin. Rather, Warwick's explanation points to the social stain that sanctions and limits her mobility. As Warwick makes clear, the social fiction of race will forever retard her progress and inhibit her social standing despite her claim to "sense as well as beauty." Although the point is punctuated by her ability to "claim whiteness" as a mulatta, and the incongruity of her appearance versus her degraded racial status, it is an argument that applies to other blacks as well. Her social status as a "negro" is already always contested by the presumption of social inferiority despite her possession of the "social capital" that would otherwise confer on her full citizenship along with the possibility of social mobility.

The importance of whiteness as social capital is revealed when Rena begins a new life with her brother John in Clarence, South Carolina. After a year of boarding school—for the purpose of "distinctly improving her mind and manners"—Rena sets out on her first public appearance as Rowena Warwick. The change in her "mind and manners" also occasions a change of name; she has remade herself in both body and mind as Rowena—the fictional heroine from Walter Scott's *Ivanhoe* whose legendary beauty and Saxon lineage make her a veritable emblem of whiteness. She has already begun to shed the old world of racial obscurity in the house behind the cedars for a new world of racial advantage and white privilege. As a woman in the vaunted tradition of the southern belle, Rena is baptized as it were into a southern cult of womanhood that not only gains her purchase to whiteness but also affords her the "protection" of southern society.[24] Appropriately, Chesnutt sets this moment of social/racial initiation in a medieval-inspired jousting tournament replete with knights on horseback and fair maidens in waiting. As Chesnutt informs the reader, the narrative of chivalry represented in Scott's *Ivanhoe* provides a model upon which the South would create its own enduring social fiction:

> The South before the war was essentially feudal, and Scott's novel of chivalry appealed forcefully to the feudal heart. During the month preceding the Clarence tournament, the local bookseller had closed out his entire stork of "Ivanhoe," consisting of five copies, and had taken orders for seven copies more. The tournament scene in this popular

novel furnished the model after which these bloodless imitations of the ancient passages-at-arms were conducted, with such variations as were required to adapt them to a different age and civilization.[25]

That this southern society should adapt a chivalric ceremony for a "different age and civilization" such as itself is suggestive of the ways in which whiteness is reproduced as normative value. Rena, who is ultimately crowned by her white suitor as "the queen of love and beauty," must adapt herself as well in order to pass into this society of white privilege. Like the performers in the tournament, she must put on the social pretense of honor, duty, and deportment. In short, she must *perform* whiteness in order to gain entry into this society of privilege. But like the tournament itself, her identity is based on an enduring social fiction that requires everyone to play along in both thought and action.

Although Rena proves to be a quick learner, she nevertheless struggles in her new identity as Rowena Warwick. Unlike her brother, who embraces the opportunistic world of whiteness, Rena is reluctant to put on the full vestment of white womanhood. At the ball following the tournament, Rena reacts to this world of white privilege as though it were a dream from which she would eventually wake up: "Her months in school had not eradicated a certain self-consciousness born of her secret. The brain-cells never lose the impressions of youth, and Rena's Patesville life was not far enough removed to have lost its distinctness of outline. Of the two, the present was more of a dream, the past was the more vivid reality."[26] The "cinderella" quality of the ball with the subtle references to the passage of time—the inevitable striking of midnight—ironically foreshadows a less-than-fairytale ending for Rena. More importantly, however, the surreal quality of the scene suggests the artificial world of whiteness into which Rena has entered.

Although whiteness is represented in the novel as artifice—as a concept born out of an enduring social fiction—it is also presented as the instantiation of social status and power. Unlike Rena, John performs whiteness with relative ease. He even evokes the ideology of white supremacy when it best suits him. Upon John and Rena's journey "down the river," into the very heart of Dixie, John fashions himself as a southern white man par excellence in the presence of the ship's captain and other well-to-do passengers:

> During the day, Warwick had taken his meals in the dining room, with the captain and the other cabin passengers. It was learned that he was a South Carolina lawyer, and not a carpetbagger. Such credentials

were unimpeachable, and the passengers found him a very agreeable traveling companion. Apparently sound on the subject of negroes, Yankees, and the righteousness of the lost cause, he yet discussed these themes in a lofty and impersonal manner that gave his words greater weight than if he had seemed warped by a personal grievance. His attitude, in fact, piqued the curiosity of one or two of the passengers. "Did you people lose any niggers?," asked one of them. "My father owned a hundred," he replied grandly.[27]

Following from the advice of his childhood mentor Judge Straight, John has built his reputation as a white man, laying brick by brick as it were the essential components of whiteness. However, when the old Judge learns from John's mother that he has taken Rena into his built world of white privilege, Chesnutt once again foreshadows the inevitable: "It is a pity," [Judge Straight] murmured, with a sigh, "that men cannot select their mothers. My young friend has builded, whether wisely or not, very well; but he has come back into the old life and carried away a part of it, and I fear that this addition will weaken the structure."[28]

Chesnutt foreshadows the inevitability of failure for both of his mulatto/a characters because they simply cannot succeed within the social framework of Jim Crow society. As Chesnutt reveals through his portrayal of both Rena and John, the cost of passing is often greater than its reward. Their assertion of whiteness, while providing a means for social ascent within a segregated society, precludes the possibility of asserting a coherent self-identity. Judge Straight's fear that John has "weaken[ed] the structure" of his new life by recovering part of his past highlights one of the tensions inherent to the experience of the passing figure. In order to pass as white, one must deny a part of himself. In turn, one must assert another self-identity that is always a false image. One must adopt a perception that is always born out of a false consciousness. John's desire to recover the past in the figure of his sister is really his attempt to ascribe meaning to a life that has become more artifice than substance. The real substance of any life must be the mutual acceptance of individuals as people and as citizens, owing to the full complexity of their being and regardless of their social status or racial/ethnic background. John and Rena belong within this society only insofar as they are presumed to be white. Therefore, the real tragedy of the novel is not merely the uncovering of their "blackness," but rather the necessity of asserting whiteness as a requirement for full citizenship.

WHITENESS AND "GOOD CITIZENSHIP"

Echoing several of Chesnutt's essays on the subject of race, *The House Behind the Cedars* makes the important correlation between whiteness as normative value and the degraded social status of black folk following the period after Reconstruction. In an unpublished essay titled "The Term Negro," Chesnutt argues that the binary conception of race in America makes a fetish of racial difference, something he believed precluded the possibility that blacks could be esteemed as anything more than second-class citizens.[29] He begins the essay with this question: "Why should any class of American citizens receive a special designation unless there is some good purpose to be subserved thereby?"[30] Implicit in Chesnutt's inquiry is an assumption that "special designations" serve only those who assign them and "subserve" those they designate. He immediately rejoins this rhetorical question with the simple assertion: "Good citizenship would rather tend toward lessening than emphasizing differences between citizens of a common country."[31] Put another way, if one is to become a "good citizen" and be assigned distinction as such, he or she must be viewed on equal terms with all other citizens. Chesnutt suspected that race could not be assigned to individuals without carrying with it the ideological baggage that privileges one racial group over another. In short, the term "Negro" would always take a subordinate position in relation to white as a racial designation.

The term "Negro" was then too reductive for Chesnutt because it did not express the variety of ways in which blacks identified themselves politically, socially, and culturally.[32] Describing the racial complexity of blacks, Chesnutt pointedly suggests that an essentializing term such as "Negro" could not possibly be a capacious enough signifier to account for an entire people possessing "an infusion of white blood which ranges from a small fraction to a proportion which renders distinctions of race imperceptible."[33] Some have held such statements to be extremely problematic. Indeed, on its face, his position would seem to privilege "whiteness" over and against "blackness," thereby making "blackness" a stain to be literally dissolved away through a process of racial amalgamation. Matthew Wilson rightly demurs by arguing that "through his scheme of amalgamation [Chesnutt] was rejecting notions of racial purity on both sides of the color line."[34] Instead, Chesnutt's observations reveal the arbitrariness of racial distinctions which proscribe difference solely on an ideological basis. Therefore, he asserts that the construction of racial identity must be "a purely personal and private matter,"[35] despite the dominant ideology of race in America. This radical assertion was tantamount to racial heresy, as it suggested that blacks could redefine ideas of race as it applied to them. Indeed, the term "Afro-American" was first coined at the turn of the twentieth century and would find wide usage several decades later, replacing "Negro" and "colored" as racial designations for blacks.[36]

In the novel, John Warwick seemingly echoes Chesnutt's position in "The Term Negro" when he insists as a young boy that he is white. When the novel flashes back to this important scene of initiation, Warwick tries to convince Judge Straight—a friend and associate of his deceased father—that he intends to pursue a career in the law. The Judge reminds him that he is a Negro, and cannot, therefore, pursue a legal career, to which Warwick (Walden) responds: "I am white . . . and I am free as all my people were before me." Because John Walden can (re)assign race to himself in the literal sense of invoking whiteness (he is white by phenotype), the Judge's response necessarily turns to the law:

> "You are black . . . and you are not free. You cannot travel without your papers; you cannot secure accommodations at an inn, you could not vote, if you were of age; you cannot be out after nine o'clock without a permit. If a white man struck you, you could not return the blow, and you could not testify against him in a court of justice. You are black, my lad, and you are not free. Did you ever hear of the Dred Scott decision, delivered by the great, wise, and learned Judge Taney?[37]

When the Judge's reasoned retort is rejoined by John's simple statement, "it may be true . . . but it don't apply to me," Chesnutt exposes the crux of the problem.[38] Chesnutt's evoking of legal statutes to support Straight's position here and then to support Warwick's claim to whiteness later, reveals both the social and legal fiction of race. The argument for slavery (as expressed here prior to the Civil War and before the abolition of slavery) as well as later arguments for segregation after Reconstruction were necessarily based on the rigid construction of racial categories. Therefore, as a mixed-race figure, Warwick embodies both a physical and rhetorical challenge to essentialist notions of racial purity and white supremacy.

In asserting his whiteness as a basis for full citizenship, Warwick echoes the reasoning behind Homer J. Plessy's historic legal challenge to segregation law in the United States. Chesnutt was undoubtedly influenced by the landmark Supreme Court decision *Plessy v. Ferguson* in 1896, a decision handed down just four years prior to publication of the novel. Like

Warwick, Plessy asserted his whiteness (he was considered an "octoroon" or one-eighth black) in arguing that his property rights were violated when he was forced to ride in a segregated rail car set aside for black passengers. Plessy believed his "whiteness" to be quite literally his property and thereby his possession to apply as he saw fit. However, rather than consider this aspect of Plessy's claim, the Supreme Court ruling instead focused on the issue of "social rights" as defined broadly to include everyone white or black. Rather than narrowly interpret the equal protection clause of the Fourteenth Amendment as providing special protection for Plessy, the court instead evoked a legal colorblindness.[39] According to the Court's majority opinion, Plessy may have been forced to ride in a Negro car against his wishes, but his social rights were not violated if there was a separate car designated for him that possessed comparable amenities.[40] Thus, the legal mandate of separate but equal was born out of this decision. Also born out this decision was a disregard for individuals like Homer Plessy who claimed a unique status as a biracial individual.[41] Paralleling Judge Straight's position that race is a matter of the law, the Court's ruling conferred absolute racial status on Plessy as a Negro. In doing so, the Court tacitly reinforced the racialist discourse of the era that defined "black blood" as contagion or contaminant when mixed with "pure white blood."[42] This pervasive ideology based on concepts of hypodescent and miscegenation made race an unassailable biological construct, impervious to legal challenges or individual preference. The so-called "one-drop rule," which designated mixed race individuals with any black ancestry as simply black, now had Supreme Court backing.

The Supreme Court's drawing of a rigid color line was also a rigid defining of blackness as essentially the inverse or opposite of whiteness. The two could not exist in one individual without the pure element of whiteness being corrupted by the impure element of blackness. Homer Plessy and others who may have easily "passed" as whites were in fact "blacks in sheep's clothing" whose corrupted racial stock made them nothing more than light-skinned Negroes. This dichotomization of racial distinctions was now even more firmly established as an organizing principle of the racial hierarchy of American society. W. E. B. Du Bois, who described the problem of the twentieth century as "the problem of the color line,"[43] understood this all too well. His concept of "double consciousness"[44] is born out of the social and psychological status of black folk who were forced to view themselves as Negroes first and as American citizens second. For Du Bois, these "two warring ideals in one dark body"[45] produced a conflict that not only alienated blacks within mainstream society, but also threatened to dissolve any viable identity they could claim for themselves as citizens.

The inevitable climax of the novel, when Rena's racial past is discovered by her white suitor Tryon, serves as both a melodramatic moment of intense despair for the two lovers and as a commentary on the incompatibility of the passing figure within the racial framework of Jim Crow society. In a penultimate moment prior to the discovery, Chesnutt foreshadows Tryon's inevitable reaction to learning that Rowena Warwick the "queen of love and beauty" is actually Rena Walden, a fair-skinned black mulatto. After reading an article on the subject of racial amalgamation in which the author warns "the smallest trace of negro blood would inevitably drag down the superior race to the level of the inferior," Tryon concludes it to be "a well considered argument, albeit a trifle bombastic."[46] Tryon's passive acceptance of black racial inferiority shades his perspective, thereby anticipating his discovery of Rena's "blackness" upon which "love and yearning had given place to anger and disgust."[47] His rejection of her is based on "the one objection which he could not overlook," the immutable blackness that prevents him from accepting her as his equal. Blackness is reified in this instance as an absolute point of distinction—a proverbial trump card that cancels the possibility that any black person may esteem herself as an equal to any other white person. The racialist perspective that motivates Tryon's rejection of Rena, therefore, also precludes the possibility of full citizenship for blacks.

NEITHER BLACK NOR WHITE

Jim Crow society rested on the ideological assumption that the racial categories of "black" and "white" could be made to narrowly define people, to predict behavior and social outcomes, and (most importantly) to delimit the inalienable rights of citizenship. In much of Chesnutt's fiction, this ideological framework creates a transcendent dilemma for his black characters, thereby limiting how far they can climb despite their social class, level of education, or individual merit. When Chesnutt makes these distinctions apparent in the novel, he reveals the ways in which black achievement and self-determination are always frustrated by the social fiction of race. In one such scene, following Rena's return to Patesville and her reentry into black society, Chesnutt describes a group of black partygoers, many of whom belong to the "privileged class of Negroes": "Many of the guests would not have been casually distinguishable from white people of the poorer class.

. . . Very few of those present had been slaves. The free colored people of Patesville were numerous enough before the war to have their own 'society,' and human enough to despise those who did not possess advantages equal to their own. . . ."[48] That these middle-class blacks are snobs who would look down their noses at poorer blacks or those born as slaves is clear enough in the passage; but it is not the primary point that Chesnutt wishes to make. Although Chesnutt distinguishes Rena well enough from them as to cast these privileged blacks in a decided negative light, he also identifies the "human" or natural strain in their social attitudes. Without licensing their haughty attitudes toward others, Chesnutt affirms their achievement as members of a privileged "society." For Chesnutt, then, part of the dilemma of segregation was that it precluded blacks from achieving any degree of exceptionalism—an ideal that reflects one of the tacit promises of American citizenship.

Rena finds herself within this social setting in the traditional position of the tragic mulatto/a figure—that is, she is neither black nor white but rather betwixt and between racial and social categories. She is unable to return to her old life in Patesville in any meaningful sense, having tasted the fruits of full citizenship as a white woman prior to the discovery of her secret. Now relegated once again to the house behind the cedars, Rena is as though an alien among her own people. She can now no more bridge the social gulf that exists between her and other black folk then she can find acceptance within white society. Despite her experience on the other side of color line, she therefore returns to an existence for which she has no place or immediate sense of belonging. Although Rena cultivates out of practical necessity a desire "to do something for the advancement" of her people, she does so with an abiding sense of resignation, as she must cast her lot with a group of people whose circumscribed existence portends her own fate.

By the novel's end, Rena is relegated in a similar fashion, as she is forced to teach in a small schoolhouse while living as a boarder among the homes of her impoverished students. She suffers the indignity of receiving less pay for her efforts than the other white teachers, and ultimately must face the prospect of marrying a man she does not love. When Tryon tries to re-enter her life, she finds herself caught between these two lovers—one she loves although he has rejected her and another she finds morally repugnant. When she encounters the two men, in a scene rife with symbolism, at the end of a crossroad, she rejects both, instead running away from them into the woods. She becomes lost and finds herself in a torrential storm. The story then ends as it must when Rena, having suffered from the exposure of storm, dies later in her mother's arms. As if confirming Warwick's earlier prediction that the stain of race can only be removed in death, Tryon decides to marry Rena and "make her white," although he is too late, arriving at the house behind the cedars just after her death. Significantly, the last words of the novel are spoken by Homer Pettifoot, "a tall, side-whiskered mulatto" who informs Tryon of Rena's death. Perhaps an allusion to Homer Plessy, whose legal claim to whiteness was invalidated by the ruling of the high court, Pettifoot's announcement that "a young cullud 'oman" has died underscores the permanently inscribed racial status of black folk within American racial ideology.

In another novel, *The Marrow of Tradition* (1901), Chesnutt writes "an educated man of his race, in order to live comfortably in the United States, must be either a philosopher or a fool; and since he wished to be happy, and was not exactly a fool, he had cultivated philosophy."[49] Put another way, black folk living under the yoke of Jim Crow segregation had to cultivate a view of race that saw it as both an enduring "social fiction" and as the systematic basis for their proscribed status as citizens. Chesnutt similarly conveys in *The House Behind the Cedars* an understanding of race and whiteness as social fictions in the service of power. It is perhaps significant that the novel once titled "Rena" evokes in its title the central image of the "house behind the cedars." It may be that Chesnutt wanted to symbolize, in this domestic space replete with vestiges of a bygone era (i.e., the old Confederate notes that now serve as wallpaper), the persistence of the past in shaping our present attitudes and beliefs. But if Chesnutt represents the past here as persistent, he also represents it as constructed. It is through this recognition of the constructedness of race and racial categories that Chesnutt believed black folk could assert their identities and thereby secure full citizenship in American society.

NOTES

1. Charles W. Chesnutt, "What Is a White Man?" 41 *The Independent* (May 30, 1889), 5–6.

2. 163. U.S. 537 (1896).

3. Charles W. Chesnutt, "What is a White Man?" in *Chesnutt: Stories, Novels and Essays*, ed. Werner Sollors (New York: Literary Classics of the United States, 2002), 837.

4. *The House Behind the Cedars* (New York: Houghton, Mifflin, 1900); *The Marrow of Tradition* (New York: Houghton, Mifflin, 1901).

5. Matthew Wilson, *Whiteness in the Novels of Charles W. Chesnutt* (Jackson: University Press of Mississippi, 2004), 4.

6. Chesnutt, "What is a White Man?," 838.

7. See Theodore Allen, *The Invention of the White Race* (New York: Verso, 1994). Also see Matthew Frye Jacobson, *Whiteness of a Different Color: European Immigrants and the Alchemy of Race* (Cambridge: Harvard University Press, 1998); David R. Roediger, *Wages of Whiteness: Race and the Making of the American Working Class* (New York: Verso, 2007).

8. Angelo Rich Robinson, "Race, Place, and Space: Remaking Whiteness in the Post-Reconstruction South," *Southern Literary Journal* vol. 35, no. 1 (2002): 98.

9. Joel Williamson, *New People: Miscegenation and Mulattoes in the United States* (New York: Free Press, 1980), 95.

10. Williamson, *New People*, 96.

11. I have in mind several of Chesnutt's other novels of passing, especially his writing in *The Marrow of Tradition*, in which he represents the plight of the black middle-class mulatto character who can neither find his place among black people nor among white society. This transcendent dilemma forces him to affirm a liminal self-identity betwixt and between racial and social categories of being.

12. Werner Sollors, "Charles W. Chesnutt's Historical Imagination," in Susan Prothro Wright and Ernestine Pickens Glass, ed., *Passing in the Works of Charles W. Chesnutt* (Jackson: University Press of Mississippi, 2010), 3–8. Also see William L. Andrews, "William Dean Howells and Charles W. Chesnutt: Criticism and Race Fiction in the Age of Booker T. Washington," 48.3 *American Literature* (November 1976): 327.

13. Keith Byerman, "Performing Race: Mixed-Race Characters in the Novels of Charles Chesnutt." In *Passing in the Works of Charles W. Chesnutt*, 84.

14. Byerman, "Performing Race," 84.

15. Eduardo Bonilla-Silva, *Racism Without Racists: Color-Blind Racism and the Persistence of Racial Inequality in the United States* (Lanham: Rowman & Littlefield, 2010), 26.

16. Melissa Ryan, "Rena's Two Bodies: Gender and Whiteness in Charles Chesnutt's *The House Behind the Cedars*," *Studies in the Novel* vol. 43, no. 1 (2011): 38.

17. Charles W. Chesnutt to George Washington Cable, November 1890. Chesnutt Papers, Fisk University Archives, Fisk University, Nashville, TN.

18. Ryan, "Rena's Two Bodies," 40.

19. Dean McWilliams, *Charles W. Chesnutt and the Fictions of Race* (Athens: University of Georgia Press, 2002), 134.

20. McWilliams, *Charles W. Chesnutt and the Fictions of Race*, 135.

21. Wilson, *Whiteness in the Novels of Charles W. Chesnutt*, 13.

22. Charles W. Chesnutt to George Washington Cable, May 28, 1890, Chesnutt Papers, Fisk University Special Collections, Box 1.

23. Chesnutt, *The House Behind the Cedars*, 284.

24. The so-called "cult of womanhood" refers to the pervasive southern ideology that elevated the "southern belle," an idealized image of white womanhood, to a valorized

albeit objectified social status within southern society. The idea that black men posed a constant threat to white womanhood whose sexual and racial purity needed to be protected at all cost became a common pretense for racial violence against black men.

25. Chesnutt, *The House Behind the Cedars*, 298.

26. Ibid., 307.

27. Ibid., 298.

28. Ibid., 297.

29. Charles W. Chesnutt, "The Term Negro," unpublished work, Fisk University, Special Collections, 2008, Box 7.

30. Ibid.

31. Ibid.

32. See Charles Chesnutt, "The Future American," in *Charles W. Chesnutt: Essays and Speeches* (Stanford, CA: Stanford University Press, 1999). Chesnutt similarly points out in this essay that blackness as a racial designation will need to be defined more broadly in the future to reflect the diversity that will come as the result of racial and social amalgamation.

33. Chesnutt, "The Term Negro."

34. Wilson, *Whiteness in the Novels of Charles W. Chesnutt*, 14.

35. Chesnutt, "The Term Negro."

36. The term "Afro-American," although already in use at the time, found mainstream currency in the writings of Thomas Fortune, a late-nineteenth-century African American journalist and social activist. See Shawn Alexander, ed., *T. Thomas Fortune, the Afro-American Agitator: A Collection of Writings, 1880-1928* (Ann Arbor: University of Michigan Press, 2010); Emma Lou Thornbrough, *Thomas Fortune: Militant Journalist* (Englewood Cliffs: Prentice-Hall, 1972).

37. Chesnutt, *The House Behind the Cedars*, 379.

38. Ibid.

39. Brook Thomas, *Plessy v. Ferguson: A Brief History with Documents* (Boston: Bedford, 1997), 12–13.

40. Ibid., 33.

41. See Chesnutt, "The Future American," 845–63. In this serial essay, published originally in three parts, Chesnutt argues that the "future American" will be of mixed racial stock. In short, he believed that racial amalgamation would shape American society in the twentieth century. Thus, he envisioned a society in which biracial individuals would challenge the very concept of race itself as a narrowly defined characteristic.

42. See Henry M. Field, "Capacity of the Negro—His Position in the North. The Color Line in New England," *Plessy v. Ferguson: A Brief History with Documents*, ed. Brook Thomas (Boston and New York: Bedford/St. Martin's, 1997), 101–19. In this excerpt from his book *Bright Skies and Dark Shadows* (Freeport, NY: Books for Libraries Press, 1970), Fields argues that "instinct" and the laws of nature, not merely social customs, made blacks unfit to live in close proximity to whites.

43. W. E. B. Du Bois, *The Souls of Black Folk*, in *The Oxford W. E. B. Du Bois Reader*, ed. Eric J. Sundquist (New York: Oxford University Press, Reprint, 1996), 107.

44. Ibid., 102.

45. Ibid.

46. Chesnutt, *The House Behind the Cedars*, 338.

47. Ibid., 361.

48. Ibid., 407.

49. Charles W. Chesnutt, *The Marrow of Tradition*, in *Chesnutt: Stories, Novels and Essays*, ed. Werner Sollors (New York: Library of America, 2002), 511.

6

MAKING WHITENESS IN REENACTMENTS OF SLAVERY

SADHANA BERY

WHITENESS IS HAUNTED BY SLAVERY. NOTWITHSTANDING THE ONGOING white insistence that the *de jure* abolition of slavery relegated it to a hermetically sealed past, a past that requires no memory, reckoning, or accountability by whites, slavery continues to haunt its afterlife. Avery Gordon writes that haunting is the "animated state in which a repressed or unresolved social violence is making itself known ... and [its] impacts felt in everyday life, especially when [it is] supposedly over and done with."[1] Slavery's haunting of the present reveals that, despite delegitimizing slavery's claim to memory and the deliberate repressing, disappearing, and forgetting of it, it has not been contained. This haunting demands recognition and reckoning in the present, for its past and its contemporary afterlife. Hartman describes the links between slavery and its afterlife: "I, too, live in the time of slavery, by which I mean I am living in the future created by it. ... If slavery feels proximate rather than remote and freedom seems increasingly elusive, this has everything to do with our own dark times. If the ghost of slavery still haunts our present, it is because we are still looking for an exit from the prison."[2] Gordon argues that haunting is a socio-political-psychological state that produces a "something-to-be-done"; that is, when whites can no longer repress and contain the haunting specters of slavery, they are compelled to account for them in the present. This paper interrogates one of the forms that the something-to-be-done, the accounting of slavery, takes: reenactments of slavery. I contend that white reenactments of slavery reckon with slavery in bad faith, violating the requirements. Gordon delineates for the something-to-be-done: "the ghost him or herself be treated respectfully (its desires broached) and not ghosted or abandoned or disappeared again in the act of dealing with the haunting ... to show what's there in the blind field, to bring it to life on its own terms (and not merely to light)."[3] I argue that whites use reenactments of slavery to discipline, manage, and re-re-press the haunting specters of slavery. Through reenactments whites engage with slavery but on their own terms, and consequently they re-legitimize their refusal to be accountable for slavery and exonerate themselves from their practices of antiblackness in slavery's afterlife.

Reenactments of slavery are a particularly promising site in which to examine whiteness because they recreate the original "ontological condi-tions," i.e., "the fundamental meaning generating conditions that frame our ways of being in the world," namely, the co-constitutive world of white supremacy and slavery, in which whiteness as racial ideology, epistemol-ogy, subjectivity, and practice was constructed.[4] In reenactments of slavery, whites perform "restored behavior" or behaviors that originated in slavery and are repeated and readapted for contemporary purposes.[5] Restored behaviors bridge temporal and spatial displacements, and facilitate the his-torical transmission and dissemination of behaviors that were established in slavery. I contend that whites re/produce whiteness and white supremacy by choosing to perform, not the behaviors of white perpetrators of slavery, but the roles of enslaved blacks, that is, those whom whites held in bond-age. In the reenactments, whites practice consumptive identifications by identifying with enslaved blacks not by acknowledging some measure of sameness between whites and blacks but by consuming the experiences and subjectivity of enslaved blacks. The white appropriation and ownership of blackness results in the obliteration of blacks as sovereign ontological subjects. Whites are empowered to ignore their responsibility for slavery and maintain white epistemological innocence when performing as slaves. They also manage to protect themselves from implication in and liability for slavery. Historical reenactments have developed into a powerful meth-od for constructing white historical memories and amnesias, shaping white knowledges of the present and envisioning the future of whiteness. The re-enactments tell us how whites construct who they were in the past, are in the present, and want to be in the future through their transactions with the specters of slavery. They inform us more about whiteness than the historical event of slavery.

I focus on reenactments of slavery in slave plantations that have been made over as living history museums because living history museums promise visitors that mimetic realism will give them an experience of the "real" past. However, reenactments subvert the claims of historical realism because they are "a form of affective history—i.e. historical representation that both takes affect as its object and attempts to elicit affect—reenactment is less concerned with events, processes or structures than with the individual's physical and psychological experience."[6] Reenactors are promised an embodied experience of slavery; their bodies "surrogate for those of historical subjects [and] become the guarantor of authentic witness" to slavery.[7] Thus, white visitors, as spectators and participants, are enabled to believe that, through their consumptive identification with the enslaved, they have experienced, learned, and transcended the trauma of slavery.[8] The "something-to-be-done" through reckoning with slavery becomes *fait accompli*.

WHITE SUPREMACY AND ANTIBLACKNESS IN SLAVERY AND ITS AFTERLIFE

"But what on earth is whiteness that one should so desire it? Then always, somehow, some way, silently but clearly, I am given to understand that whiteness is the ownership of the earth forever and ever, Amen!"[9] As Du Bois observes, the ontology of whiteness exists only within and is constituted by the apparatus and practices of white supremacy. White supremacy is not an aberration or unconscious deviation from "white civilization"; it is both, the spectacular and the routine workings of white regimes and white subjects. It re/produces the white nation, positions whites as its naturalized governors, and normalizes white mastery by racializing belonging and ownership of the nation as exclusively white.[10] Slavery is at the core of the nation's socio-political system, including its foundational "rights of man," which were constructed during slavery by whites to secure their property rights in enslaved blacks. These include the right to liberty, personhood, and property, equality before the law, freedom of movement and speech, the right to bear arms to protect life and property, and the state's (often violent) protection of these rights. These "rights" continue to be sustained *de facto* for whites and denied to blacks in the afterlife of slavery. Slavery was and continues to be the template for white domination through antiblackness.

During slavery, white supremacy transformed the enslaved into the ultimate tool for the material and psychic benefit of whites. The slave's human status was alienated, creating the condition of black human nothingness, a condition that is perpetuated post-slavery through racist antiblackness.[11] Slavery made the bodies and personhood of blacks into property for whites. The "propertization" of black bodies made them into commodities that could be legally "transferred, assigned, inherited, or posted as collateral," and even transformed them into currency for the exchange of other commodities.[12] Patterson explains that whites imposed social death on enslaved blacks, making them human nonpersons as the terms of their inclusion in the society. To avoid physical death, enslaved blacks had to give up their social personhood, to live and be treated as the "living who are dead."[13] The black subject was made into "an object in the midst of other objects" with "no ontological resistance in the eyes of the white man."[14] Whites created a zone of non-being for blacks, i.e., an existential reality that demands black existence and presence but simultaneously constructs blacks as outside of humanity. "To see him as black is to see enough. Hence to see him as black is not to see *him* at all. His presence is a form of absence."[15] By claiming that whiteness is the normal and normative mode of humanness, white supremacy negates the existence of black humanness.

White supremacy's core of antiblackness and its production of blackness as social death continue in the ongoing afterlife of slavery. As Hartman explains: "Slavery had established a measure of man and a ranking of life and worth that has yet to be undone. If slavery persists as an issue in the political life of black Americans ... it is because black lives are still imperiled and devalued by a racial calculus and a political arithmetic that were entrenched centuries ago."[16] Today, black bodies, personhood, and rights continue to be captive and subject to white interests and desires. Foucault states that this terror, white racism, is "the basic mechanism of power, as it is exercised in modern States" and that it creates the break in the domain of life between what must "live and what must die."[17] White supremacy is predicated on the belief that the white "right to take life [is] imperative," promising whites that "the very fact that you let more die will allow you to live more."[18] White supremacy is productive, not only repressive or oppressive; it produces whiteness. The white construction of blackness as the absolute alterity of whiteness produces community, solidarity, and sanctity for whiteness. "The security of (white) belonging accompanies the re-racialization of whiteness as the intensification of anti-blackness" and guarantees whites impunity for antiblack acts.[19]

The foundational elements of slavery established by white supremacy are incorporated into white reenactments of slavery. The reenactments reanimate black social death and non-being, the commodification, consumption, and fungibility of black bodies, and reinforce the singular, essentialized, and timeless identity whites constructed of blacks that fuses slave, social death, human non-being, and blackness. They legitimize the white strategic ignorance of white supremacy's endowment of power and prosperity for whites and its devastating consequences for blacks. Reenactments of slavery also socialize whites into the cognitive, emotive, political, economic, cultural, and social workings of whiteness. They reaffirm the ascendancy of white interests and desires. Whites use the reenactments to make claims of racial empathic identification, racial reformation, and redemption, without endangering their racial dominance. They (seemingly) minimize their self-ascribed moral superiority by engaging with slavery and gesturing toward the (always conditional and situation specific) moral superiority of enslaved blacks; but they do this to ultimately affirm the hegemonic normativity of white morality and whiteness as humanness.

MAKING WHITENESS: SLAVE PLANTATION MUSEUMS

Living history museums assert that their primary purpose is pedagogical, changing historical ignorance into historical knowledge, by immersing visitors in material, discursive, and embodied reconstructions of the past that are based on diligently researched, documented, and authenticated facts. Yet, despite the abundance of evidentiary facts, slave plantation living history museums excluded slavery and the enslaved in their constructions of an exclusively white, elite, and celebratory "colonial" history. The valorization of white history requires whiteness to be hyper-visible and fetishized and for the enslaved to be disappeared. Even the most frequently used terms of reference for these places, namely, heritage sites, colonial living history museums, colonial plantations, plantation museums, and tourist plantations, occlude slavery by not naming it, or, at best, only implying it with "plantation."[20] Museum historians justified the absence of slavery by citing the lack of documented and verifiable "facts" that could indisputably testify to the "real" experience of slavery. The institutions and their historians subjugated and rejected the knowledges and evidence of slavery by delegitimizing, disqualifying, and burying them. Foucault urges that this power/truth-effect be interrogated: "What types of knowledges are you trying to disqualify? What speaking subject, what discursive subject, what subject of experience and knowledge are you trying to minorize?"[21]

Even when slavery finally began to be included, white interpreters "tended to avoid or gloss over it. They were able to justify their discomfort, while avoiding the taint of explicit racism, because they believed that black history was, as they often complained, 'undocumented'—it verged on fiction; it never quite had the same just-the-facts authenticity as the stories they could tell about the elite white inhabitants."[22] Paradoxically, the rhetoric of historical realism was used to disappear all but the least discomfiting (for whites) representations of slavery. Despite those acts of occlusion, slavery could not be fully repressed or contained, and its haunting demanded a presence, a reckoning, a something-to-be-done in the spaces where it had been perpetrated.

Slave plantation museums create a codependent and mutually valorizing relationship between visitors' whiteness and a reconstructed moral white American history that recreates "for the average citizen (who is clearly assumed to be white) the color, the pageantry, and the dignity of our national past."[23] Minimizing slavery at slave plantation museums produces a celebratory white "colonial" history that resonates with white visitors' desires and subjectivity.[24] Alderman and Modlin's study of current online promotions of North Carolina slave plantations museums found "no plantation devoted more than 0.9% of its total text to slavery and related words."[25] The accord between minimization of slavery and white visitors' interests is demonstrated in a study of Laura Creole Plantation that asked visitors to rank their interest in slavery in comparison to architecture, civil war narratives, furnishings, and landscape/grounds, and discovered that white visitors always rated slavery as least interesting.[26] To enhance the experience of white visitors and indulge their race-class aspirations, slave plantation museums treat them as members of the slave plantation's elite ruling class and ensure that the "white middle class tourists receive cues that they have things in common with the planter and his family."[27] Tour guides use emotionally evocative discourses to describe "human" life experiences (birth, death, marriage) and affective states (sorrow, joy, pain) shared by slaveowners and white visitors. The constant merging, and reciprocal bolstering, of the whiteness of the "planter class," the idealized white past, and white visitors succeeds in disguising, naturalizing, and normalizing white supremacy in the past and present. When advertisements for the slave plantation museums ask visitors to imagine, "Who would you be here?" it is apparent that they are exclusively hailing whites because only whites could feel gratification by imagining themselves as a part of the slave plantation.

White ontology requires the presence of blacks but as an absence; that is, blacks cannot exist as fully human. Consequently, when slavery is included at the slave plantation museums, it is through an "inventory discourse" of property that enumerates the number of slaves and their purchase prices.[28] To disguise the presence of enslaved blacks and to maintain the illusion of a southern plantation without slaves, museums frequently depict African

Americans from the slave-era as servants or workers. Tours and reenactments that focus on slavery are segregated by location (often located at a distance from the main museum), time of event (outside normal museum hours, only during certain months, or as "special events") and require purchase of a separate ticket. At some slave plantation museums, such as Robert E. Lee's Arlington House, visitors want slavery interpreted at the slave quarters and not at the plantation house.[29] White visitors usually prefer slaves not be inside the main house during regular tours so that they can sustain their veneration of the planter class. At others, white visitors want to see enslaved black reenactors work at "easier" domestic jobs inside the plantation house rather than in the fields where bondage, forced labor, and the production of profit cannot be disguised. At all times, the enslaved must be depicted as "happy, well-fed, well-clothed blacks working in the fields or around the large plantation house."[30] At Hampton Plantation, tour guides talk about "servants that stole and drank liquor . . . and regimens such as whistling that were put in place by slaveholders to prevent their 'servants' from pilfering."[31] This discourse of enslaved blacks as thieves seamlessly merges with, and affirms, contemporary white discourses that essentialize blacks as always already criminals. The construction of black criminality is relocated, in time and space, to the afterlife of slavery.

The making of slave plantations into financially and subjectively successful tourist sites for whites requires museums to "selectively and seductively shape the past into embraceable and restorative national legacies" that are pleasurable and consumable for white visitors.[32] To accomplish this, slave plantation museums must fulfill white desires of nostalgia and fantasy. The past that is recreated at these sites, a world of genteel cultured white gentry and docile slaves, evokes a "mood of nostalgia [that] makes racial domination appear innocent and pure. . . . It uses a pose of 'innocent yearning' both to capture peoples' imaginations and to conceal its complicity with often brutal domination."[33] White desires to identify with "colonial elites" are facilitated by representations of slavery's agents as innocent, unknowing, and benevolent. White visitors reassure themselves that they are "good whites" by defining slaveowners as "good whites." A white visitor to Colonial Williamsburg commented, "I am so happy that Mr. Wythe . . . didn't really relish owning humans." She then replicated that ideology of benevolent white supremacy in her own family history, reporting that "Her father 'cared for his servants' just as her grandmother 'took very good care of her slaves' and just as Mr. Wythe cared for his slaves."[34] White nostalgia for the idealized white past represented in slave plantation museums is not simply a remembering of the past; rather, it is wanting and willing the past to become the present. Contemporary white fantasies of a white nation and white supremacy are displaced on the past, and then the "past" becomes the object of present-day white yearning. White visitors use the slave past in paradoxical ways: they remember the past fondly even though they "know" that it was built on slavery; they momentarily empathize with the suffering of the enslaved but do it consumptively and identify it as their own suffering; and they do not feel the obligation to account for the legacies of slavery in the racist present. Whites use nostalgia to resolve these paradoxes, and for them, "Nostalgia becomes a particularly appropriate emotion to invoke in attempting to establish one's innocence and at the same time talk about what one has destroyed," but without the burden of accountability.[35]

Reenactments of slavery at slave plantation museums are a particular method of accessing history based on affective experience, emotive identification, evocations of morality, and fantasy role-playing. The premise underlying reenactments is that "bodily epistemology is a representational strategy that uses the body of a present-day protagonist to register the traumatic slave past."[36] The embodied experience of history, that is, "the body (as) a site of knowledge production" conveys to spectators and participants that they have actually "lived" the past.[37] The epistemological and authenticity claims of reenactments depend on their artificial analogies of past and present, them and us. Reenactments collapse time, by reenacting the past as present and the present as identical to the past. "Paradoxically, it is the very ahistoricity of reenactment that is the precondition for its engagement with historical subject matter."[38] Reenactments "privilege a visceral, emotional engagement with the past at the expense of a more analytical treatment."[39] By promoting the affective "experiencing" of the past through bodily consumptive identification, reenactments do not force whites to learn about or confront slavery; emotion replaces thought. As Crumrin observes, reenactments "devolve into a sort of 'history as therapy' . . . in a self-help sort of way."[40] When whites choose to "play" slaves in reenactments, their bodies do not become the sites for the production of critical and transformative knowledges; rather, they reinforce dominant white epistemologies and ideologies. Whites elide reckoning with slavery as a part of their heritage by choosing to not perform the roles of white perpetrators of slavery.[41] Consequently, reenactments of slavery provide whites with an emotional and redemptive experience of slavery that allows them to evacuate, once again, the system of slavery and its ongoing afterlife.[42]

Whites can get the validation, reassurance, and comfort they seek from reenactments of slavery only if they sustain white epistemic colonization of black experiences and white epistemological and moral ignorance. Lewis Gordon theorizes epistemic colonization: "If the one who experiences, plays no role in the interpretation of the experience, then a form of epistemic colonization emerges . . . colored folk offer experience that white folks interpret."[43] Epistemic colonization requires the exclusion of black interlocutors from interpretations of slavery. By primarily summoning and affirming whites, reenactments require black epistemologies of slavery to be subjugated, marginalized, and discredited. This is illustrated at Historic Brattonsville, South Carolina, a living history museum, described on its website as a "Revolutionary War Site" and not as a slave plantation with more than one hundred and forty slaves.[44] The tombstone of Bratton's first recorded slaves testifies to an exclusively white narrative of slavery: "Sacred to the Memory of WATT Who died Dec. 1837 During the War he served his master Col. W. Bratton Faithfully and his children With the same fidelity Until his death. Also Polly his wife who died July 1838 Who served the same family With equal faithfulness."[45] The inscription is a testament to the white need to make the brutality of slavery invisible by constructing and disseminating a narrative of benevolent slavemasters and "loyal slaves." Brattonsville forbids black reenactors from interpreting slavery through the lens of black epistemology and experience. However, black reenactors conceptualized their enactments as "podium(s) for the truth" and rejected the museum's scripts that made them sound like "happy slaves."[46] One of the reenactors said: "When people leave these events, they leave applauding, laughing, and saying 'Thank you for the show.' We should see tears come out of their eyes."[47] To counter the white (mis)interpretation of slavery, black reenactors started including information about the brutality of the white perpetrators and horrific experiences of enslaved blacks, including narratives about the "pit" into which whites threw enslaved blacks to punish them, slave coffles, whippings, rapes, and slave breeding farms. The response from white visitors and management was swift. Visitors complained that the new scripts were offensive, especially the mention of rape during the nostalgic Christmas Candlelight Tour. Managers agreed, noting, "angry people are not going to learn anything," and awarded precedence to the interests of the white visitors over the black epistemic interpretation of the black experience of slavery. Several black reenactors were fired or quit when they refused to go back to the "happy scripts."

The exclusion of black interlocutors in the interpretation of slavery is critical for the preservation of white strategic ignorance. Mills argues that white ignorance, a type of non-knowing, is a deliberate epistemological practice that is "not the innocent unawareness of truths to which there is no access but a self- and social shielding from racial realities."[48] Epistemological ignorance has co-constituting relationships with other dominant white epistemologies, especially epistemologies of blindness and disassociation. As an epistemology, white ignorance is a "way of knowing and being that is predicated on superiority, which becomes normalized and forms part of one's taken-for-granted knowledge."[49] White ignorance is not innocent; it is caused by "white racism and/or white domination" and inextricably linked to the interests of white supremacy.[50] Whites have an investment in remaining ignorant, of knowing the "world wrongly," because that facilitates and legitimizes white abdication from their responsibility for slavery. Reenactments of slavery often combine epistemological ignorance with white moral ignorance, which Mills theorizes as "not merely the ignorance of facts with moral implications but moral non-knowings, incorrect judgments about the rights and wrongs of moral situations themselves."[51]

At Colonial Williamsburg, antagonism between black and white interpreters over the interpretation of slavery fused white epistemological and moral ignorance. Black interpreters wanted to include the documented sexual exploitation of enslaved black women by the slavemaster, George Wythe.[52] White interpreters refused, wanting to retain the virtuous and moral iconic status of Wythe, and claimed that the black interpretation lacked factual evidence and was politically motivated. White interpreters complained, "To be honest with you, I wish it was fact. It would make it much easier," and "you need something that you can talk about that's *fair* to talk about. And the George Wythe story . . . isn't the story to tell."[53] White interpreters deployed strategies of epistemological ignorance (absence of facts) and strategies of moral ignorance (incorrectly judging the issue of morality implicated in the sexual exploitation of enslaved women as an unfair depiction of slavemasters) to discredit the epistemological and moral knowledge of black interpreters.

A white reenactor/guide in the Follow the North Star program at Conner Prairie provides another example of the amalgamation of epistemological and moral ignorance. When asked which post on the Underground Railroad she most liked to reenact, she chose the poor white farming family, explaining, "The Merricks are an Indiana family that's barely scraping along.

No thanks to the slaves that have stolen all their jobs. Despite everything, they agree to help the slaves."[54] By constructing historically inaccurate representations of slavery, "slaves steal white jobs" and whites sacrifice to help slaves, the reenactor/guide practiced, and produced for the visitors, white epistemological and moral ignorance. The historical knowledge that slave plantation museums want to teach is hostage to the white desires and interests of the institutions, their staff, and the visitors.

MAKING WHITENESS: REENACTING SLAVE AUCTIONS

Reenactments of slave auctions reveal the historical transmission and dissemination of the behavioral vortex of the original slave auctions. The first reenactments of slave auctions are instructive in exposing the displaced and restored behaviors that continue to be enacted in contemporary culture. They also divulge the appeal and usefulness of slave auction reenactments for white supremacy and whiteness.

The earliest recorded slave auction reenactments were performed while slavery was still ongoing (1848–60) by the white abolitionist Henry Ward Beecher.[55] Held at his church in New York, for audiences that regularly numbered two thousand, the theatrical performances reenacted the spectacle of the selling and buying of enslaved Africans. Beecher reproduced the technologies of the original slave auctions, including the public display of black subjects, re-commoditizing them as objects to be sold and bought, and re-establishing their social death. Beecher instructed his congregation that if they did not buy the black women they would be forced back into sexual slavery. By deploying sexual slavery, Beecher reproduced the eroticism that was integral to slave auctions and constructed black women as sexual objects whose sexuality was subject to the power of white men, both those who "commit high crimes against the flesh" and those who "save" them from sexual violation.[56] For the reenactment Beecher stood at his pulpit "playing" the auctioneer, exhorting white buyers to increase their bids, and promising them religious salvation in return. Amidst much noise, clamoring, and hysterical crying, white buyers, both men and women, competed with each other to buy the "slaves" and, if successful, paid for and claimed their human purchases to great applause.

Masquerading as "reenactments" or "mock auctions," these religious-marketplace performances disguised what were, in fact, real auctions, the public sale of human flesh, of enslaved black women who had escaped from slavery but would be remanded back into it unless their slave master was paid for his "property." Beecher held the slave auctions ostensibly to raise money to buy the "freedom" of the young women who hovered precariously between freedom and re-enslavement. However, there is a question of which, their freedom or their auction, was more important to Beecher, because in many cases he had already raised the money before "selling" them in the auction and in the case of nine-year-old child Sally/Pinky, he refused to "save" her unless she came North and participated in the "mock" auction. Subject to Beecher and his white congregation's financial power, racial supremacy, and religious aspirations, the black women were forced back into situations of un-freedom, beholden and obligated to whites, and had to live lives mapped for them by their new northern white masters and mistresses. The white sentiment of ownership was unambiguous, as evidenced by Sally/Pinky's name being changed to Rose Ward, the names of her buyer and Beecher.

Beecher "saved" the previously enslaved but now free black women by giving their purchase money to the slave masters from whose bondage these women had recently escaped. Consequently, Beecher funded the slave trade and system of slavery in the name of abolition. Beecher did not honor the young women's struggles in escaping slavery or their aspirations for freedom by facilitating their journeys to Canada but chose to resell them into the guardianship of whites, re-binding them to the desires and dictates of whites. He promised his white congregants that by paying for these women they "had the opportunity to free themselves, saving their eternal souls from the state of sin," thereby binding white redemption and salvation to ownership of blacks.[57] Sally/Pinky's bill of sale is still displayed as a treasured item in the church.

Beecher's "mock" auctions normalized and legitimated the practice of selling and buying blacks as commodities. They were not transgressive but, in fact, re/produced white supremacy by not disrupting white beliefs and practices of their legal and customary right to own and subject blacks. The self-deception integral to whiteness enabled Beecher and his congregants to reconfigure their enactments of power and domination as morality and benevolence, reproducing the original "white man's (and woman's) burden." The success of the auctions rested on efficaciously evoking white empathy, consumptive identification, pity, and benevolence.

It is telling that the only recorded auctions were of very light-skinned black women, their epidermal "whiteness" facilitating the white congregation's racial identification of, and with, them as whites.[58] The perceived likeness encouraged whites to empathize not with racial difference, but with racial sameness, and to regenerate beliefs of white female purity, sanctity, and fragility and the white male imperative to protect and save them from becoming "white slaves" and sexual slavery. As Nathans writes, "Beecher's performance allowed spectators to read not the biography of the slave, but the autobiography of themselves as both victim and savior."[59]

Critical elements of the behavioral vortex of Beecher's reenactments are historically transmitted to contemporary reenactments of slave auctions in slave plantation living history museums. The continuity of the restored behaviors, notwithstanding temporal and spatial displacements, discloses that white ontology continues to depend on black subjection and the white power to enforce it.

Indeed, as Walter Johnson asserts, "The history of the antebellum South is the history of two million slave sales."[60] Slave auctions were constituted by an extreme imbalance with on one side enslaved black subjects, and on the other the white apparatus of slavery including state officials, banks, police, state and private militias, slavetraders, businesses that owned and operated the slave markets, specialists who processed black subjects into desirable products, slaveowners, insurance companies, law firms, commercial and entertainment zones, tourists, brothels, slave coffles, slave pens, auction blocks, auctioneers, money lenders, and managers who organized the spectacle. The slave auctions created and thrived on Manichean categories of white entertainment and black abjection, white triumph and black degradation, white amusement and black terror, white self-making and black social death, white mobility and black entrapment. How do slave plantation museums reenact this horrific history of slave auctions, especially when their mission is to create programs that are "not so real that it drives away potential guests" and experiences that are "entertaining, educational and, above all, positive"?[61] They do so by conforming to the racial expectations, ideologies, and comfort, of the predominantly white visitors and not the concerns of black visitors.[62] The disregard for black visitors' epistemic, experiential, and subjective needs has resulted in a dramatic decrease in black visitors and black reenactors at slave plantation museums. For example, at Colonial Williamsburg, the site of a slave auction reenactment in 1994, black visitors dropped from 4 to 2 percent.[63] Respect for the "comfort zone" of white spectators was apparent at the slave auction reenactment in St. Louis in 2011. After being sold, the "slaves" were crowded into a cart to transport them to the plantations but reenactors were instructed, "Be careful not to drive the cart off with the slaves in it. That would just be too terrible" for the audience.[64] The slave auction was truncated after only thirty minutes, when an "officer" announced that the federal judge had ordered the auction be stopped. The creating of emotional comfort for white visitors depended on historical falsifications and occlusions that mocked the goals of black organizers "to teach the history of our mothers and grandmothers so that every one of you will never forget what happened to them."[65]

Slave auctions are strategic choices for reenactments of slavery because they are finite, dramatic, and emotional. White acknowledgment and engagement with a singular episode of unimaginable white cruelty and black suffering during slavery, rather than reckoning with the systemic and continuous white subjections of enslaved black subjects, is more conducive to the contemporary maintenance of whiteness. By constructing slave auctions as "unimaginable" they are rendered "unreal," and in so doing the need to account for their brutality is obviated. This also endorses the deliberate and active refusal to "know" that the forms of black subjections constructed during slavery continue into the present. Whites can claim that the "past is the past" and that, once they have made the goodwill gesture to witness the reenactment of the slave auctions and empathize with the enslaved, they can reasonably be exempt from further expectations, demands, and obligations.

The reenactments of slave auctions are rewarding for whites because they elide most of the white apparatus of slavery. White reenactors perform the roles of auctioneers, bailiffs, sellers, and buyers, but their performances principally facilitate the main drama of enslaved blacks being sold and bought. White spectators expect slave auctions to focus on the staging of spectacular and extreme black suffering. This desire to view the visual, aural, and bodily suffering of enslaved black subjects is part of the "long and complex history of white enjoyment to be found in black suffering as an 'American spectacle,' a national pastime."[66] Reenactments present the violence of the slave auctions as intense but nonetheless endured, and therefore endurable, by enslaved blacks. By imagining the violence as endurable, the "violence becomes neutralized by becoming part of the socially endurable," is alienated from its specificity, and gets transformed into "human" and universal violence.[67]

In reenactments of slave auctions, black suffering becomes fungible, assimilated by whites as their suffering. Through the empathic consumption of black suffering, white spectators are enabled to believe that their suffering can, in actuality, surrogate for black suffering. With this simplistic and consumptive identification, based on the negation of black suffering, whites define black enslavement and its subjections as inherently knowable, uncomplicated, and transparent, and they eliminate black subjection's specificity and magnitude. Most importantly, whites make a second surrogation: they assume that their experience of enslavement *is* the experience of enslaved black subjects. Thus, they not only consume black suffering as their own, but they also surrogate their suffering for the suffering of enslaved black subjects. Through this double surrogation, whites thrust blacks, both enslaved and black reenactors, into the zone of non-being, where they are present not in their full humanity but as vehicles for white emotional catharsis. They negate the integrity of black ontology and subjectivity, by demanding black presence but decomposing it, through consumption, into an absence. The double surrogation reinforces black social death in the afterlife of slavery because it does not acknowledge or value the subjective work of black reenactors who, Auslander notes, "strive for 'emotional authenticity,' summoning up affective states of horror, fear, anguish, and subjection."[68] The effortless consumption of black subjectivity enables whites to not be obliged to think about the distressing embodied experiences of black reenactors. Rex Ellis, one of the first black reenactors at Colonial Williamsburg, said about reenacting a slave before a "live and sometimes antagonist audience. . . . Putting on the costume remained a burden as the years wore on. Walking the streets of the historic area became a test of mental fortitude. People were not interested in what the characters had to say; instead we feared they were using our portrayals to confirm their prejudices. The more we got into character—the greater our misery and discomfort."[69]

During the slave auction reenactment at Colonial Williamsburg, four enslaved subjects were sold to differing responses by the largely white audience: sale of an enslaved black woman to her husband, a free black man (audience cheered); sale of an enslaved young black man (no special reaction from the audience); and the sale of a couple to two different slavemasters (audience cried and protested). At the reenacted slave auction in St. Louis, the sale of two children and the sale that separated an old woman and her daughter elicited the most emotional responses. White spectators react most strongly to reenactments of enslaved families being torn apart, especially the separation of mothers and children and spouses. Familial separations evoke strong feelings because they readily align with common white experiences. Crumrin states, "In a world of divorce, broken families, and relocation for economic reasons, the modern person can easily relate" to reenactments of familial separation.[70] The focus on family reflects Freeman Tilden's strategy for museums: "Any interpretation that does not relate what is being displayed or described to something within the personality and experience of the visitor will be sterile."[71] These reenactments also resonate with white ideologies of familial whiteness, especially, white maternalism, white men as protectors of their families and especially of white women, and the innocence and preciousness of white children. Even though whites do not extend these attributes of familial integrity and bonds to black subjects, especially in the afterlife of slavery, they are able to assimilate the enslaved black subjects' familial experiences of loss as their own. White supremacy defines white subjectivity as the measure of "human" and normative subjectivity and by surrogating their loss for black bereavement, whites disappear a specifically black experience of suffering into a de-racialized, universal, and human (that is, white, which is constructed as human and not racialized) loss. Once converted into de-racialized human suffering, the traumas of slavery need not be attributed to white acts of supremacy or cruelty.

During slavery, slave auctions were sites of entertainment and often organized as theatrical performances, replete with costumes, semi-nudity, processions, dance, and music. Many whites went to them not to buy slaves but for amusement and sociability.[72] Opponents of contemporary reenactments of slave auctions worry that reenactments will also be experienced as entertainment and that the "re-creation might be inaccurate or sensationalized for entertainment."[73] This fear is not unfounded, because the audience at these reenactments is mostly a "touring and vacationing public" who go to slave plantation museums on sightseeing vacations and expect to have fun. In fact, the crowd that viewed the slave auction reenactment at Colonial Williamsburg was largely whites, tourists, reporters, and students, many wielding video cameras.[74]

White expectations of entertainment at reenactments of slave auctions are consistent with the amusement, joviality, and profanity with which they treat artifacts that are symbols of slavery's most brutal subjections. Stephen Hanna documents that in Fredericksburg, Virginia, the original slave auction block still rests at its historical site with a plaque that states, "Fredericksburg's Principal Auction Site in Pre-Civil War Days for Slaves and Property."[75] This has become a popular tourist site and white tourists are often seen laughing and teasing while taking pictures of their partners and children standing on the block. In Colonial Williamsburg, the restored Raleigh Tavern is a popular site for entertainment and fun, for visitors to eat and drink. In all the merriment, the history of the tavern as an auction site for the selling and buying of enslaved blacks is rendered invisible and silent.[76] Displayed on the grounds at Colonial Williamsburg is a pillory, a device used to punish enslaved blacks. A photograph shows two white men with their heads inserted into the pillory, playfully enacting the punishment of slaves, as another white man gets his camera ready to take their photograph.[77] The auction block, the pillory, and the tavern are powerful witnesses to the subjection of enslaved blacks but whites conceal that subjection by repurposing them for entertainment.

Slave plantation museums, visitors, and the media validate and measure the success of slave auction reenactments by attesting to their production, and public display, of emotion. Beecher's "mock" slave auctions produced a "crowded church filled with sobbing, hysterical women, with shining-eyed, trembling-handed men."[78] Colonial Williamsburg's slave auction reenactment encouraged and drew out emotional responses, even from protestors. Mr. Jack W. Gravely from the NAACP, had opposed the reenactment, saying, "You cannot portray our history in twenty-one minutes and make it a sideshow"; but, by the end of the reenactment, with tears in his eyes, he said: "Pain had a face. Indignity had a body. Suffering had tears."[79] If affective demonstrations are the gauge for the efficacy of slave auction reenactments, then the pedagogical function has been subordinated to a "visceral, emotional engagement with the past at the expense of a more analytical treatment."[80] The emotional "experience" of slavery drowns the potential for epistemological interrogation and transformative political work. For whites, the collective emotional effervescence becomes an ontological condition for the articulation and affirmation of, and re-commitment to, individual and collective white identity. Immersion into a deliberately constructed and regulated melodramatic episode of slavery produces emotional effervescence but does not result in understanding, interrogating, or ending contemporary antiblack racism.

Whites have remade the narrative of slavery into a narrative of blackness. In this transformation slavery is only about black history, black experiences, and black subjectivity. For reenactments of slavery to be emotionally gratifying for contemporary whites it is necessary that white acts during slavery, other than those by "good whites," be made invisible. White interpreters even ascribe the act of owning slaves to free black slaveowners, using this to "deflect or avoid discussions of the immoral and racist nature of enslavement."[81] This is the whitewashing of slavery, not in the usual sense of whites making black history invisible, but of whites "washing out" the white apparatus and practices of slavery.[82] Cultural representations of slavery, including reenactments, camouflage whiteness. White constructions of slavery as the history and domain exclusively of blacks result in whites never having to acknowledge that slavery is a foundational part of white heritage and a principal producer of white wealth. The whiteness of slavery has been marginalized, deflected, disguised, minimized, or simply made invisible. Whiteness is represented at slave plantation museums, but only in the service of "protective reverence" for the slaveholding colonial elites and not as the apparatus of slavery.[83] By absenting whiteness as the productive and regulating force of slavery, whites conceal centuries of white labor, including the deployments of white desire, will, agency, and creativity that constructed, and continue to re/produce, the white supremacist nation. By not compelling white spectators to identify with the whites at slave auctions, the reenactments enable whites to abdicate the legacy, accountability, and culpability of their racial group as perpetrators of and profiteers from slavery. This dis-identification provides whites an escape from recognizing that their whiteness is historically derived from white practices of slavery. The acknowledgment that whiteness is rooted in slavery is important not only as a historical gesture but also because white supremacy displaces the behavioral vortex of slavery to the afterlife of slavery, where it is evident in contemporary practices of whiteness that reproduce the negation of full humanness for blacks. As Steve Martinot and Jared Sexton note, "the passive apparatus of whiteness . . . in its mainstream guise actively forgets that it owes its existence to the killing and terrorising of those it racialises for that purpose, expelling them from the human fold in the same gesture of forgetting."[84]

In his study of New Orleans, Roach demonstrates that the spectacle and behavioral vortex of slave auctions was reproduced post-slavery, in the 1880s, in legally sanctioned prostitution. Storyville was a district created by the city for entertainment, commerce, and brothels where black women and girls were placed on "front-parlor tables and gaveled to the top bidder" as objects for white male sexual pleasure. It became a local tradition for fathers to initiate their sons into sexual "manhood" at Storyville in the same way that slaveowners had initiated their sons by raping enslaved black women. In the present, Roach locates the slave auction's displaced transmission in New Orleans's Superdome, where NFL football is the vehicle for the "spectacles—the commoditization of flesh in an economy of ever more specialized greed—that display immensely valuable black bodies sweating for white people who still unblinkingly call themselves 'owners.'"[85] Reenactment of slave auctions are even more directly reproduced in the (inter)national televised "draft" in professional basketball and football that reduces black men to their physical coordinates and sells them as "property," both *de jure* and *de facto* to team owners. The congruence of past and present commoditization of black bodies is articulated only too clearly in the words of a guide at Colonial Williamsburg who, after informing the tour group that the most expensive slave at Williamsburg was valued at one thousand pounds, asked them "if the master would mistreat such a valuable property" and then answered his own question: "No, he'll treat him like an NFL quarterback."[86]

MAKING WHITENESS: REENACTING THE UNDERGROUND RAILROAD

Conner Prairie, a living history museum in Fishers, Indiana, was recreated as a functioning "Northwest Territory Settlement" that promised visitors a "back to the frontier" experience.[87] David Lowenthal argues that heritage museums "customarily bend to market forces"; and when visitors to Conner Prairie dwindled because, as the museum's curators noted, "the past we presented was boring," Conner Prairie introduced "controversial" programs "intensifying the experience for more entertainment."[88] One of the new programs was Conner Prairie's celebrated and multi-award-winning reenactment of the Underground Railroad, "Follow the North Star." This is a second-person reenactment in which visitors are full participants who, through embodied role-playing, "become" the people represented in the historical drama. Like other living history museums, Conner Prairie assumes that bodily surrogation—that is, acting like a fugitive slave—produces for all reenactors an authoritative and authentic experience of "real" enslavement. At Conner Prairie the majority of the visitors and staff are white and most groups that reenact the Underground Railroad are all white or, in very rare cases, include one or two black participants. It is telling that Conner Prairie allows visitors, whose racial demographic is overwhelmingly white, to perform only the roles of enslaved blacks and not of the whites who were central to slavery.[89] This ensures that white visitors never embody, experience, or identify with, their racial group's practices of white supremacy and black subjection in constructing and sustaining slavery. Through acting as enslaved blacks, whites practice the restored behaviors of slavery; whites commodify, control, and exercise their right to use black bodies and personhood to fulfill white desires.

The surrogation of black bodies by white bodies did not originate in contemporary slave reenactments. Its historical lineage can be traced through the evolution of black minstrel shows, in which blackface "functioned as one method of repeatedly obliterating the black body, substituting in its stead not only the white body but also the white man's parodic imitation-black-body."⁹⁰ Minstrel acts, much like the idealized historical representations in slave plantation museums, represent life on antebellum slave plantations as praiseworthy. Lott argues that minstrel acts obscure the terror of slavery by presenting it as "amusing, right, and natural."⁹¹ Both minstrelsy and Follow the North Star use black commodification to "make 'blackness' into a marketable thing of white interest."⁹² For blackness and slavery to be profitable without being emotionally discomforting for whites, Follow the North Star is segregated from the main museum and takes place at a different location and time and with a separate fee.

This segregation would seem peculiar because the most popular special event at the museum is "Civil War Days," which one would assume addresses slavery. However, Conner Prairie advertises Civil War Days as a "fun" day with "Battle reenactments! See, feel and smell the Civil War! Let your imagination run wild! If you visit you can milk a cow, make 1800s pancakes, explore our Nature Walk with binoculars, march in infantry drills, shoot a Civil War–era musket, cool off in the Water Cannon Splash Play Area!"⁹³ Conner Prairie divorces the Civil War from slavery and integrates it into the museum's dominant historical narrative of white "homesteading" and nation building.⁹⁴ Consequently, slavery is dismissed as integral to, and formative of, national history.

Follow the North Star promises participants that the "authentic" experience of a fugitive slave's life will "affect [them] in ways that reading a book or watching a movie about it cannot." The program wants participants to believe that they are "central actors in a drama, taking on a whole new identity, as well as the risks that identity entails, [to] think about slavery in a deeper way by making [them] identify with enslaved peoples."⁹⁵ Each visitor is given the identity of an enslaved black subject, so that they can "Become a runaway slave on the Underground Railroad, fleeing from captivity, risking everything for freedom." As fugitive slaves, they travel along the Underground Railroad having "authentic interactions with costumed characters" who play a "variety of characters such as, a belligerent Southern, a reluctantly helpful farm wife, a former fugitive headed South to try to rescue family, a Quaker family and a free black family." The museum alerts visitors that they will "Leave the comfort of the world you know" and cautions them: "Follow the North Star is not for everyone. You should be prepared to take on the role of a runaway slave; you'll be walking outside on rough terrain in all kinds of weather, told to keep your eyes focused downward and spoken to in an abrupt manner." Each reenactor is given a strip of white cloth that

they can display if they find the experience of being a fugitive slave too discomforting and want out. One participant commented, "It was my escape
route. It's a nice idea, a simple accessory capable of transforming its wearer
from a frightened slave into a calm, detached observer."[96] The embodied
reenacting of the traumatic journey to freedom comes with the guaran-
tee of ontological distance for whites, that when the consumptive "experience" exceeds the limits of white comfort they can end it and become white
again. This ontological distance is not a possibility for black participants, as
Bethany, the only black student in a school group, questioning if her white
classmates perceived the reenactment as a game, said, "Would they really
even care after they went through it? After all this was not their families'
experience. But if this was still happening, I'd be their slave."[97]

In Follow the North Star's second-person reenactment of slavery, whites
enact a complete consumption of enslaved black subjects through full
bodily surrogation. This form of consumptive identification, complete dispossession of the black subject's body and personhood and transference of
its sovereignty to white participants, is a white supremacist practice that
Sullivan calls white "ontological expansion": "Taking on another race . . .
might seem like a white person's respect for people of color and non-white
lived experience. But it often is merely another example of white people's
assumption that any and all spaces . . . are open for white people to legiti-
mately move about [and it is] a gesture closer to colonialism than one of
respect."[98] Contemporary slave reenactments assert that bodily enactment
of slavery helps whites know, and empathize with, the import of slavery's
trauma. However, these claims of bodily epistemology negate the fact that
bodies, both white and black, have a historico-racial schema constituted
by very specific racial histories. The claim that whites can experience black
enslavement through inhabiting enslaved black bodies rests on some core
principles of white supremacy: one, that whites, uniquely and singularly,
are not constituted by their historico-racial bodily schema or they can ef-
fortlessly shed it and replace it with a un-raced bodily schema; two, blacks
are confined to only those experiences that are made available by their historico-racial bodily schema, their racial corporeality, making them "black"
but no more than black or, as Fanon said, being "sealed into that crushing
objecthood"; and three, that whites can violate black bodily integrity by inhabiting it and through that "obliterative assimilation" can experience black
bondage as black slaves.[99]

However, white bodily consumption of blacks cannot replicate the specific bodily epistemology of black enslaved subjects nor make the trauma

of slavery cognitively and emotively knowable or experienced by whites. White assumptions that black identities can be "tried on," that "anyone can be anyone," are symptomatic of the delusional nature of the white racial contract. Mills states, "[O]n matters related to race, the Racial Contract prescribes for its white signatories an inverted epistemology, an epistemology of ignorance" that creates for its white signatories "an invented delusional world, a racial fantasyland, a consensual hallucination."[100] This "invented delusion" can never be disproved because it does not exist; but precisely because it cannot be disproved, the white desire to make it a reality makes practices of whiteness formidably powerful.

The white performance of the Underground Railroad gives whites permission to appropriate experiences of black suffering, the heroism of fugitive slaves fleeing to freedom, and the white "compassionate people who helped the travelers." This enables whites, both visitors and staff reenactors, to be victims, heroes, and saviors, all identifications that evoke sympathy and admiration and do not cause guilt or demand accountability. Rather than develop "genuine self-/social criticism" and responsibility for their racial group's past and present subjugations of blacks, the guise of white empathy frees whites from the burden of critical inquiry. Sheltered within these affective and "epistemically comfortable situations," whites are enabled to retain their identification as innocent and unknowing of white supremacy, while simultaneously claiming empathic solidarity with the suffering imposed by white supremacy on enslaved black subjects.[101] White empathy and consumptive identification via the appropriation of black suffering promote white illusions of subjective commonality, assuage guilt, and do not disrupt past or existent racial relations of power. Lewis Gordon explains that the white person who declares that he has immersed himself into blackness does that "in order to protect himself from blackness," that is, to evade the black judgment of whiteness: "The eyes that are evaded are the eyes that matter, the eyes that judge."[102] The consumptive identification, and through that the obliteration, of ontological blackness by white reenactors makes white bodies (disguised as black through immersion into blackness) "the point of view that determines authority and reality."[103]

The surrogation of black bodily experience, epistemology, and subjectivity by white bodies and feelings minimizes the black experience of slavery's trauma and creates a false equivalence between the very real black suffering and the totally imagined suffering of white reenactors. The belief that imagined suffering is real suffering serves a double purpose; it is used to justify white refusals to be accountable for slavery and its afterlife and to achieve white desires for racial reassurance and redemption. In the ongoing re/pro-duction of white identity, some whites seek to re/form themselves as "good whites," that is, non-racist, though not necessarily anti-racist, whites.[104] For them, Follow the North Star is a "safe space" for their personal transfor-mation, a space that privileges white thoughts, feelings, and experiences over those of the communities they oppress. White acts of redemption use technologies of empathic consumptive identification and emotional cathar-tic release to claim that by suffering the black trauma of slavery they have transcended their whiteness.[105] Reformed and redeemed white ontology is sought, paradoxically, through the restored behaviors of slavery, namely, the repeated consumption of black subjects. This amounts to "an act of mas-tery" and not acts of "interrogating historical injustices" or instigating de-mands for transformative changes, by reckoning with slavery.[106] The pub-lic performances of white redemptive fantasies are always from positions of white autonomy and dominance and do not threaten the supremacy of whiteness. They allow whites to monitor and regulate their own racism as a matter of choice.

White enjoyment of reenactments of slavery is produced by complicity between white visitors and slave plantation museums. Conner Prairie mar-kets Follow the North Star as a real-time adventure: "Follow the North Star requires that both interpreters and participants commit to the adventure." It is no wonder that visitors respond to their experiences of the Underground Railroad as fun, awesome, exciting, and scary. One participant likened it to a thriller saying: "I'll leave whether we escaped a mystery. I wouldn't want to spoil the experience for you."[107] Other problematic responses by visitors who had just "lived" as fugitive slaves included degrading slavery to their experience of enforced "bodily discomfort" of a "cowed posture, kneeling, squatting, hands limp at our sides, eyes downcast"; responding with trivial examples when asked what they had learned from the experience, such as, "rubbing onions and pepper on our feet [to] throw dogs off our scent"; and racist responses which the staff "diffused as a joke."[108] Another common re-sponse was the deracialization of slavery and transformation of it into a human experience, "understanding a fragment of a fragment of what makes the soul tick was a valuable and powerful experience." Most reports on the experiences of white participants dwell, sympathetically, on whites feeling dehumanized and humiliated by their subjection and instances of white participants responding to the abuse of slave hunters with verbal and physi-cal aggression. It is telling that there are no reports of black participants re-sponding with violence. White antagonistic responses, for example, whites shouting at slavehunters, "who do you think you are" and "You can't treat me like this!" and physically threatening them, are symptomatic not of slave resistance but of white assumptions of being powerful, autonomous, and free from subjection. They respond as whites to being treated as blacks. White supremacy grants whites the power to choose to sympathize with blacks subjected to white antiblackness, in slavery or the present, while ensuring that whites will not be treated like enslaved or free blacks. Whites can play at being black but always from the security of their absolute supremacy.

Rex Ellis decries the enjoyment that whites derive from reenactments of slavery: "It is difficult at best to . . . have people view the exhibits, hear the interpretation and leave the museum with smiles on their faces. If they leave the museum laughing and joking, it is possible that the message has not been delivered or that the museum has been in some way misguided or mistaken in the implementation of its interpretive plan."[109] I argue that rather than interpreting white gratification as the result of an unforeseen mistake by the museum, it is better understood as the slave plantation museum's conscious practice of providing white visitors with reenactments of slavery that confirm their white ontology. This is evidenced in the white overvaluation of the Underground Railroad as the story of slavery and the neglect of black slave resistance, including the revolts lead by Nat Turner, Denmark Vesey, and Gabriel Prosser, the Battle of Negro Fort, and the 1811 German Coast revolt. The Underground Railroad is, by far, the most popular dramatization and reenactment of slavery. Yet, the number of enslaved blacks who achieved their freedom through the Underground Railroad is minimal when compared to the numbers of enslaved blacks that perished in slavery. The Underground Railroad's prominence lies in its confirmation of white ideologies that mystify and justify white supremacy during slavery and its afterlife. Though the Underground Railroad is an example of black agency and resistance, in the white imagination the "escape" to freedom is realized only through the aid of white operators and white abolitionists who help fugitive slaves at considerable risk to themselves and their families. This scenario affirms that white morality and sacrifice enabled black freedom and veils the fact that whites held blacks in bondage. In the contemporary white imaginary, if enslaved blacks could escape, then the white apparatus of slavery could not have been as totalizing and powerful as it is condemned (by blacks) to have been. Just as critically, whites imagine that if one enslaved black could escape, then all enslaved blacks could escape, if they really desired freedom. All that escape required was individualism, enterprise, a "real" desire for liberty, and the embrace of the unknown, in fact, all the qualities whites ascribe to themselves in their narrative of nation building. That more enslaved blacks did not (want to) escape confirms for whites the slave plantation museums' representations of the enslaved as happy, loyal, grateful, and appreciative of their benevolent slave masters and mistresses. The similarity between this interpretation and the pro-slavery argument (the enslaved blacks lived better and more cared-for lives than free white industrial workers in the North) demonstrates the merging of the past, present, and the past that is not yet past, in epistemologies and practices of whiteness.

RECKONING WITH GHOSTS

Slave forts, slave ships, slave auction sites, and slave plantations are the iconic sites of slavery. They are peopled with the ghosts of slavery and it is there that their haunting is most insistent, agitated, and closest to the surface. At one of the sites, slave plantation museums, compelling questions emerge about who is looking for the ghosts, which ghosts are they looking for, and what do they want to do with them? Because white supremacy has consigned slavery to being the history and heritage of blackness, we are left to seek only the ghosts of enslaved blacks, to decry their absences and count their presences. But what about the ghosts of whites who peopled and executed the apparatus of slavery? The "colonial elites" and "good whites" represented at slave plantation museums are not the white ghosts that need to be reckoned with, because they are the apparitions that disguise the ghosts of the white perpetrators of slavery, which are the ghosts that need to be made present and not disappeared. They are the ghosts that have to be brought to light, not on their terms, because those are always the terms of white supremacy, but on the terms of enslaved blackness and contemporary anti-blackness. If they are not accounted for, then there is no accounting for slavery. The reenactments of slavery discipline the ghosts of slavery, subverting the something-to-be-done from acts of accounting for the actions of whites to acts of re-consuming blackness in the furtherance of white supremacy. For whites, the reenactments as the something-to-be-done should "ideally force [whites] to feel that changing the world that produces these stories is now a condition of one's own survival" and to create a "regime of justice that does not exist yet."[110] However, white supremacy and white ontology depend on not implicating, or accounting for, whites in slavery and its afterlife and on rejecting the demands of the ghosts of enslaved blacks for a reckoning and an accounting of their loss, which is not yet lost.

NOTES

1. Avery F. Gordon, "Some Thoughts on Haunting and Futurity," *Borderlands* 10, no. 2 (2011): 2.

2. Saidiya V. Hartman, *Lose Your Mother: A Journey Along the Atlantic Slave Route* (New York: Farrar, Straus & Giroux, 2007), 133.

3. I am using "bad faith" in the Sartrean sense of bad faith being self-deception, insincerity, un-freedom, and a lack of authenticity. Gordon, "Some Thoughts," 3.

4. Toula Nicolacopoulos and George Vassilacopoulos, "Racism, Foreign Communities and the Onto-Pathology of White Australian Subjectivity," in *Whitening Race*, ed. Aileen Moreton-Robinson (Canberra, Australia: Aboriginal Studies Press, 2004), 32.

5. Joseph R. Roach, "Slave Spectacles and Tragic Octoroons: A Cultural Genealogy of Antebellum Performance," *Theatre Survey* 33, no. 2 (November 1992): 168.

6. Vanessa Agnew, "History's Affective Turn: Historical Reenactment and Its Work in the Present," *Rethinking History* 11, no. 3 (September 2007): 301. For discussions of affective history, see Ian McCalman, "The Little Ship of Horrors: Reenacting Extreme History," *Criticism* 46, no. 3 (Summer 2004): 477–86; Jason Endacott, "Reconsidering Affective Engagement in Historical Empathy," *Theory and Research in Social Education* 38, no. 1 (2010): 6–47.

7. Scott Magelssen, "'This is a Drama. You are Characters': The Tourist as Fugitive Slave in Conner Prairie's 'Follow the North Star,'" *Theatre Topics* 16, no. 1 (2006): 20.

8. I am using "trauma" to denote the horrific experiences that slavery created for the enslaved and not the psychological condition that results from the repression of the experience and its delayed and displaced repetition that continues without resolution.

9. W. E. B. Du Bois, *Darkwater: Voices From Within the Veil* (Mineola: Dover, 1999), 18.

10. Ghassan Hage, *White Nation: Fantasies of White Supremacy in a Multicultural Society* (New York: Rutledge, 2000); Charles W. Mills, *The Racial Contract* (Ithaca: Cornell University Press, 1997); Tomas Almaguer, *Racial Faultlines: The Historical Origins of White Supremacy in California* (Berkeley: University of California Press, 1994); Ian Haney Lopez, *White by Law: The Legal Construction of Race* (New York: University of New York Press, 1996).

11. Lewis R. Gordon, *Bad Faith and Antiblack Racism* (Amherst: Humanity Books, 1999).

12. Cheryl I. Harris, "Whiteness as Property," *Harvard Law Review*, 106, no. 8 (1993): 1720. For commoditization of blacks, see Joseph Roach, *Cities of the Dead: Circum-Atlantic Performance* (New York: Columbia University Press, 1996).

13. Orlando Patterson, *Slavery and Social Death: A Comparative Study* (Cambridge: Harvard University Press, 1982).

14. Frantz Fanon, *Black Skin, White Masks* (New York: Grove Press, 1967), 109–10.

15. Lewis Gordon, *Bad Faith*, 99.

16. Hartman, *Lose Your Mother*, 6.

17. Michel Foucault, *Society Must Be Defended* (New York: Picador, 1997), 255.

18. Ibid.

19. Steve Martinot and Jared Sexton, "The Avant-Garde of White Supremacy," *Social Identities* 9, no. 2 (2003): 176.

20. "Plantation" continues to denote sites of wealth and prestige and is used to name exclusive sites like gated communities and resorts. In the literature, I found only three authors who name the museums "slave plantations." See Christine N. Buzinde and Carla Almeida Santos, "Representations of Slavery," *Annals of Tourism Research* 35, no. 2 (2008): 469–88; Christine N. Buzinde and Iyunolu F. Osagie, "Slavery Heritage Representations, Cultural Citizenship, and Judicial Politics in America," *Historical Geography* 39 (2011): 41–64.

21. Foucault, *Society Must Be Defended*, 10.

22. Richard Handler and Eric Gable, *The New History in an Old Museum: Creating the Past at Colonial Williamsburg* (Durham: Duke University Press, 1997), 84. Interpreters or guides are museum staff members who teach history to the public.

23. Verne Chatelain, head of the National Park Service, quoted in Cary Carson, "Colonial Williamsburg and the Practice of Interpretive Planning in American History Museums," *Public Historian* 20, no. 3 (Summer 1998): 21.

24. Jennifer Eichstedt and Stephen Small, *Representations of Slavery: Race and Ideology in Southern Plantation Museums* (Washington: Smithsonian Institution Press, 2002). Eichstedt and Small delineate four strategies used by slave plantation museums: symbolic annihilation and erasure of slavery, trivializing and deflecting experiences of enslavement, segregation of knowledge, and complication of the master narrative.

25. Derek H. Alderman and E. Arnold Modlin Jr., "(In)visibility of the Enslaved Within Online Plantation Tourism Marketing: A Textual Analysis of North Carolina Websites," *Journal of travel and Tourism Marketing* 25, no. 3-4 (2008): 265–81.

26. David Butler, Perry Carter, and Owen Dwyer, "Imagining Plantations: Slavery, Dominant Narratives, and the Foreign Born," *Southeastern Geographer* 48, no. 3 (2008): 288–302.

27. E. Arnold Modlin Jr., Derek H. Alderman, and Glenn W. Gentry, "Tour Guides as Creators of Empathy: The Role of Affective Inequality in Marginalizing the Enslaved at Plantation House Museums," *Tourist Studies* 11, no. 3 (2011): 10.

28. Ibid., 5.

29. James Oliver Horton, "Slavery in American History: An Uncomfortable National Dialogue," in *Slavery and Public History: The Tough Stuff of American History*, ed. James Oliver Horton and Lois E. Horton (Chapel Hill: University of North Carolina Press, 2006), 48.

30. Zora Martin, "Colonial Williamsburg: A Black Perspective," *Roundtable Reports* (June 1973). www.jstor.org/stable/40478194.

31. Buzinde and Osagie, "Slavery Heritage," 59.

32. Buzinde and Santos, "Representations," 470.

33. Renato Rosaldo, "Imperialist Nostalgia," *Representations* 26 (Spring 1989): 107–8.

34. Handler and Gable, *The New History in an Old Museum*, 109.

35. Rosaldo, "Imperialist Nostalgia," 108.

36. Lisa Woolfork, *Embodying American Slavery in Contemporary Culture* (Chicago: University of Illinois Press, 2008), 2.

37. Rosemarie A. Roberts, "Dancing with Social Ghosts: Performing Embodiments, Analyzing Critically," *Transforming Anthropology* 21, no. 1 (April 2013): 5.

38. Vanessa Agnew, "Introduction: What is Reenactment?" *Criticism* 46, no. 3 (Summer 2004): 328.

39. Alexander Cook, "The Use and Abuse of Historical Reenactment: Thoughts on Recent Trends in Public History," *Criticism* 46, no. 3 (Summer 2004): 491.

40. Timothy Crumrin, Associate Director for Research at Conner Prairie, in David Thelan, "Learning from the Past: Individual Experience and Re-Enactment," *Indiana Magazine of History* XCIX (June 2003): 169.

41. Mark Auslander, "Touching the Past: Materializing Time in Traumatic 'Living History' Reenactments," *Signs and Society* 1, no. 1 (Spring 2013): 174.

42. For other discussions of reenactments as affective performances, see Woolfork, *Embodying*; Scott Magelssen, *Living History Museums: Undoing History Through Performance* (Lanham: Scarecrow Press, 2007); Stephen Gapps, "Mobile Monuments: A View of Historical Reenactment and Authenticity from Inside the Costume Cupboard of History," *Rethinking History* 13, no. 3 (September 2009): 395–409.

43. Lewis R. Gordon, "Through the Hellish Zone of Nonbeing: Thinking through Fanon, Disaster, and the Damned of the Earth," *Human Architecture: Journal of the Sociology of Self-Knowledge*, Special Double-Issue V (2007): 6.

44. http://chmuseums.org/brattonsville/.

45. http://chmuseums.org/african-american-history-hb/.

46. Ellen Barry, "Slavery: A Hard Truth to Portray," *Los Angeles Times*, June 4, 2005.

47. Ibid.

48. Charles C. Mills, "White Supremacy as Sociopolitical System," in *White Out: The Continuing Significance of Racism*, ed. A. W. Doane and E. Bonilla-Silva (New York: Routledge, 2003), 45.

49. Aileen Moreton-Robinson, "Whiteness, Epistemology and Indigenous Representation," in Moreton-Robinson, ed., *Whitening Race*, 76.

50. Charles W. Mills, "White Ignorance," in *Race and Epistemologies of Ignorance*, ed. Shannon Sullivan and Nancy Tuana (New York: State University of New York Press, 1997), 20.

51. Ibid., 22.

52. George Wythe's sexual exploitation of his slave, Lydia Broadnax, is well documented, including the existence of a son, Michael Brown.

53. Handler and Gable, *The New History in an Old Museum*, 86–92.

54. www.connerprairie.org/plan-your-visit/special-events/follow-the-north-star (emphasis mine).

55. Auslander, "Touching"; Jason Stupp, "Slavery and the Theatre of History: Ritual Performance on the Auction Block," *Theatre Journal* 63, no. 1 (March 2011): 61–84.

56. Horstene Spillers, "Mama's Baby, Papa's Maybe: An American Grammar Book," *Diacritics* 17 (Summer 1987): 67.

57. Auslander, "Touching," 165.

58. The argument that the white congregation racially identified their whiteness with the "light-skin/whiteness" of the women being auctioned is made by Stupp, "Slavery and Theater" and Auslander, "Touching."

59. Heather S. Nathans, *Slavery and Sentiment on the American Stage, 1787-1861: Lifting the Veil of Black* (Cambridge: Cambridge University Press, 2009), 197.

60. Walter Johnson, *Soul by Soul: Life Inside the Antebellum Slave Market* (Cambridge: Harvard University Press, 2003), 17.

61. Guest Experience manager Michelle Evans, quoted in Carl R. Weinberg, "The Discomfort Zone: Reenacting Slavery at Conner Prairie," *OAH Magazine of History* (April 2009); Woolfork, *Embodying*, 188.

62. Handler and Gable, *The New History in an Old Museum*; Butler, Carter, and Dwyer, "Imagining Plantations"; Eichstedt and Small, *Representations of Slavery*.

63. "Slavery is a Tough Role and a Hard Sell at Colonial Williamsburg," *Washington Post*, March 8, 2013. Retrieved from ProQuest Newspapers.

64. Auslander, "Touching," 179.

65. Christy Coleman, Director of the African American Department at Colonial Williamsburg, quoted in Horton, "Slavery in American History," 50.

66. Christina Sharpe, "Blackness, Sexuality, and Entertainment," *American Literary History* 24, no. 4 (Winter 2012): 328.

67. Saidiya Hartman, *Scenes of Subjection: Terror, Slavery, and Self-Making in Nineteenth-Century America* (Oxford: Oxford University Press, 1997), 34.

68. Mark Auslander, "'Give Me Back My Children!' Traumatic Reenactment and Tenuous Democratic Public Spheres," Religion and Culture Web Forum paper, Marty Martin Center for the Advanced Study of Religion, University of Chicago, 11. http://divinity.uchicago.edu/martycenter/publications/webforum/archive.shtml.

69. Rex Ellis, "Living History: Bringing History into Play," *American Visions* 7, no. 6 (December-January 1992): 2.

70. Crumrin, in Thelan, "Learning from the Past," 170.

71. Tilden quoted in Handler and Gable, *The New History in an Old Museum*, 175.

72. Horton, "Slavery in American History"; Roach, "Slave Spectacles."

73. Magelssen, *Living History Museums*, 120.

74. Woolfork, *Embodying*, 114–15.

75. Stephen P. Hanna, "A Slavery Museum? Race, Memory, and Landscape in Fredericksburg, Virginia," *Southeastern Geographer* 48, no. 3 (2008): 316–37.

76. Martin, "Colonial Williamsburg," 2.

77. Handler and Gable, *The New History in an Old Museum*, 98.

78. Paxton Hibbens quoted in Stupp, "Slavery and the Theatre," 75.

79. "Tears and Protest at Mock Slave Auction," *New York Times*, October 11, 1994. Retrieved from ProQuest Newspapers.

80. Cook, "The Use and Abuse of Historical Reenactment," 491.

81. E. Arnold Modlin Jr., "Tales Told on the Tour: Mythic Representations of Slavery by Docents at North Carolina Plantation Museums," *Southeastern Geographer* 48, no. 3 (November 2008): 276.

82. David Butler, "Whitewashing Plantations: The Commodification of a Slave-Free Antebellum South," *International Journal of Hospitality and Tourism Administration* 2 (2001): 163:75. Butler's argument that plantation museums whitewash history is

restricted to signify only the absence of enslaved blacks and not, as I argue, the absence of white perpetrators of slavery.

83. Stephen Eddy Snow, *Performing the Pilgrims: A Study of Ethnohistorical Role-Playing at Plimouth Plantation* (Jackson: University of Mississippi Press (1993), 34.

84. Martinot and Sexton, "Avant-Garde," 179.

85. Roach, "Slave Spectacles," 186.

86. Handler and Gable, *The New History in an Old Museum*, 114.

87. Conner Prairie is notable for its symbolic annihilation and reinvention of American Indian history at the site, which had been the home of the Delaware. I address this in a forthcoming paper.

88. Magellsen, *Living History Museums*, 75.

89. Magelssen, "This is a Drama," 20.

90. Susan Gubar, *Racechanges: White Skin, Black Face in American Culture* (New York: Oxford University Press, 1997), 56. For other studies of black minstrelsy, see Eric Lott, *Love and Theft: Blackface Minstrelsy and the American Working Class* (New York: Oxford University Press, 1993); David R. Roediger, *The Wages of Whiteness: Race and the Making of the American Working Class* (New York: Verso, 1991).

91. Eric Lott, "Love and Theft: The Racial Unconscious of Blackface Minstrelsy," *Representations* 39 (Summer 1992): 44. See, Hartman, *Scenes of Subjection*, for an analysis of minstrelsy's roots in antebellum performances by enslaved blacks at the command of whites for white entertainment and amusement.

92. Lott, "Love and Theft: The Racial Unconscious of Blackface Minstrelsy," 23.

93. All information about Conner Prairie, unless otherwise noted, is from the museum's promotional materials located at www.connerprairie.org/plan-your-visit/special-events/follow-the-north-star, www.connerprairie.org/, and www.facebook.com/connerprairie.

94. The separation of the Civil War from slavery is a common theme in reenactments and memorials of the Civil War. See Paul A. Shackel, "Public Memory and the Search for Power in American Historical Archaeology," *American Anthropologist* 103, no. 3 (Sep. 2001): 655–70; David Blight, *Race and Reunion: The Civil War in American Memory* (Cambridge: Harvard University Press, 2001); Dwight T. Pitcaithley, "A Cosmic Threat: The National Park Service Addresses the Causes of the American Civil War," in Horton and Horton, *Slavery and Public History*, 169–86.

95. Weinberg, "The Discomfort Zone," 63.

96. *NUVO News Indianapolis*, "It's Intense: Follow the North Star Challenges the Participant," October 30, 2002 www.nuvo.net/indianapolis/its-intense/Content?oid=1202800#.Ugqfnrtej4g.

97. Susan Ray, "Underground Railroad Reenactment Reveals Heroes as Well as Villains," *Los Angeles Times*, December 20, 1998.

98. Shannon Sullivan, *Revealing Whiteness: The Unconscious Habits of Racial Privilege* (Bloomington: Indiana University Press, 2006), 159–60.

99. Fanon, *Black Skin*, 109.

100. Mills, *Racial Contract*, 18.

101. Allison Bailey, "Strategic Ignorance," in Sullivan and Tuana, ed., *Race and Episte-mologies*, 77–94.

102. Lewis Gordon, *Bad Faith*, 118.

103. Ibid.

104. I define *non-racist* as an individualized and passive mode of being that is satis-fied with assuming nonparticipation in racism and *anti-racist* as an active resistance against racism. Non-racist and anti-racist have fundamentally different goals and prac-tices premised on radically disparate understandings of white supremacy, racism, and antiblackness.

105. For the relationship between the denial of white privilege, redemption, and fan-tasy, see Leslie G. Roman, "Denying (White) Racial Privilege: Redemption Discourses and the Uses of Fantasy," in Michelle Fine et al., *Off-White: Readings on Race, Power, and Society* (New York: Routledge, 1997), 270–82.

106. Agnew, "History's Affective Turn," 302.

107. Piper Lynch, "My Night as a Runaway Slave," http://voices.yahoo.com/conner-prairie-interactive-history-park-night-as-7713890.html.

108. Magelsson, "This is a Drama," 26–28.

109. Rex Ellis quoted in Magelssen, *Living History Museums*, 122.

110. Lauren Berlant, "Trauma and Ineloquence," *Cultural Values* 5, no. 1 (January 2001): 44.

7

ABOUT SCHMIDT'S WHITENESS
The Emotional Landscapes of WASP Masculinity

TIM ENGLES

LOUIS BEGLEY IS A JEWISH AMERICAN HOLOCAUST SURVIVOR WHO emigrated from Poland to the United States in 1947 at the age of fourteen. As an adult, Begley worked his way through anti-Semitic barriers into Harvard College and Law School, and then into a successful career in a top-tier New York City law firm.[1] While doing so, Begley undoubtedly found it necessary to carefully scrutinize the ways and mores of the WASP elite, especially those of the men who primarily formed his clients, colleagues, and competitors. Given the barriers faced by mid-twentieth-century Jewish professionals and the acumen regarding human psychology and behavior required to overcome them, who better than a successful and literarily inclined Jewish American professional to dramatize the subtle attitudes and projected feelings of those whose ranks he successfully fought to join? Born in 1933 as Ludwik Begleiter, Begley did not begin publishing fiction until the age of fifty-seven. His first novel (with Alfred E. Knopf, which has published nearly all of his subsequent novels), the award-winning *Wartime Lies* (1991), describes a young Holocaust survivor who avoids Nazi persecution by pretending to be Catholic, a story that echoes Begley's own early travails.[2] Begley has since turned primarily to American scenes and characters, and his fourth novel, *About Schmidt* (published in 1996, and the basis for an eponymous 2002 film), which examines the late-life crisis of a retired WASP lawyer, is an acute, deeply observed portrait of privileged, late-twentieth-century white masculinity in crisis. His novel thus joins the ranks of numerous besieged-white-male narratives of the 1990s, yet it crucially distinguishes itself from most of them by exposing the emotional states commonly inculcated by the construction of whiteness typically depicted in this brand of fiction as reactionary, rather than justified. Thus, the novel can be read as a counternarrative to the more standard depictions of white masculinity as an essential, normative status, revealing instead the ideological fissures that threaten to undermine hegemonic whiteness.

Some of Albert Schmidt's depicted internal states, which other white male narratives of the time also illustrate ad nauseam, include anger, grief, and despair, emotions often felt by the privileged when confronted with a changing social order. As Sally Robinson explains in her landmark study of an array of eighties and nineties novels written by white American men, such narratives gave voice to an emerging conviction that the rise of identity politics among disempowered groups, and the consequent highlighting of unmarked white masculinity, constituted an unwarranted attack on white men. Such responses coalesced into a new "identity politics of the dominant," as expressed by such cultural narrative producers as literary authors, filmmakers, TV show writers, and politicians, all of whom repeatedly cast the supposedly "disenfranchised white man" as a "symbol for the decline of the American way."[3] This widely reiterated narrative ironically appropriated the liberationist claims of the minoritized, reformulating "what had once been an unquestioned privilege . . . into a liability," and casting the average white male in essentialist terms as a newly restrained repository of imminently and justifiably violent sexual energy.[4]

Writing in the midst of this milieu as a Jewish American achiever of elite access and stature, Begley in *About Schmidt* critiques the popular trope of white male victimhood so often present in contemporary narratives that revolve around the central image of the besieged white American male. My reading of the novel examines Begley's psychological appraisal of his protagonist as a figure who displays emblematic racialized and masculinized feelings commonly induced in late-twentieth-century denizens of insular WASP enclaves by a salient white supremacist legacy. Aside from xenophobic and paranoid responses to ethnic and racialized others, other feelings, including racially inflected sensations of lust, possessiveness, and entitlement, are more difficult to detect and trace to their sources, both in the novel and in many of the habitually self-contained male WASPs on whom Schmidt is modeled.

Any era's manifestations of United States whiteness are of course formed and shaped by both local and national influences; in *About Schmidt*, elite workplaces, families, and neighborhoods receive insightful and at times satiric scrutiny, particularly the legal profession and one of the depicted region's most exclusive enclaves of respite and social interaction, the Hamptons on New York's Long Island. These locations, along with broader sociohistorical contexts, comprise the extant structures that encourage Schmidt

to repress many of his emotions, and then when they resurface, to chan-
nel them into gendered and racialized reactions and behaviors. My analysis
is thus in alignment with Jonathan Flatley's study of depictions in earlier
modernist literature of potentially productive melancholic states, a scholarly effort to map sociohistorical forces that shape emotions in order to better
grasp "the lived, affective and very unfixed, half-articulated way that most
of us experience our lives most of the time."[5] Socially constructed whiteness is of course one such shaping force, and reading *About Schmidt* as a
diagnostic portrait of a particular, historically contextualized form of whit-
ened subjectivity can help us understand the emotionally driven reactions
of privileged people, who often feel beleaguered by growing numbers of
racial and/or ethnic others. While Schmidt ultimately achieves release from
forces that he perceives as being arrayed against himself, Begley portrays
this liberation not as the inevitable and legitimate result of undeserved
impositions on white men like Schmidt, but rather as another destructive
symptom of a sociopolitically situated whiteness—the stunted WASP male
pathology that frames and prompts Schmidt's psychological and emotional
choices.

PROPRIETARY WHITE MASCULINITY

In interviews, Begley has expressed admiration for the themes and methods of various modernist writers, many of whom deployed deeply psychological modes of storytelling and character development.[6] Unsurprisingly,
About Schmidt's third-person narrative relates events from deep inside the
perspective of its protagonist, Albert Schmidt, a sixty-year-old man who
instructs seemingly everyone but his daughter to call him by the ironically
suggestive diminutive "Schmidtie," but whom the third-person narrator
simply calls Schmidt.

   As the novel opens, Schmidt has recently retired from corporate finance
work for Wood & King Associates, and his wife Mary, a relatively high-pro-
file fiction editor, has died several months earlier.[7] Having sold off a large
Manhattan apartment, Schmidt now lives in a Bridgehampton house that
is technically owned by his deceased wife—more on how that important
financial arrangement came about in a moment. His daughter Charlotte,
who lives in New York City, has recently informed him of her plans to marry Jon Riker, a young Jewish American lawyer at Schmidt's former firm.
In a conventionally restrained WASP manner, Schmidt recoils from such a

supposedly mixed union. Upon meeting Jon's parents, Schmidt recoils further, hastening his plans to flee from the house that Charlotte and Jon had
hoped to share with him on their weekends and vacations, and pursuing a
relationship with a half–Puerto Rican waitress, Carrie, who is one-third his
age. Other significant characters include Jewish American Gil Blackman,
who is Schmidt's former Harvard College roommate, current confidant,
and lifelong best friend (at least in Schmidt's mind), and Mr. Wilson, or
"the man," as Schmidt continually calls him, even after learning his name.
This character is a wildly animated, "black-faced" homeless white man who,
Doppelgänger-like, repeatedly shadows and pesters Schmidt.

Primary questions driving the novel's plot include just who "the man" is;
whether Schmidt will settle into amicable relations with his daughter and future in-laws; why he reacts as he does to his new situation and to the people
he knows; and whether Schmidt will change enough to accept and embrace
the life that could be his, that of a respected, successfully retired professional
and proud, supportive, and loved father. In a reaction to the 2003 film version of his novel published in the *New York Times*, Begley summarized his
novel's intended themes: "Schmidt's frightful and, I believe, lifelong loneliness; the devastating realization that we can botch a relationship that matters
to us above all others—in the event, that between Schmidt and his daughter—even though we have worked hard to make it succeed and believe with
some reason that we have done a good job; [and] the way in which our fears
of the Other and prejudices against the Other imprison us."[8]

In the novel's opening section, Schmidt struggles with his daughter's
engagement announcement and with new living arrangements in the
Bridgehampton house. These early domestic scenes establish the protagonist as a geographically and sociohistorically situated exemplar of certain white masculine feelings and proclivities, particularly a presumptive
sense of ownership. Sherrow O. Pinder points out that "At the beginning of
American history, the distinction between who could *have* property and
who could *be* property was paramount."[9] As many other historians have
explained, the social script for respectable, successfully performed white
American masculinity long called for property ownership, in terms of both
land and people. The latter included not only slaves, but also wives and
children. While people are no longer a legally sanctioned form of property,
remnants of the perceived perquisites of ownership linger in the habits and
feelings of a self-declared WASP like Schmidt, who clearly views his daughter's impending marriage to a Jewish American in terms of loss—the loss of
"his" daughter—instead of as a gain of more family members.

On the novel's first page, Charlotte tells her father during breakfast of her decision to get married. At this news, Schmidt openly sheds tears, something he remembers not having done since learning of another imminent loss, that of his wife Mary several months earlier to cancer. As Charlotte strokes his hand, Schmidt tells her that he cannot explain his uncharacteristically emotional display, then attributes it to "happiness. Or because you are so grownup. I'll stop now, I promise."[10] By WASP dictates and mores, crying and other naked displays of emotion are rarely acceptable forms of behavior, and the emotions that provoke them should be squelched or hidden when they arise.[11] Indeed, the one instance in which Schmidt explicitly self-identifies as a WASP occurs during another emotionally vulnerable moment with Jon's mother, Renata. As Schmidt writes a diary entry included in the novel about a day that he spent lying sick in bed, he recalls admitting to Renata, "I love my daughter," and then adds in an aside to his diary, "I keep all note of pathos out of my voice. It helps to be the last of the Wasps."[12]

As Schmidt receives his daughter's news of her decision to wed, his repressed confusion about his emotions may be sincere. However, as the novel progresses, Begley gradually suggests that the array of conflicted feelings prompting Schmidt's outburst have their roots in common WASP conceptions of a proper man's expressed relations to others. In particular, these mores dictated that the primary mark of propriety is a relationally heightened level of success, and the primary mark of heightened success is possession, not only of material property, but also, in a way that resonates historically with the possessive foundations of racial whiteness, of people.

As Charlotte enters the kitchen, Schmidt is immersed in some dismaying figures listed in the *New York Times* related to his financial holdings. Upon hearing Charlotte's announcement, Schmidt "put aside the paper [and] looked at his daughter, so tall and, it seemed to him, painfully desirable in her sweat-soaked running clothes. . . ."[13] For a daughter to seem not only desirable to her own father, but "painfully" so, strikes an odd note, but Schmidt's twinge of desire for a far younger woman becomes more characteristic of him as the novel progresses. In a particularly perceptive review of this novel, Thomas R. Edwards notes the pointed similarity of the names of three young women whom Schmidt finds desirable: "'Charlotte' sounds just a little like 'Corinne,' the name of the French-Asian *au pair* girl with whom he went to bed [during his forties], and quite a lot like 'Carrie,' the young woman he gets deeply involved with as the book goes on."[14] While Begley may seem to be depicting with these three "C's" a latent incestuous desire on Schmidt's part, this opening moment—with its conjunction of Schmidt's money, "his" daughter, and perceived threats to both—establishes him more pointedly as a white American man whose very identity is grounded in a racially informed, masculine possessiveness. The impending "loss" of Charlotte to marriage means losing something desirable (and to a Jewish man, no less), a self-affirming possession of sorts so valued that Schmidt feels a pain akin to that of unrequited lust; possession itself, Begley suggests, is a source of excitement for Schmidt, one with a resemblance to sexual excitement that becomes more apparent when that to which Schmidt feels a proprietary right is a woman.

Schmidt's possessive conception of his daughter is further established as an animating proprietary white male habit when he feels resentment over not having been asked by Charlotte's fiancé for her hand in marriage: "couldn't Riker have gone to the trouble of coming to Charlotte's father to ask for her hand?"[15] Schmidt feels disrespected in this way, a reaction that echoes a particularly Anglo-Saxon tradition of marriage stretching back to the medieval era. Anglo-Saxon mores long dictated that a daughter's prospective husband approach her father in a courtly manner and request the daughter's "hand" in marriage. The request was not merely an effort on the suitor's part to seek paternal approval of himself; it was also a financial transaction, since a daughter was a form of paternal property destined to become another man's property, as a wife. As Carl Holliday noted in 1919, in his study of Anglo-Saxon marital customs: "The etymology of the very name 'wedding' betrays the character of the second stage in the development of matrimony. The 'wed' was the money, horses, cattle, or ornaments given as security by the Saxon groom and held by trustees as a pledge and as proof of the purchase of the bride from her father. . . . [A] handsome daughter has always been considered a decidedly marketable product."[16] This is not to deny, of course, that many other cultures have also treated daughters as transferable property in marriage rituals. Rather, in this particular tradition, and as Schmidt's feelings illustrate, remnants of the Anglo-Saxon conception of impending marriage as a masculinized exchange of property lingered with greater than average salience among the American WASP elite, given their occupancy in the upper realms of a social hierarchy that resembles feudal English stratification in more ways than one. Begley depicts WASP whiteness as an ideology with myriad restrictive, status-producing manifestations, including marital conceptions that resonate historically in terms not only of gendered possession but also of race.

Throughout the novel, Schmidt's latent anti-Semitism functions as a means of maintaining a pure, unmitigated sense of whiteness, or WASP-ness, as it were, for himself as well as for his future progeny. Accordingly, certain thoughts and feelings on Schmidt's part suggest that he resents what he sees as an impending loss of his daughter not only to another man, but also to a Jewish man, and to his Jewish family. Other characters at times indicate their awareness of Schmidt's genteel bigotry, but only his daughter eventually becomes fed up enough to confront him about it directly. As sociologist Jessica Holden Sherwood notes in her study of attitudes and mores among the members of exclusive country clubs in the northeastern United States, "Polite indirection is characteristic of the WASP style of interacting. . . ."[17] Begley's portrayal of Schmidt's obstinate denial of his own anti-Semitism suggests that evasive indirection may also be characteristic of the WASP style of interacting internally with oneself, especially about one's own less than admirable traits. While Begley depicts Schmidt interacting with many other characters, he spends most of the narrative on his protagonist's internal divagations and avoidances. A persistent thorn in Schmidt's psyche is his daughter's impending marriage to Jon Riker. Again, a WASP of Schmidt's generation was likely to feel such a union as the "loss" of a daughter, and an attendant feeling is that since she must be released into adulthood, she should at least marry someone "like us." As Sherwood also notes of wealthy, northeastern elite values, "a family is conventionally expected to be ethnically homogenous."[18]

Schmidt's identification of himself as "the last of the Wasps" is a grudging recognition that in terms of race and ethnicity, his insular, monochromatic environment is changing. One irony of the novel is that, with a name like Schmidt, his own family's entrée into White Anglo-Saxonism is technically tenuous, as well as quite recent (as is his wealth); indeed, while Schmidt thoroughly enacts the WASP masculine mores of his era, his claim to Anglo-Saxonism is little more genuine than claims to such a status by a Jewish American would be. Nevertheless, although Schmidt has worked extensively with Jewish colleagues, his daughter's impending marriage still *feels* like an incursion, and Schmidt doesn't quite know why. "Decidedly there was nothing wrong with Jon Riker," the narrator says at one point in Schmidt's internal voice, without directly stating that Schmidt somehow feels the marriage is wrong.[19] Rather than admit, even to himself, that his feelings are anti-Semitic, Schmidt instead focuses on certain characteristics he remembers being displayed by Jon. As I will explain, he does so because whiteness functions, especially at psychic levels, as a normalized set of values, rather than as what it also is—an ideology in the service of power.

Recollection of actual Jewish American forays into elite northeastern United States settings reveals that although Schmidt thinks he is judging Jon's candidacy for son-in-law by a list of objective criteria, what he actually focuses on are stereotypes that northeastern white elites had come to associate with Jewish Americans who sought professional and social advancement. These stereotypes constituted an exclusionary strategy of WASP whiteness as it reproduced itself within institutional structures. As Karen Brodkin notes in her study of Jewish American assimilation, elite colleges and universities of the mid-twentieth century were converting from finishing schools and sites of social connection for scions of the WASP elite to a "newer professional training mission": "Pressures for change were beginning to transform the curriculum and to reorient college from a gentleman's bastion to a training ground for middle-class professionals needed by an industrial economy."[20] As Begley illustrates in his later novel *Matters of Honor* (2007), which traces the adulthood path of a professionally successful Jewish immigrant much like himself, competing well academically became a viable mode of advancement for Jewish Americans (particularly those of Ashkenazi descent, and thus lighter skinned) who lacked the generationally transferred social connections of elite whites, and often as well the precise sorts of manners, interests, vocabulary, and other markers of insider status.[21] An attendant and greater barrier was the elite white perception of Jews; as Brodkin writes, "The Protestant elite complained that Jews were unwashed, uncouth, unrefined, loud, and pushy."[22] Such perceptions of a Jewish Other led to de facto forms of discrimination in educational institutions, including admission applications that asked for religious affiliation, "a fixed class size, a chapel requirement, and preference for children of alumni. . . ."[23] Faced with such barriers, doing all that one could to prove one's suitability for a professional field, especially in academic terms, was a common strategy on the part of besieged Jewish students. An unfortunate consequence was that such hard work reinforced the elite white perception of Jews as fundamentally different—as "pushy," but also as too driven, and too narrowly focused, to fit in well with the more "well-rounded" white elites.

Begley spends several early pages depicting Schmidt's efforts to sort out his feelings against Jon. His protagonist's rationalizations reflect with nuanced precision several preconceptions that were commonly held against Jews by northeastern white elites during the mid- to late twentieth century, dramatizing in the process ways in which hegemonic whiteness is often normalized for its bearers as a set of proper, practical mores and values. Accordingly, Schmidt's thoughts and feelings here demonstrate a common lack of self-awareness regarding one's own racism, which white Americans often characterize instead as reasonable, supposedly accurate perceptions of mere differences from an unspecified (though actually, specifically white) norm. Schmidt's first demurral is that although Jon is "an excellent young lawyer, almost certain to become a partner . . . he works much too hard."[24] Schmidt dwells further on this supposed characteristic of his future son-in-law, recalling that when he and Riker traveled together for their firm, Riker continued working during night flights while Schmidt "struggle[d]" to stay awake over "some contraband belles lettres."[25] Schmidt repeatedly finds time for classic European novels, but does so more dutifully than enthusiastically; the suggestion is that Schmidt regards the habit of reading literature as a distinguishing mark of a conventionally complete and polished man like himself. Accordingly, Jon's apparent disinterest in such supposedly edifying and broadening fare constitutes a mark against him (Schmidt only recalls Jon reading one book, "the first volume of Kissinger's memoirs").[26] What clearly makes this supposed disinterest in the arts more risible, and even noticeable, for Schmidt is Jon's Jewishness; because he sees Jon primarily in terms of his ethnicity, especially since Jon has been dating his daughter, his feelings against the young man's encroachment upon Schmidt's familial property of sorts are channeled through the lens of anti-Semitic sentiment. Schmidt himself is described as having worked excessively hard to achieve prominence in his profession, and the long hours he spent working away from home are identified as another source of estrangement from his daughter; readers can easily imagine him ironically overlooking or even embracing such traits in a gentile suitor.

By the late twentieth century, with organizations like Schmidt's former firm of Wood & King having (according to him) "filled up with Jews since the day he had himself gone to work there," continued elite white resistance to perceived Jewish incursions had become less overtly discriminatory.[27] Begley's depiction of Schmidt's inner workings here suggests again that habitual politeness and restraint can engender self-deception about one's own inclinations and actions. For Schmidt, the pathological result is repeated detours from his bigoted feelings into a focus on his own actions towards Jewish people, or rather, the lack thereof: "To the best of his recollection, no matter how deeply or far he looked, Schmidt was sure he had not once in his life stood in the way of a Jew."[28] The truth of this claim remains indiscernible, but what Begley stresses here is Schmidt's feelings about Jewish people as simply different from himself, and at a deeper level, both inferior in some ways and alarmingly superior in others. As a self-professed member of the WASP elite, Schmidt seems especially inclined to resent the apparent expectation that he adapt to the somewhat different, and supposedly Jewish, ways of Jon's family, so accustomed are people of his sort to the opposite, that is, Jewish assimilation into "normal" (for him, elite white) ways. By this point, thoughts and feelings about the impending "loss" of his daughter have risen to the point of anger, as a broader, racialized structure of feelings diverts Schmidt's emotions into a focus on supposed, and supposedly objectionable, Jewish difference.

Nevertheless, Schmidt can never admit, even to himself, that he harbors these culturally instilled prejudicial inclinations. He continues to insist that his passive (rather than actively discriminatory) inaction toward Jews he has known are what count, even after Charlotte calls him out during a heated telephone conversation about her wedding plans: "At Wood & King, it was a standard joke: Schmidt's last stand against Zion! That's why they never let you near the management of the firm. Half the firm would have walked out the door! . . . Sure you helped Jon make it, but you held your nose doing it." "When have I ever stood in the way of a Jew?" Schmidt answers incredulously, again stressing his supposed passive tolerance in order to deny his bigotry.[29]

Schmidt's anti-Semitism becomes more pronounced as the novel progresses, and as I will argue later, his denial of these feelings leads not only to the severance of relationships that could have been positive for him; it also leads to the channeling of those feelings into other, ultimately injurious relationships. Schmidt's possessive stake in the Bridgehampton house, or his technical lack thereof, is somewhat more complicated, and it too serves to flesh out another sector in his structurally racialized inclinations.

Having rather blindly hashed out his resentment against Jon as he strolls about the house's yard, and ending up little more than angry in the process, Schmidt descends into the cellar, where he makes a momentous decision. A longstanding aggravation has been the fact that this house does not technically belong to Schmidt. Rather, his wife Mary inherited it from an aunt who had to be persuaded against leaving it to Charlotte, who was only four years old at the time. The aunt nevertheless instructed Mary to leave it to Charlotte when she herself died. Instead, Mary left Schmidt a "life estate" in the house, meaning that when he died, Charlotte would then legally inherit it.[30] This decision was reached because Charlotte would not be able to afford taxes incurred by inheriting the house, but she will be able to pay them when Schmidt dies, with money inherited from him. The upshot for Schmidt of this convoluted plan is the expectation that he "continue to be a slave to a house that would never be his own."[31] Schmidt decides instead to move out and set up his own, smaller "shack" in Sag Harbor. He makes this dubious domestic decision with Charlotte and Jon continually in mind, despite the emotional distance from them it will inevitably create, and despite fears of financial insecurity due to the loss not only of a large amount he would pay for Charlotte's gift taxes, but also of the annual interest income from that money, and of the money to be spent on a new home.

Schmidt goes through these tortuous financial and residential calculations for two reasons, both influenced by his status as an elite, and thus extensively propertied, white American man of his time and place. The first is that he resents the intrusion of a Jew into his family life, as well as the expectation that he and his daughter form a marital union with a Jewish family. The second is that Schmidt considers such a situation even less tolerable because he cannot commandeer it from the ground base of a home that he himself actually owns:

> Damn the taxes and the loss of income. He would give the house to Charlotte and move out. Living under the same roof with Jon Riker married to Charlotte during vacations, all summer weekends, and however many other weekends in the year they would want to use it might have been contemplated if it were on his own terrain, in a house that was really his, where he made the rules. But never in a fake commune, where he felt the obligation to consult those two about calling the plumber, repainting the house blue, or ripping out a hedge![32]

Schmidt attributes his feelings to the potential living situation, which he disparages as a "fake commune," but what he also exhibits is an instantiation of elite white privilege: an overwhelming sense of entitlement that drives him as it forms not only his outlook but his identity as well. To own one's home outright upon retirement has of course been a longstanding and central component of the American Dream, for people of all races and ethnicities. Nevertheless, Schmidt's feelings and decision here reflect as well the shaping influences of a lengthy history of class-bound racial formation that exacerbates such common American possessive presumptions.

As numerous historians of racial formation have explained, possessive white supremacy is a consistent historical continuum that reproduces itself generationally. In terms of material property, early contact between Native Americans and those who later dubbed themselves "white Anglo-Saxons" soon melded with religious conceptions of humanity's responsibility for utilizing what they saw as the God-given gifts of land, flora, and fauna to form colonial conceptions of proper usage of land as just that—usage, via farming especially, a practice white elites and other "settlers" accused Native Americans of failing to perform (despite abundant evidence to the contrary).[33] White appropriation of land thus became a collective racial responsibility. As Cheryl Harris notes in her groundbreaking work on whiteness as itself a form of property, "being white automatically ensured higher economic returns in the short term, as well as greater economic, political, and social security in the long run."[34] As George Lipsitz and others have demonstrated, numerous subsequent methods of limiting land and other forms of ownership primarily to white men has resulted in vast racial disparities in terms of material and financial possession.[35] In the 1800s, generationally transferred ownership of real estate become a distinguishing hallmark of white Anglo-Saxons, an affiliation that took on salience greater than mere whiteness, as an exclusionary nationalized identity, when waves of non-British European immigrants arrived, most of whom had to work their ways gradually into whiteness. In the early 1900s, atomized homeownership became a naturalized ideology, and whether a family rented property, or lived in newly available public housing, or if one could eventually afford it, in one's own small, relatively landless home, became a key marker not only of class difference, but also of ethnic differences within the hierarchized category of whiteness.[36]

The end of slavery and other subsequent changes have of course erased de jure white claims to exclusive or preferential residential ownership. However, de facto modes have remained, and as Begley's depiction of Schmidt's feelings about the Bridgehampton house and surroundings illustrate, longstanding white conceptions about oneself in relation to real estate ownership remain as well. And yet, few contemporary white Americans feel disturbed by ongoing racial disparities in home ownership, let alone by their resonant historical roots. One reason those who possess especially disproportionate amounts of unearned or more easily gained property fail to perceive such disparities as unjust is because ownership of land and housing, and the relative lack of such ownership by nonwhite Americans, still seems and feels right to them. In her study of "whiteness as possession," Shannon Sullivan examines "the possessiveness of unconscious habits of white privilege," noting that such ownership habits "manifest an 'appropriate' relationship to the earth, including the people and things that are a part of it":

> The appropriate relationship is one of appropriation: taking land, peo-
> ple and the fruits of others' labor and creativity as one's own. Failure
> to embody this proper relationship with the world marks one as a
> subperson, as a quasi-thing that is then legitimately available for, seen
> in need of, appropriation by full persons. . . . Whiteness as possession
> describes not just the act of owning, but also the obsessive psychoso-
> matic state of white owners. . . . The benefits accrued to white people
> through this process include not merely economic gain, but also in-
> creased ontological security and satisfaction of unconscious desires.[37]

As I will explain, several of Schmidt's possessive "unconscious desires" do indeed come to be satisfied, and the structured racial order in which he lives helps focus those desires toward ultimately damaging pursuits. In the novel's early description of Schmidt's thoughts on the Bridgehampton house, he demonstrates more pointedly the desire for what geographer Steven D. Farough terms "the dominant standpoint of white men, sovereign individuality."[38] This perspective includes a sense of self in terms of socio-geographic spaces that seems to its bearers independent and non-racial. However, it depends on conceptions of other types of people living in less desirable spaces: "To be sovereign, or free, means that only those who are in positions of privilege or 'supreme rank or power' may possess a consistent sense of self-determination. The outcome of sovereignty is a subjective sense of 'complete independence,' a distinct separation between the individual and the social world, where the person is self-governing and autonomous."[39] And yet, to be a sovereign individual is not to be truly independent, because the very concept depends on self-defining conceptions of others, including, in the case of elite white American men, the conception of oneself as an owner of that which others (usually darker or ethnic others) do not own.

In this novel's socio-geographic setting, some of these other people leave their own places of residence in such communities as Sag Harbor to work for people like Schmidt. During his stroll around what amounts to an al-most feudally conceived estate, Schmidt notes with satisfaction the "chatter-ing Ecuadoreans" he has hired for yard work.[40] Later, he repeatedly refers to a group of women who arrive for weekly housecleaning as "Polish" or "Po-lacks," and as he ventures outside of the house, he continually surmises the apparent ethnicities of other people as well. Again, as a more or less landed WASP, Schmidt's attention to ethnicity, and to its seemingly appropriate locations as far from his own, establishes the classed and raced differences of such others from himself, thereby asserting his own difference, and supposed superiority, in the process. Begley's attention to Schmidt's conception of hierarchically indicative geographical arrangements furthers the portrait of Schmidt's historically resonant, representatively elevated self-conception. Schmidt enjoys his house's expansive yard because its meticulous orderliness strikes him as aesthetically pleasing, but also because its size provides "the feeling of open space."[41] This feeling of owned openness enhances Schmidt's sense of achieved individualism, but again, this is a "sovereign" individualism because his open space primarily exists as such for him not merely because it is relatively empty, but also because that expansive and expensive emptiness constitutes a barrier between himself and other, supposedly lesser people. When Schmidt recalls, for instance, that his neighbor might sell some land for subdivisions, and that developers could "put up two or three houses," thereby destroying his feeling of open space, he soon hits upon a solution for maintaining his individualized sense of spatial isolation: "it would not be difficult to plant out whatever monstrosities they might build."[42] As cultural geographers Nancy and Jack Duncan point out, "aesthetic appreciation of residential landscapes is an issue that primarily preoccupies the affluent."[43] However, such appreciation is not merely a matter of aesthetics: "A seemingly innocent pleasure in the aesthetic appreciation of landscapes and efforts to maintain and protect them can act as subtle but highly effective excluding mechanisms for reaffirming class and race identities."[44] In sum, keeping other, lesser people out of one's residential space and sightlines is a common, largely unconscious elite white male desire, a sense of landed possessiveness that indicates habitual conceptions of others in subordinated relation to oneself, and thereby one's own vaunted self-conception as well.

WHITE WORLD-TRAVELING

Prior to depicting Schmidt in flight from his future in-laws and his own daughter, toward a self-involved and ultimately numbing relationship with Carrie, a sexually abused, twenty-year-old waitress, Begley further cements the racialized underpinnings of the sociohistorical and geographically resonant context in which Schmidt is situated by temporarily sending him into an allegorical idyll of privileged, pampered exile. After spending Thanksgiving and another evening with Charlotte, Jon, and Jon's parents, Schmidt declines an invitation to spend Christmas with them, falsely implying that it feels too soon after the death of his wife to spend a family holiday with anyone but himself. He then visits best friend Gil and his wife, Elaine, who help him decide how to spend the holidays. They hit upon the idea of sending Schmidt to "our Amazon island," a small patch of ground in Brazil containing an airstrip, a guest house, and "silent" native servants who move "like polite shadows."⁴⁵ What all three characters demonstrate in this conversation, and by their visits to this island, is described well by Sullivan as a racially informed "ontological expansiveness": "As ontologically expansive, white people consider all spaces as rightly available for their inhabitation of them."⁴⁶ Sullivan elsewhere describes a specific example of this unconscious white way of being and acting as "white world-traveling," an entitled sense that not only should all spaces be entirely available for one's touristic consumption, but also that the inhabitants of nonwhite communities should be hospitably adaptive to white middle-class ways of being, rather than the reverse.⁴⁷

Readers are prompted to think of Schmidt's Brazilian idyll in allegorical terms when Gil twice refers mistakenly to the German ex-patriot who oversees the island, a man whose name Elaine says is "something like Oskar Lang," as "Herr Schmidt." "My Doppelgänger," Schmidt replies in a metanarrative mode.⁴⁸ As I will explain, another character, "the man," better fills the novelistic role of Schmidt's ontologically suggestive double; nevertheless, when Schmidt later arrives and settles into the house as the island's only guest, the parallels between "Oskar Lang" and Schmidt become significant. According to Elaine, Lang has an unnamed "native" wife whom he appreciates with a paternalistic combination of sexism and racism. "He kept on pointing out to Gil that white women's breasts fall as they get older," Elaine says, "while his Indian woman has boobs that stayed small and hard. Like *mein* fist, only nice, so nice and small, was how he put it!"⁴⁹ Schmidt has also been engaging in increasingly vigorous appreciation of a darker woman, the half–Puerto Rican Carrie, whom he too finds especially alluring because of the racialized differences between her body and those of most of the (white) women he has known.

Schmidt, Gil, and Elaine clearly share a collective investment in whiteness that structures their experiences of themselves in relation to racialized others. However, because white supremacy has largely morphed into a hegemonic state, they register no understanding of how their privileged ability to enjoy such a vacation is enabled by their positioning within an on-going colonialist set of relations, between people who became "white" and those whom they declared inferior and exploitable because of their darker differences. These hierarchical relations are echoed by the very arrange-ment of this island and its "Caboclo servants, very silent, moving like polite shadows. You only see them when you want something, and they seem to know it without being called."[50] That such people would have other lives apart from their work for wealthy white people, and would likely under-stand much about such visitors because they need to watch them carefully, never seems to occur to these three white Americans.

Upon arrival, Schmidt does make some effort to assess the local context of his vacation, by reading Joseph Conrad's novel *Nostromo* (1904), "since he decided that if he were going to South America he might as well test his theory that Conrad had fixed in it completely and forever the essence of that continent . . ."[51] Aside from fatuously believing that anyone, let alone a Westerner, could capture some singular "essence" of such a highly varie-gated continent, Schmidt never considers consulting the insights of South American authors. His attempts to analyze the place (though not his own current relation to it) via Conrad apparently fail; as he basks in the sun on the island house's deck, his concentration on the book wanes because he "has been overcome by intense, rather stupid happiness. He feels good all over. . . . Nature is beautiful and good . . ."[52]

Nevertheless, as at other moments in the novel, pangs of something like privileged, WASP guilt also arise here for Schmidt, along with a twinge of interest in probing within himself for the source of that guilt. Earlier, on the way to a Thanksgiving dinner with Jon's parents, such feelings also arise when Schmidt stops at the exclusive Harvard Club, where he makes his way to a restroom, adjusts his hair and clothing, and then leaves for the Rikers' apartment. As he approaches their home, Schmidt has no particular con-scious reason for stopping at the club. That this WASP male has an under-lying need to bolster himself, precisely as a racially sanctioned member of the Ivy League–educated elite (one who at the moment resents the incur-sion into his family and world of Jewish people) is suggested by his self-assessing pause in front of the restroom mirror. The mirror tells him that he "looked worse than even the sour person wearing his own clothes he had glimpsed returning his own stare from a Fifth Avenue window."[53] Of course, time changes everyone fortunate enough to reach Schmidt's age of sixty, but this brief Harvard Club visit itself, and what drives Schmidt to make it, suggest just how this man does not know himself. Since readers know by this point that Schmidt looks down, as it were, on the Rikers merely because they are Jewish, he clearly pauses at this bastion of elite privilege not to partake of its amenities, but rather to reassert his position, as a member of the WASP elite, in relation to the Rikers.

That his self-conception is the point here, and that it is ever ironically relational, becomes more evident when thoughts of less privileged others very briefly occur to him: "There's enough fancy stuff on me to lodge and feed a homeless family for a month."[54] Another pang of this sort arises as Schmidt basks in his stupor of "happiness" on the Amazonian island, when he idly imagines "barefoot, brown boys and girls tirelessly playing soccer in the village perhaps half a mile away with a bundle of rags tied with a string [who] will never get to kick a leather ball or learn to read."[55] At these moments, such thoughts, not only of perceived Others, but also of his highly privileged positioning in relation to them, subside quickly, as Schmidt performs habitual internal retreats, from a better understanding of his social positionality and from his emotions (in this case, something like sympathy), into a numbed, isolated distance from others. Accustomed to thinking of his Others, especially women and ethnic or darker people, as the emotional ones, and thus of himself as rational and controlled, Schmidt continually retreats from the possibility of a more mature understanding of his own highly raced and gendered emotions. He instead pursues internal numbness, especially during encounters in which he is confronted with his Others, through such palliatives as a superficially stupefying vacation, alcohol, and later in the novel, sex and money.

THE WHITE MANCHILD

Since Begley depicts his protagonist as a committed male WASP who lacks self-awareness, Schmidt represents an ostensibly respectable, successful insider who in a sense is not yet a fully mature adult. Not only does he make remarkably selfish and immature choices in his relationships; he does so because the broader structures of feeling in which he operates, and in which he has been raised, have stunted his emotional capacities and responses. Again, early relational constructions of white masculine identity account for much of this problem. As the white race developed its collective self-conception in relation to others, a European claim of limited emotional capacities in nonwhite people arose. In this sense, *About Schmidt* initially reads as a sort of late-life bildungsroman, a "novel that recounts the development (psychological and sometimes spiritual) of an individual from childhood to maturity, to the point at which the protagonist recognizes his or her place in the world."[56]

A key character in this regard is the seemingly minor figure of a person whom Schmidt continually refers to as "the man," even after learning his name. Deployed by Begley as Schmidt's Doppelgänger, this person represents the "darker" racialized and sexualized aspects of Schmidt's psyche, and he functions as well, like other traditional Doppelgängers, as the potential bearer of a message to Schmidt about these deleterious sides of himself. That Schmidt ultimately fails to receive this message, and thus to mature emotionally, has much to do with his adherence to the scripted role he plays as the self-identified "last of the Wasps."[57]

Schmidt first encounters this man after falling asleep on a bus while trying to read another European literary classic, Anthony Trollope's 1855 novel *The Warden*.[58] Significantly, Schmidt is on his way home after the Thanksgiving dinner at which he has met Jon's parents for the first time. Jon's mother, Renata, is a psychiatrist, and she has pulled Schmidt aside for a long, inquisitive chat. As Renata asks Schmidt increasingly personal questions, she warmly takes his hand. Schmidt is unaccustomed to such open intimacy with women, except in sexual encounters. Accordingly, he considers trying to fondle Renata's breast, then tells her, "I want to kiss you."[59] She rebuffs him, apparently uninterested in sex because her actual goal—acceptance and affection from Schmidt toward her son and his union with Charlotte—occurs at a more emotional level, a realm from which Schmidt habitually flees. Schmidt abruptly ends the conversation by telling Renata of his plans to give his life estate in the Bridgehampton house to Charlotte as a wedding gift and of moving into his own house, thereby withdrawing, both literally and symbolically, from the newly formed family that would include Renata's family. Schmidt, then, is briefly attracted to Renata not as a friendly and caring future fellow parent-in-law, but rather in a more adolescent manner as a sexualized and exoticized (because of her Jewishness) female. The stage that is Schmidt's internal emotional landscape has thus been set for the entrance of another key character, "the man," a self-reflecting figure who immediately emerges as if from Schmidt's dreaming unconscious.

On an otherwise empty bus that evening, this shambolic white man invades Schmidt's personal space, and indeed his personhood itself, by sitting right next to him. Both this man and Schmidt have fallen asleep when the latter is awakened by a "stench."[60] In their study of racialized aesthetics in suburban New York environs, geographers Duncan and Duncan note that in such ostensibly tolerant settings, "the Other is not so different from me as to be an object. . . . But at the level of practical consciousness they are affectively marked as different."[61] Because tolerating racial difference (if not embracing it) had become a polite white norm by Schmidt's time, racial difference is no longer perceived in essentialist terms, and explicitly naming it has become censured as well. An affective result is that members of other racialized groups "threaten to cross over the border of the subject's identity because discursive consciousness will not name them as completely different. . . . The face-to-face presence of these others, who do not act as if they have their own 'place,' a status to which they are not confined, thus threatens aspects of my basic security system, my basic sense of identity, and I must turn away with disgust and revulsion."[62] In order to function as Schmidt's Doppelgänger, this man's difference from Schmidt is marked in terms of class rather than race. As Begley depicts Schmidt confronting the reality of the person slumbering noisily beside him, he underlines the man's flagrant corporeality to comedic, satiric effect:

> He shifted in his seat and broke wind. It was expelled in ample bursts, followed by a liquid rumbling in the stomach. . . . The cloacal odor was unbearable, but different from the stench that had interrupted Schmidt's sleep and continued to nauseate him. Was the man hiding a piece of carrion in his pocket, had he a suppurating wound on his feet or somewhere under his clothes? It seemed impossible that an accumulation of dirt and sweat alone could account for such fetor.[63]

Humor arises in this scene, not from the man's abject corporeality but rather, as emphasized by such recondite vocabulary as *cloacal, carrion, suppurating*, and *fetor*, from Schmidt's appalled reaction to it. Again, as an apparent "hobo," this man is Otherized with disgust in classist terms, but Schmidt's revulsion also springs from a literal invasion of himself, via his senses. Schmidt's rising panic as he awakens the man and tries to get past him is thus a reaction to the breaching of his "basic security system," and the man also represents a threat to Schmidt's "basic sense of identity," a threat that grows as Schmidt repeatedly encounters this character during a time in his life when reconfigurations of his social and internal affective landscapes are taking place. Eventually, this man's exteriorized and blatant rejection of genteel white decorum functions as a parallel for the novel's protagonist, an indicator for readers if not for Schmidt himself, of his internal, and thus behavioral "filth."

Begley emphasizes this threat of self-recognition by detailing this character's suggestive physical similarities to his protagonist. Schmidt is wearing his dead father's tweed jacket, and this man, who is "as tall" as Schmidt, is "dressed in a threadbare tweed suit of the same shade."[64] Schmidt, a self-declared WASP with a discordantly German name, is mirrored as well in his perception of this man's "good English or German face"; the man also wears a tie and carries a cane, with which he swaggers foppishly at other points in the novel, a mocking echo of Schmidt's own rather pompously inflated masculinity and class status.[65] In this sense, this man's seemingly parodic appropriation of genteel whiteness, despite his otherized "hobo" status, threatens to disrupt the idealized racial narrative that Schmidt tenuously maintains for himself. As a traditionally deployed Doppelgänger, "the man" represents resurgent sides of Schmidt that he actively represses from his own conscious awareness; accordingly, Schmidt presses past this person with an excuse about having "to go to the can this very minute," takes another seat far from the man, then scurries to his car and locks himself inside.[66]

Later in the novel, Schmidt encounters this person several more times. In one scene, while Schmidt chats with Carrie in O'Henry's, her place of employment, this man appears outside the restaurant's window. He winks at Schmidt, gives him the finger when Schmidt doesn't respond, then leaves obediently when Carrie shakes her fist and waves him away. At another point, after dining with Gil and Elaine and hearing their suggestion of a trip to Brazil, Schmidt drives home with Gil. As his headlights shine on the house, he notices a figure on the porch, "like a melting snowman, squatting on top of the steps. Its exposed buttocks were fat and exceedingly white."[67] Schmidt recognizes this figure, who pulls up his pants and scurries away, as the same man. What he does not recognize is the symbolic import of that which the man has left literally on his doorstep, "the fruit of the white buttocks."[68] Significantly, Schmidt scoops up the feces, throws it away, and continues to more or less ignore both this person and the question of why he has taken an interest in Schmidt, paralleling his disavowal of all the disturbing clues about himself and his structurally informed emotions that this figure does deliver to alert readers.

Those attuned to common usages of the Doppelgänger figure will be primed by these encounters with "the man" to watch for an internal change in Schmidt, which would manifest as him recognizing, and then grappling with, that which this abject figure represents, that is, the unacknowledged content that has backed up, as it were, in his own constipated psyche. These parts of himself—his sexism, racism, and classism—are not components of self that a late-twentieth-century WASP male faced with a changing social order is likely to acknowledge, perhaps even to himself. As Thandeka writes in her analysis of common modes of white shame: "Experiences of shame are self-exposures that lower one's own sense of personal esteem and respect. They are snapshots of embarrassing features of the self. Looking at these uncomplimentary mug shots, one feels shame, as in the feeling 'I am unlovable.'"[69] And yet, as Schmidt continually demonstrates, shame, disgust and other ugly feelings about himself nevertheless arise, provoking his actions in ways that the more conscious and socially sanctioned side of himself guiltily recognizes at times as reprehensible. When interpreted in this light, "the man" represents the man performing behind the social imposture of "Schmidtie," and whether Schmidt will recognize this mirrored image of himself, thereby advancing in maturity, becomes the novel's central question.

REPRESSED WHITE-MALE SHAME

After discarding the mess on his porch, Schmidt enters the house with Gil and tells him about having seen the same man at O'Henry's, and about odd feelings that this man has repeatedly triggered in him, including "revulsion," "panic," and a suspicion that this man is trying to "terrorize" him.[70] After Gil leaves, Schmidt, who often imbibes heavily, pours himself another drink as he ponders what to do about the man, and the odd feelings that this person inspires. "Shame and paralysis!" he thinks, as he ponders whether to call the police.[71] Were Schmidt to analyze his strong yet confused reactions to the man more fully, he might wonder why these feelings arise. Readers, of course, are invited to perform this analysis themselves. Given the hints here of connections made in traditional psychoanalysis between abject bodily functions and shame, as well as the probing conversations that Schmidt twice endures with Jon's psychiatrist mother, Renata, an interpretation of "the man" as the bearer of a message about the denied parts of Schmidt's self—his bigotry, possessiveness, and misdirected, exoticizing sexual desire, especially—becomes appropriate. In rather traditional Freudian terms, "the man" functions at the narrative level as the return of Schmidt's repressed. Schmidt has spent a lifetime denying to both himself and others his own destructive feelings and characteristics. That he may well continue to ignore his occasional, resultant shame is suggested here, and elsewhere, by how he anesthetizes himself whenever budding sensitivity arises within him, in this case with alcohol, which clouds and diverts his thoughts about "the man" onto other subjects. Schmidt also turns to sex and money for similar reasons.

A more direct connection between Schmidt and this man arises one night when Carrie unexpectedly arrives at Schmidt's house for the first time. As Schmidt begins a sexual relationship with her, Carrie reveals that she met the apparently homeless man when she was fourteen years old, and that he has been following her ever since. The topic arises when Schmidt asks Carrie who the love of her life is, and she reveals that this man was once a chemistry teacher named Mr. Wilson: "An old guy like you. He broke me in."[72] Mr. Wilson (we never learn his first name) began having sex with Carrie after he walked in on her during a sexual encounter with a fellow student in a classroom. Whether Carrie is attracted to Schmidt because she now simply prefers "old guys" or because, like many people who have been sexually abused, she unconsciously seeks reminders and repetition of her abuse, is a question the novel does not answer.[73]

Within the framework of Begley's anatomization of Schmidt's culturally induced inclinations, it is significant that Schmidt never questions Carrie's attraction to himself. He has pursued her for several months by dining at O'Henry's, where Carrie always serves him, and now that she has arrived literally at his doorstep—the same place where Mr. Wilson left his abjecti-fied message of sorts for Schmidt—he instead revels in the feeling that he now possesses her. When Carrie asks what he likes about her, he replies, "It's what you said, you belong to me."[74] Begley underlines how strongly the feeling of possession drives his representative WASP male protagonist when Schmidt also ponders to himself at this moment how his life has changed: "Here was an aspect of unemployment and nearly total loneliness he had not previously examined, let alone apprehended: they set one free! . . . There was [only] Charlotte's wedding reception to be held in June, and the need, which was turning into a wish, to move into another house."[75] The "need" Schmidt had felt to move into another house, and away from one that he did not technically own, is weakening into a "wish" because he now feels that he possesses Carrie. This feeling compensates for the possessive lack Schmidt had felt before, as he considered the looming "loss" of his daughter and the expectations that he live in and be "a slave to a house that would never be his own."[76]

Begley's primary point about the culturally induced inclinations and feelings instilled in Schmidt because of his social positionality as a WASP male is that they steer him toward further loss and destruction. At this point in the novel, because it simply feels wrong to "lose" his daughter to a Jewish husband, Schmidt is gradually alienating and driving away both his daughter and his future in-laws. Similarly, the satisfaction he now takes in believing that he possesses Carrie blinds him to not only what he really sees in her—an objectified entity for him to possess—but also to who she is, and to the significance of who else she shares her life with, especially Bryan, a young man who lives in nearby Sag Harbor: "I've kind of been with him since I got this job [at O'Henry's]."[77] This news "[goes] through Schmidt like an icicle," but his persistent, self-bolstering possessiveness pushes him to ignore how this relationship may well be more significant to her than the one she has with Schmidt, and to feel that she still "belongs" to him: "Nothing mattered. He had to keep her body. She said she belonged to him."[78] Indulging this narcissistic desire distracts Schmidt from thinking about what Bryan really means to Carrie, and thus about what he himself could mean to her.

Nevertheless, Schmidt's relationship with Carrie is not portrayed as an entirely negative manifestation of his self-absorbed WASP male possessiveness, and Begley clearly does not cast a disapproving authorial eye merely because of the socially inappropriate age gap. To the contrary, Begley has stated that he meant for the union to represent a possibility for Schmidt to break out of his numbed loneliness. In his commentary on the film based on his novel, Begley writes of the filmmakers' decision not to include Carrie: "I missed the theme of the redemptive and regenerative power of Eros, embodied in my novel by Carrie, the personage I care for most among all that I have created. . . . her love for Schmidt, and the torrid sex between them, ripen him and open the possibility that he will become a freer and wiser man."[79]

By emphasizing here both a pent-up sexual force in his protagonist and the potential of a sexist, one-dimensional caricature of a conveniently available female to provide release, Begley would seem to echo in this regard other American "male liberationist" writers of his time. As Robinson notes, these writers typically portrayed a dominant white masculinity in crisis, with central characters who are "wounded by their power, their responsibilities, and indeed, by patriarchy itself."[80] A problem with many such texts is that, unlike Begley in *About Schmidt*, their authors lose sight of how social relations nevertheless both empower and influence white men. Schmidt does revel in sexual release with Carrie, and he does become temporarily enlivened by it, but his primary interest in her, possessive sex, soon becomes another numbing palliative, which both soothes him and distracts him from the impending severance of any positive connection with his daughter Charlotte.

As a representative male WASP who continually represses powerful feelings, Schmidt battens down the complex emotions provoked by the loss of his wife Mary and by Charlotte's engagement. Begley highlights Schmidt's anesthetic use of both alcohol and Carrie during a telephone conversation with Charlotte about her wedding plans, including the expected services of a rabbi. Carrie has quietly situated herself in his lap, but as Schmidt struggles to express his objections to a Jewish wedding, and as his emotions rise accordingly, he notices that the warm glow of sex and a nap is fading: "The novocaine was wearing off. He nudged Carrie off his lap."[81] Carrie then prepares a drink for Schmidt, and as Charlotte presses her father on the prejudice that he is again obliquely but obstinately expressing, he thinks, "The effect of one hundred proof bourbon on an empty stomach was marvelous."[82] Confronted with an emotional eruption that pushes him to acknowledge, just as his daughter is doing, his own true bigoted and possessive self, Schmidt's habitual repression asserts itself. After offering the evasive (and common white) assertion that he cannot be harboring discriminatory feelings against Jews because he has openly socialized with many of them,[83] Schmidt abruptly ends the conversation, then turns immediately to Carrie for condolence, and then for more sex, this time on the kitchen table. His refusal to acknowledge certain emotions, let alone to consider their sources, continues, and the gap between himself, his daughter, and the possibility of wider familial contentment increases. Thus, where Begley differs from the essentialist politics of many of his era's white male storytellers is by maintaining a critical focus on broader forces that influence common white male feelings. Although a man in Schmidt's situation might find some sort of life-affirming release in a new sexual relationship, Begley's protagonist remains sadly responsive to sociohistorical forces that have shaped his emotions and actions, warping how he regards and reacts toward not only Carrie, his daughter, and his future in-laws, but also himself and his own general future.

As the novel approaches its conclusion, Schmidt meets again with Jon's mother, Renata. He requests that they meet at "his club," the Harvard Club, a spatial choice that suggests how being energized by Carrie has solidified not into a new appreciation for life and the people around him, but rather into his habitual mode of privileged and possessive white masculinity. Prior to consummating his relationship with Carrie, Schmidt had found Renata bearable and even alluring, but he now thinks of her as a "meddling witch."[84] As they talk it becomes clear that Charlotte is quite happy to join their Jewish family, and also to move further from what remains of her own family, that is, her father. Renata relays to him Jon and Charlotte's proposal that, contrary to his own idea regarding the Bridgehampton property—that he pay her gift taxes so the house will be hers right away, rather than when he dies—he instead buy out her portion and keep the house himself. Schmidt agrees, reasoning to himself that he can quickly sell it, and that he "wouldn't be selling the Schmidts' ancestral homestead. Someone must have sold that long ago."[85] Charlotte and Jon are instead thinking of buying property north of New York City, and they will also hold the wedding reception at a restaurant in Manhattan, instead of in Bridgehampton, where Schmidt had hoped it would be. That he has lost all shreds of his daughter's affection seems obvious to all but Schmidt, who suppresses, beyond even his own awareness, his sense of loss in order to focus instead on being sure that he understands the financial matters at hand, and what the various arrangements will cost him in those terms. When he later reads a letter from Charlotte that further explains her wishes regarding the house and the wedding, he quickly writes back, mostly to assert again his own financial agreements and refusals, the latter including a notice that he will keep the family silverware that Charlotte has requested. His own curtness is clearly further prompted by Charlotte's explanation in her letter that she will likely convert to Judaism. Upon finishing his letter, Schmidt's racialized tendency to suppress his feelings results in another: "Shouldn't I send a copy of the letter to Renata? . . . In the end, he didn't do it; he felt too ashamed."[86] Once again, Schmidt does not understand his sense of shame, let alone examine it. Readers can surmise that for a moment he feels something akin to disgust for his actions, and ultimately for himself, not only because he has driven away his daughter, but also because he let his anti-Semitism cause that to happen.

Begley suggests in these moments that while the feeling of racialized shame is often confusing, searching for its roots can prove enlightening, particularly in regards to how one conceives of oneself. Schmidt's ultimate failure is his refusal to take the opportunity for personal understanding and growth provided by the provocation of surprising emotions. Were such a person to do so, he might uncover the sources of his anti-Semitism in his early training as a member of the de facto WASP community, which has no doubt expressed to him in countless ways its disdain for and fears of Jewish people, effectively embedding such feelings within him and creating an illusory psychic split between "his" people and "them."

That Schmidt will continue refusing to face the roots of his own emotional confusion is conclusively suggested in what I read as the climax of this novel's largely internal drama—Schmidt's killing of the person he only ever refers to as "the man." After attending a party thrown by fellow Hamptons residents who are no longer, and clearly never really were, his friends, Schmidt races home toward Carrie. He hits a lengthy patch of dense fog, "an immense, unending bottle of milk," out of which rises none other than the man.[87] Like a deus ex machina, the car kills this message-bearing adversary, freeing Schmidt from an irritating and vaguely frightening presence, and freeing him as well, at a symbolic and subliminal level, from the various forces that have been pushing him to confront the repressed characteristics within himself that this mirroring double figure represents. Just as Schmidt has refused to recognize this person with his name, "Mr. Wilson," he also refuses to recognize the actual "man" that he himself is. In this sense, then, this novel's protagonist refuses to grow up; he remains "Schmidtie," instead of becoming Albert Schmidt. In these ways, Begley exposes the subtle machinations of white supremacist forces that animate the members of an elite demographic. These are ongoing sociohistorical forces that bolster an inequitable social order and discourage recuperative human connection.

In the novel's denouement, Schmidt finds himself being nursed at the Bridgehampton house after the car accident by Bryan, the young man whom Carrie has said she is "kind of seeing." Schmidt remembers his plans to sell the house after buying out Charlotte's share, since the cost of upkeep would be beyond his remaining means. It becomes clear that Bryan and Carrie are involved in illegal drug trafficking, and when they smoke hashish in front of him, he refuses to partake, preferring his own habitual anesthetics. He remains largely unconcerned about what the true relationship and motives of this pair might be, and fixated instead on Carrie's continued claims that she actually "belongs" to him. In the novel's final pages, Schmidt receives a letter regarding the death of his stepmother, who had been living in Florida. In a traditional O'Henry twist, the letter reveals that she has left him a great deal of money, both from his long-dead father and from her own deceased family members.[88]

Schmidt now has no need to sell the Bridgehampton house, and having just acquired another one in Florida, he instantly sees a way to vanquish this young man, whom he cannot help but think of as a rival for Carrie's body and affections. Bryan has portrayed himself as something of a jack-of-all-trades, so the novel closes with Schmidt offering to hire him for extensive renovations on the Florida house, a move that would leave Carrie with

Schmidt. Thus, while Begley provides an ostensibly happy ending, careful readers will deduce that, as Victoria N. Alexander writes, "Schmidt's world, like King Lear's, is presided over by irrational gods."[89] Given the course of Begley's penetrating, incisive depiction of both his protagonist's representatively distorted WASP-male emotional landscapes and an obstinate refusal to explore them, Schmidt seems likely to go on harming himself and others, influenced as he continues to be by racially influenced inducements into enacting material and corporeal possessiveness, and thus into continuing the narcissistic self-assertion enabled by such blithe uses and abuses of others.

NOTES

1. Allan Hepburn, "Lost Time: Trauma and Belatedness in Louis Begley's *The Man Who Was Late*," *Contemporary Literature* 39.3 (1998): 380; James Atlas, "Louis Begley, The Art of Fiction," *Paris Review* 172 (Summer 2002): 162; www.theparisreview.org/interviews/392/the-art-of-fiction-no-172-louis-begley.

2. Louis Begley, *Wartime Lies* (New York: Alfred A. Knopf, 1991).

3. Sally Robinson, *Marked Men: White Masculinity in Crisis* (New York: Columbia University Press, 2000), 3, 2.

4. Robinson, *Marked Men*, 5.

5. Jonathan Flatley, *Affective Mapping: Melancholia and the Politics of Modernism* (Cambridge: Harvard University Press, 2008), 25. See also Frederik Tygstrup, who writes that if we understand the self as socially situated in such a way that discernible structures like whiteness and masculinity tend to provoke predictable emotional responses, then "we can study the self in different historical situations and chart different historically contextualized emotions," and we can also trace "how [such] subjectively felt emotions taint the perception of outer stimuli . . ." (195). "Affective Spaces," in Daniela Agostinho et al., ed., *Panic and Mourning: The Cultural Work of Trauma* (Boston: Walter de Gruyter GmbH, 2012), 195–210.

6. Atlas, "Louis Begley," 162. Begley's admired modernists include Henry James, Marcel Proust, F. Scott Fitzgerald, Ernest Hemingway, Joseph Conrad, Thomas Mann, and Franz Kafka, about whom Begley has written a biography, *The Tremendous World I Have Inside My Head: Franz Kafka: A Biographical Essay* (New York: Atlas, 2008).

7. When pronounced, the firm's name sounds like "wooden king," suggesting Schmidt's lack of human emotional display, as well as his elevated but rickety pose of self-assuredness. In Alexander Payne's 2003 film version of the novel, Schmidt's job is changed to actuary at an insurance company with a similarly suggestive name, Woodman of the World. *About Schmidt*, DVD, directed by Alexander Payne (2002; Burbank, CA: New Line Entertainment, 2003).

8. Louis Begley, "My Novel, the Movie: My Baby Reborn; 'About Schmidt' Was Changed, But Not Its Core," *New York Times*, January 19, 2003. Online, n.p.

9. Sherrow O. Pinder, *Whiteness and Racialized Ethnic Groups in the United States: The Politics of Remembering* (Lanham: Lexington Books, 2011), 33. Emphasis in original.

10. Louis Begley, *About Schmidt* (New York: Alfred A. Knopf, 1996), 4.

11. As Tad Friend writes in his probing memoir about his own declining WASP family: "I am fiercely but privately emotional. . . . I ended up spending my inheritance and then some on psychoanalysis. I was in trouble, but it was nearly impossible for anyone who didn't know me well to tell, and I made it nearly impossible for anyone to know me well" (13–14). Tad Friend, *Cheerful Money: Me, My Family, and the Last Days of Wasp Splendor* (New York: Little, Brown, 2009), 13–14.

12. Begley, *About Schmidt*, 143.

13. Ibid., 2.

14. Thomas R. Edwards, "Palm Beach Story," *New York Review of Books* (October 31, 1996), 65.

15. Ibid., 10.

16. Carl Holliday, *Marriage Customs Then and Now* (Boston: Stratford, 1919), 9, 11.

17. Jessica Holden Sherwood, *Wealth, Whiteness, and the Matrix of Privilege: The View from the Country Club* (Lanham: Lexington Books, 2010), 43.

18. Ibid., 43.

19. Begley, *About Schmidt*, 10.

20. Karen Brodkin, *How Jews Became White Folks: And What That Says About Race in America* (New Brunswick: Rutgers University Press, 1998), 31.

21. Louis Begley, *Matters of Honor* (New York: Alfred A. Knopf, 2007).

22. Brodkin, *How Jews Became White Folks*, 30.

23. Ibid., 31.

24. Begley, *About Schmidt*, 10.

25. Ibid., 13.

26. Ibid.

27. Ibid., 14.

28. Ibid., 13.

29. Ibid., 204–5.

30. Ibid., 18–19.

31. Ibid., 19.

32. Ibid., 23.

33. See Reginald Horsman, *Race and Manifest Destiny: Origins of Racial Anglo-Saxonism* (Cambridge: Harvard University Press, 1981); Charles C. Mann, *1491: New Revelations of the Americas Before Columbus* (New York: Vintage, 2006); Ronald Takaki, *A Different Mirror: A History of Multicultural America* (Boston: Little, Brown, 1993).

34. Cheryl I. Harris, "Whiteness as Property," *Harvard Law Review* 106, no. 8 (June 1993): 1713.

35. George Lipsitz, *The Possessive Investment in Whiteness: How White People Profit from Identity Politics* (1998; Philadelphia: Temple University Press, 2006); Melvin Oliver

and Thomas Shapiro, *Black Wealth/White Wealth: A New Perspective on Racial Inequality* (New York: Routledge, 2006).

36. David R. Roediger, *Working Toward Whiteness: How America's Immigrants Became White: The Strange Journey from Ellis Island to the Suburbs* (New York: Basic Books, 2005); Richard Ronald, *The Ideology of Home Ownership: Homeowner Societies and the Role of Housing* (New York: Palgrave Macmillan, 2008).

37. Shannon Sullivan, *Revealing Whiteness: The Unconscious Habits of Racial Privilege* (Bloomington: Indiana University Press, 2006), 122.

38. Steven D. Farough, "The Social Geographies of White Masculinities," *Critical Sociology* 30, no. 3 (2004): 243.

39. Ibid., 244.

40. Begley, *About Schmidt*, 6.

41. Ibid., 5.

42. Ibid., 5.

43. James Duncan and Nancy Duncan, "Aesthetics, Abjection, and White Privilege in Suburban New York," in Richard H. Schein, ed., *Landscape and Race in the United States* (New York: Routledge, 2006), 160.

44. Ibid., 160. See also Eduardo Bonilla-Silva and David G. Embrick, "'Every Place Has a Ghetto . . .': The Significance of Whites' Social and Residential Segregation," *Symbolic Interaction* 30, no. 3 (Summer 2007): 323–45.

45. Begley, *About Schmidt*, 156–57.

46. Sullivan, *Revealing Whiteness*, 144.

47. Shannon Sullivan, "White World-Traveling," *Journal of Speculative Philosophy* 18, no. 4 (2004): 303. Sullivan acknowledges her debt to María C. Lugones for the term and concept of "world-traveling."

48. Begley, *About Schmidt*, 158.

49. Ibid.

50. Ibid., 157.

51. Ibid., 172.

52. Ibid., 173.

53. Ibid., 91.

54. Ibid., 93.

55. Ibid., 173. As Timothy J. Lensmire writes, "People of color are central to the drama of White lives. . . . White people are *always already in relationships with people of color (even if imagined) and always already 'know' them.*" Timothy J. Lensmire, "White Men's Racial Others," *Teachers College Record* 116, no. 3 (2014): 26, emphasis in original.

56. Ross Murfin and Supriya M. Ray, *The Bedford Glossary of Critical and Literary Terms* (Boston: Bedford/St. Martin's, 2003), 39.

57. Begley, *About Schmidt*, 143.

58. As Begley suggests in his description of Schmidt as a man whose prejudices "imprison" him ("My Novel, the Movie," n.p.), the Trollope title, *The Warden*, indicates Schmidt's figurative status as both prisoner and warden; as a WASP male, he has usually followed dictates for a person like himself that entail "proper" containment of perceived

desires and impulses. Others are perceived in a binary mode as "other" because they supposedly fail to contain, or imprison, themselves in these ways.

59. Ibid., 117.

60. Ibid., 118.

61. Duncan, "Aesthetics, Abjection," 172.

62. Ibid.

63. Begley, *About Schmidt*, 119.

64. Ibid., 119.

65. Another repressed side of Schmidt's self, his family's forgotten ethnicity, is represented by both this Doppelgänger with a "good English or German face" and the Doppelgänger-like figure of the German Amazonian island proprietor, whom Gil mistakenly dubs "Herr Schmidt." As Russell A. Kazal notes in his study of formations of German ethnicity and assimilation in Philadelphia: "No other large immigrant group in the twentieth century saw its country of origin twice go to war with the United States; none, correspondingly, faced such sustained pressure to forgo its ethnic identity for an 'American' one; and none appeared to mute its ethnic identity to so great an extent." As Kazal also points out, degrees of German assimilation took different forms in different times and places, and in accordance to differing affiliations within the German immigrant population. Those who were Protestant rather than Catholic, for instance, often assimilated into whiteness more readily, a difference that would help to account for the accelerated movement of German descendants like Schmidt toward a self-declared WASP identity. Russell A. Kazal, *Becoming Old Stock: The Paradox of German-American Identity* (Princeton: Princeton University Press, 2004), 11.

66. Begley, *About Schmidt*, 120.

67. Ibid., 162.

68. Ibid., 164.

69. Thandeka, *Learning to Be White: Money, Race and God in America* (New York: Continuum, 1999), 12.

70. Begley, *About Schmidt*, 168.

71. Ibid.

72. Ibid., 212.

73. As Bessel A. van der Kolk notes regarding the repetition compulsion initially conceptualized by Freud, "Many traumatized people expose themselves, seemingly compulsively, to situations reminiscent of the original trauma. These behavioral reenactments are rarely consciously understood to be related to earlier life experiences." Bessel A. van der Kolk, "The Compulsion to Repeat the Trauma: Re-enactment, Revictimization, and Masochism," *Psychiatric Clinics of North America* 12, no. 2 (June 1989): 389. See also M. S. Levy, "A Conceptualization of the Repetition Compulsion," *Psychiatry* 63, no. 1 (Spring 2000): 45–53.

74. Begley, *About Schmidt*, 199.

75. Ibid., 198.

76. Ibid., 19.

77. Ibid., 210.

78. Ibid.

79. Begley, "My Novel, the Movie," n.p.

80. Robinson, *Marked Men*, 130.

81. Begley, *About Schmidt*, 203.

82. Ibid., 205.

83. Schmidt echoes here a "standard semantic move" of defensive, white American "post–Civil Rights racial discourse," a move perhaps most commonly iterated in the phrase "Some of my best friends are black." Eduardo Bonilla-Silva, *Racism without Racists: Color-Blind Racism and the Persistence of Racial Inequality in the United States* (Lanham: Rowman and Littlefield, 2006), 57.

84. Begley, *About Schmidt*, 216.

85. Ibid., 229.

86. Ibid., 242.

87. Ibid., 266.

88. As Steven G. Kellman writes, "The fact that Schmidt dines regularly at a local Bridgehampton restaurant named O'Henry's should alert the reader to a reversal of fortune on the final page." Steven G. Kellman, *The Translingual Imagination* (Lincoln: University of Nebraska Press, 2000), 99. William Sydney Porter (1852–1910) published over six hundred short stories under the pen name of O. Henry; their most remembered feature is surprise endings.

89. Alexander, Victoria N., "Louis Begley: Trying to Make Sense of It," *Antioch Review* 55, no. 3 (Summer 1997): 302.

8

HEGEMONIC WHITENESS
From Structure and Agency to Identity Allegiance

MATTHEW W. HUGHEY

THE STUDY OF WHITENESS IS FAR FROM NEW. AN EXPLICIT YET EM-
bryonic interest in whiteness stretches back to at the least William J. Wilson's 1860 essay "What Shall We Do with the White People?" Since that time,
there has been an array of influential studies that have interrogated the social meanings and makeup of white racial identity.[1] Sociologists France W.
Twine and Charles Gallagher maintain that three waves of research characterize scholarship on whiteness.[2] The first wave of these inquisitions cen-
tered on the privilege and power of white racial identity contrasting with
the ongoing construction and *de jure* and *de facto* marginalization of people of color.

The second wave of scholarship on whiteness explored the observation
that whites generally have a lower degree of self-awareness about race and
their own racial identity than do members of other racial groups. In interviews with white respondents, various scholars found that when asked
about the meaning of whiteness, most replied along the lines of "I've never
really thought that much about it."[3] Such data bolstered scholars' assertions
that the power of whiteness stemmed from its mundane normality. Hence,
it has been widely accepted that whiteness, in a US context, is generally synonymous with social normativity and an unconscious set of privileges.

While the invisibility and normality of whiteness is an important insight, it is crucial neither to overemphasize white racial unconsciousness
nor paint whiteness as a monolith in terms of attitudes, resources, or interactive patterns. The third wave of whiteness studies has done well to
emphasize the changing and fluid character of white racial identities and
their intersection with an array of subject positions across the social axes
of gender, class, sexuality, and nationality.[4] So also, the meaning of whiteness varies spatially (by location), temporally (by historical eras and within

the individual life span), contextually (by the relative culture), differentially (by power), and intersectionally (by combination with class, gender, sexual orientation, and so forth).[5]

These three paradigms have now established that whiteness is a powerful and ever-morphing social category. However, these three models tend to rely on conventional social scientific models that bifurcate "structure" and "agency" into rigid independent and dependent variables. "Structure" models examine how differently stratified resources affect white worldviews and political persuasions; "agency" models analyze how whites employ various discourses and attitudes to navigate the world. I argue that this developing "third wave" should also examine white racial *identity* and its attendant *identity expectations* as the key site where structural forces and acts of volition convene and synthesize. To better understand how whiteness is continually constructed, research must highlight patterned sets of expectations, obligations, and accountabilities that govern the racial identity performances of whites across varying material resources, professed attitudes, and political sensibilities. Without such a move, recent sociological research may mask, mystify, or marginalize the social, psychological, and cultural mechanisms that simultaneously constrain and enable the formations of white racial identity, and thus white actions.

As a resolution to this dilemma, I expand upon my previous work with a variety of data—white activist discourse, film reviews, historical events, etc.—to examine how whiteness is continually (re)crafted from an allegiant pursuit of an ideal type of white racial identity.[6] In a wide array of settings, whites often hold eerily similar understandings of an ideal or "hegemonic" form of white racial identity thought idyllic, proper, and desirable. As sociologist Amanda Lewis wrote: "Whiteness works in distinct ways for and is embodied quite differently by homeless white men, golf-club-membership-owning executives, suburban soccer moms, urban hillbillies, antiracist skinheads, and/or union-card-carrying factory workers. . . . In any particular historical moment, however, certain forms of whiteness become dominant."[7]

While the meanings of an idealized and dominant white racial identity are reformed in localized interactions, it is clear that local settings do not exist in isolated vacuums. Rather, the processes by which actors come to interpret white racial identity are guided by larger sets of shared expectations and authoritative meanings. In this sense, adherence to racialized expectations of what it means to be "white" is not entirely reducible to local context. While a range of "whitenesses" exist, white actors across formally different settings hold similar notions of an ideal and hegemonic whiteness. And this shared understanding constitutes a net of expectations that simultaneously constrain and guide the ongoing formation of one's white racial identity throughout everyday social interactions.

From this perspective, "hegemonic whiteness" is neither essential nor innate, but appears "natural" and "common-sense." All racialized individuals are compelled to adhere to culturally valorized mythologies taught in social interaction, and which over time are accepted as *a priori* reality. For example, throughout an average young white male's formative years, he is encouraged to adopt a special vision of white manhood as strong, autonomous, rational, neutral, objective, and meritocratic—characteristics that commonly (yet never exclusively) characterize a dominant, idealized, or hegemonic form of masculinity and whiteness. And it is from these shared schemas, internalized as the natural and existential background of who one is (and should be), that a host of actions are simultaneously enabled and constrained.

Building on the concept of "hegemonic whiteness," I argue that meaningful racial identity for whites is produced vis-à-vis the reproduction of, and appeal to, racist, essentialist, and reactionary inter- and intra-racial distinctions:

> (1) *Inter-racial Difference and Superiority*: positioning whites as essentially different and superior from those marked as nonwhite.

> (2) *Intra-racial Distinction and Marginalization*: marginalizing practices of being white that fail to exemplify dominant white racial ideals and expectations.[8]

Within the context and setting of an array of cases, I aim to show how hegemonic ideals about white racial identity are collectively shared and function as seemingly neutral yardsticks against which white discourse and action are measured.

This theoretical contribution gestures toward at least three new vantage points of white racial identity today. First, we may substitute the mechanisms of identity formation and interactive expectations for the linear and one-way dichotomy of both independent/dependent variables and structure/agency. Second, we can better conceptually navigate between the long-term staying power of white privilege on the one hand, and the multifarious manifestations of the experience of whiteness on the other. And third, this work holds the potential to map the various dimensions of hegemonic whiteness as they are used and marshaled toward differing utilitarian and symbolic ends across differing settings and cultural milieu.

THE TUSKEGEE EXPERIMENTS

Between 1932 and 1972 the US Public Health Service (PHS) conducted experiments in Tuskegee, Alabama, that evaluated the natural progression of untreated syphilis in hundreds of poor, rural black men who thought they were receiving free health care from the US government. As a result, many died painful deaths from the progression of the disease. The genesis and continuation of this racist and class-exploitive program can be explained by way of the theory of hegemonic whiteness.

The program was first conceived by the Public Health Service, a group then composed of a segregated core of white male physicians eager to put to use their knowledge of germ theory, sanitation, basic research, and public education to fight and conquer disease—and the growing cases of, and moral panic over, syphilis made the disease an easy target.[9] With the backing of federal and philanthropic funds, the PHS launched six pilot studies throughout the rural, black, and impoverished South. One such study was launched in Macon County, Georgia, in 1930, wherein the PHS would attempt to stamp out syphilis in the area. Their agenda would prove difficult; 35 percent of the black men tested in the area had syphilis. By 1931, due to their underestimation of the spread of the disease, coupled with the financial effects of the Great Depression, the PHS program would run out of money. They had only treated 1,400 patients, and many of those did not receive the full course of treatment.[10]

Back in Washington, D.C., many of the doctors in the PHS wished to salvage some research from the area. Dr. Taliaferro Clark proposed they return to Macon County to study the six-month effect of *untreated* syphilis. Clark wrote: "Macon County is a natural laboratory; a ready-made situation. The rather low intelligence of the Negro population, depressed economic conditions, and the common promiscuous sex relations not only contribute to the spread of syphilis but the prevailing indifference with regard to treatment."[11]

Clark was interested in studying the difference in the disease between blacks and whites, as the dominant medical theories of the time were firmly embedded in eugenics and racist ideology. Blacks were thought to be inherently syphilitic and to have smaller brains that could not control their sexual lust. Clark seemed unclear and skeptical of such thought and turned to the historically black institution, the Tuskegee Institute, which had both the trust of the local black community and federal funding that could be put to use to continue the new PHS project. Soon, the PHS was advertising free medicine for black men suffering from "bad blood." They quickly recruited four hundred black men and duped them into believing they would be treated for illness. However, the PHS intended to only watch and catalogue the progression of the disease.[12]

This program could only get off the ground with two concurrent processes. First, the white male doctors in charge of the program were professionally, personally, and racially invested in its success. For example, after the six-month trial period proposed by Dr. Clark had expired, the findings promised accolades and prestige to scientists that would continue the work. Given that the profession of research doctor in the PHS was itself heavily racialized as an elite type of "white man's work," physicians' participation in, and support of, the program was a strong social expectation from peers and family members. To critique the program, to decline participation, or to fail to enthusiastically support the goals of the Tuskegee experiment was not just a mark of personal or professional stigma, rather, it meant that one was not the right type of white man. In the social context of the PHA, the ideal white man was the rational and logical man who did not allow emotion or empathy to distract or "bias" him and who knew how to manage, control, and manipulate his social world—particularly through the exercise of scientific domination on the bodies of darker-skinned men. White men who were not in this position nonetheless aspired to be. Herein is the social creation of intra-white symbolic boundaries.[13]

The second process of boundary construction dovetails with the first. The white administration of the PHA was entrenched in a cultural logic of white superiority in which the black male participants in the Tuskegee experiment were subhuman, thus rationalizing the violently dangerous and deceptive experiments upon them. Participants were told that spinal taps were treatment, thus demonstrating the direct lie of the PHS. They were given placebos and told that the medicine would cure them of their "bad blood." The end point of these experiments was autopsy. Such lethal deception of hundreds of black men who had syphilis could only be rationalized via the belief in whites' genetic, moral, social, and certainly legal difference and superiority over blacks. Such beliefs were undergirded by both Congress, to whom the PHS reported and who consistently green-lighted the program to continue, and within the larger scientific community via published papers. The first publication from the Tuskegee experiments was published in 1936 in the *Journal of the American Medical Association*.[14]

These two social practices—the professional marginalization of lesser whites that would not support the PHS program, and the scientific experimentation upon blacks thought less than human—provided an identity to which whites could aspire. This white ideal subject position was institutionally buttressed until the end of the Tuskegee experiments in 1972, and effectively undermined potential whistleblowers who knew of both ethical wrongdoing and of easily administered remedies such as the introduction of penicillin in the 1940s.[15] As such, an ideal and material interest in performing a competent and rational white subject position, in terms of policing and protecting both inter- and intra-white racial boundaries, were the necessary social processes that reproduced white racial superiority and identity.

RACIAL CODE WORDS

"Stupid nigger go play basketball, hockey is a white sport," so tweeted a spectator after Joel Ward—a black member of the Washington Capitals hockey team—scored a Game 7 overtime goal in April 2012 to eliminate the defending Stanley Cup champion Boston Bruins.[16] Other tweets included "4th line black trash," "white power," and "The fact that a nigger got the goal makes it ten times worse."[17] As these examples of overtly racist speech demonstrate, recent years have borne witness to the collectively shared myth that blacks and basketball (and whites and hockey) fit hand in glove, and that never the twain should meet. That is, the myth that blacks and hockey are akin to oil and water, and that whites are somehow more naturally predisposed to the game, has reached a dominant, even "common-sense" status. And the expression of these sentiments can function to produce and promote the wielder of that discourse as a competent, belonging, and rational speaker. That is, the usage of racial code words, unlike the above antebellum-style examples, can be used to speak about race in ways that do not promote a racist identity.[18]

Racial code words prove important interactional resources.[19] Code words may be intentionally used against members of certain racial groups in order to discriminate against them in subtle, but no less efficacious ways. For example, sociologists John Farley and Gregory Squires cite an anonymous home insurance agent who asked homeowners, "Do the kids in the neighborhood play hockey or basketball?"[20] Such questions are one way that people skirt around the issue of race in seemingly color-blind fashion, but with the effect of reproducing structural patterns—in this case residential segregation and insurance discrimination. Code words may also unintentionally reproduce racialized—even racist—patterns. Political scientists Jon Hurwitz and Mark Peffley discovered that when whites were surveyed about their support for spending money on prisons, they were less likely to support prisons that housed "inner city criminals" than prisons who housed "criminals." Given that "inner city" and "urban" are cultural synonyms for black and brown populations, the mere introduction of the term shaped whites' racial preferences for punitive policies.[21]

Code words reproduce not just the social world but the identity of those who circulate in those worlds and speak those words. Overall, people constantly (re)make the meaning of their racial identity in specific social settings and in relation to others with whom they interact.[22] Those interactions carry significant, collectively shared expectations about how, what, and where members of a specific racial group should and should not act, say, and go. Racial code words provide the necessary cues as to how to navigate those expectations. Code words operate as intentional tools for guarding racial resources and spaces (e.g., segregating housing) or as unintentional devices for shaping or recalling racial preferences (e.g., policy implications).

The use of code words in real-life settings is vital because it enables one to deploy signal terms in order to pursue or avoid certain racialized agendas and outcomes that do no comport with the dominant expectations of one's racial group. Physical and/or social-psychological abuse or discomfort has been, and continues to be, used to police the color line.[23] Hence, the use of code words to discover the specific racial demographics or expectations of a particular place can be an efficient strategy for avoiding social stigma.

It would be a gross oversimplification to state that the improper use of racial code words only differently constrain or enable the white actors who use them. Rather, discourse is as much generative and performative as it is utilitarian. That is, discourse creates the subjects that purport to speak it. Racialized speech is not merely a description of the world, its usage is an opportunity for ordering in-group hierarchy, strengthening and testing solidarity, and for chasing particular notions of whiteness thought "ideal." In this sense, the use of racial code words allows whites—as members of a still-salient racial group—to subtly yet expertly navigate the expectations of the racial category to which they belong.

Through discursively marking the ontological difference between white and nonwhite as a division between superior and inferior, respectively, and by marginalizing practices of being white that fail to exemplify dominant white racial ideals and expectations, both inter- and intraracial boundaries are temporarily solidified in common everyday speech and serve as the mortar and bricks that build the social structures of racial segregation. This discourse is an important part of white identity formation, as supposedly "polite" yet poignant racial distinctions are drawn in ways that situate the rationality, morality, and superiority of the speaker. Sociologist Judith Howard said it best: "Identities are thus strategic social constructions created through interaction, with social and material consequences. . . . At the most basic level, the point is simply that people actively produce identity through their talk."[24]

WHITE SAVIORS ON SILVER SCREENS

In the 1980s Hollywood birthed the cinematic genre that many call "White Savior Films." The character of the "White Savior" is a protagonist with a decidedly upright character that enters a black, Latino, Asian, or Native context in which the nonwhites struggle through the social order. By the film's end and through the sacrifices of the White Savior, the nonwhite "others" were transformed and redeemed.[25] In the 1980s, the United States bore witness to a cadre of films in this genre.[26] During the 1990s and into the twenty-first century, Hollywood and US audiences demonstrated an increased appreciation of films in this category.[27]

The White Savior film is an important cultural device and artifact of our modern "post-racial" era because it helps repair the myth of white supremacy and paternalism in an unsettled and racially charged time. The films show whites going the extra mile to help people of color who cannot or will not help themselves, thus establishing social order, teaching nonwhites right from wrong, and framing the white savior as the only character able to recognize these moral distinctions and act upon them. In a climate where many whites believe they are unfairly victimized, white fatigue with hearing of racial matters, and a latent desire to see evidence of inter-racial reconciliation and amity, films that showcase messianic white characters assisting down-on-their luck nonwhite characters deliver a touch that resonates. These interracial depictions of friendly and cooperative race relations thus eschew any blatant message of white supremacy while relying on an implicit message of white paternalism and anti-black stereotypes of contented servitude, obedience, and acquiescence. Whiteness emerges as the kind and fatherly de facto savior of the dysfunctional racial "others" who are redeemable so long as they assimilate into white society via their obedience to their white benefactors of class, capital, and compassion.

For example, in *The Last Samurai*, protagonist Nathan Algren, played by Tom Cruise, is captured by Japanese samurai. Having once been dispatched to kill them, Algren comes to respect the samurai. As a consequence, he teaches them military tactics in order to beat the Western trained military forces of Japan of which he was once a part. His new Japanese friend Higen, played by Sôsuke Ikematsu, asks Algren:

> HIGEN: Will you fight the white men, too?
> ALGREN: If they come here, yes.
> HIGEN: Why?
> ALGREN: Because they come to destroy what I have come to love.[28]

Sentimental dialogue finds great expression in these films. The discourse labors to drive home the point that a true and authentic interracial and intercultural friendship has been established, which obscures the larger pattern of the white intruder *qua* savior instructing the "primitive" peoples on how to live (and in the case of *The Last Samurai*, how to die). In the end, all the samurai—including his newly found best friend "Katsumoto" (Ken Watanabe)—are killed. Yet, Algren seems to have both taught the Japanese about Western modernity as well as reminded them to be true to their own historical origins:

> EMPEROR MEIJI: You were with him [Katsumoto], at the end?
> ALGREN: Hai. Your Highness, if you believe me to be your enemy, command me, and I will gladly take my life. [...]
> EMPEROR MEIJI: I have dreamed of a unified Japan; of a country strong, independent, and modern. And now we have railroads, and cannon, Western clothing. But, we cannot forget who we are or where we come from. [...] Tell me how he [Katsumoto] died.
> ALGREN: I will tell you how he lived.[29]

While *The Last Samurai* was based loosely on the Satsuma Rebellion of Japan in 1877, many other White Savior films claim more realistic roots. In that vein, many of these films explicitly state they are "based on a true story." Such appellations lend to audiences' belief in righteous white paternalism and that people of color should be grateful for white assistance. Moreover, such labels demonstrate that Hollywood seems to hold greater interest in the narratives of heroic whites saving people of color than in the stories about people of color helping their own communities or resisting the racist status quo.

For example, *The Blind Side* stars the White Savior Leigh Anne Tuohy, played by Sandra Bullock, and the to-be-saved African American Michael Oher, played by Quinton Aaron. The film is based on Michael Lewis's book that examined the real life of Michael Oher.[30] As Lewis tells the story, Oher rose from an impoverished ghetto in Memphis to become offensive tackle for the Baltimore Ravens. In the film, Oher is depicted as a mute, docile, slow, yet ever-grateful character who was homeless until the Tuohys, a wealthy white Republican family in Mississippi, took him in.

Interestingly, the real-life Michael Oher took issue with his representation in the film in his own book.[31] While Oher maintained his appreciation for what the Tuohys did for him, he writes:

> I felt like it portrayed me as dumb instead of as a kid who had never had consistent academic instruction and ended up thriving once he got it. Quinton Aaron did a great job acting the part, but I could not figure out why the director chose to show me as someone who had to be taught the game of football. Whether it was S.J. moving around ketchup bottles or Leigh Anne explaining to me what blocking is about, I watched those scenes thinking, "No, that's not me at all! I've been studying—really studying—the game since I was a kid!" That was my main hang-up with the film.[32]

Here Hollywood ignores the intersectional structure of educational and racial inequality. That is, it disregards what Oher calls his lack of "consistent academic instruction." Instead, the White Savior motif emerges not just in terms of saving Oher from homelessness, but in creating a fictional dolt of a character in which white children like S.J., played by Jae Head, have to instruct Oher on the basics of football. With that narrative in place, there is no aspect of his life left unsaved by his white messianic adopted family. Such saving graces adorn the Oher character throughout the film. In one scene Leigh Anne Tuohy gives Oher his own bed:

TUOHY: John says all the pro athletes use futons if they can't find a bed big enough, so I got you one of those. Of course the frame was heinous; was not about let that in my house, but I got you something nicer.

OHER: It's mine?

TUOHY: Yes sir. . . . What?

OHER: Never had one before.

TUOHY: What, a room to yourself?

OHER: A bed.

The sentimentalism is ripe, if not over the top. Who could not feel respect and empathy for a person that gives an adult their first bed and safe place to sleep?

In 2011 *The Help*, based on the best-selling book of the same name by Kathryn Stockett, grossed over $166 million in the first month of its release. The film is based on the real lives of people who lived in Mississippi in the 1960s. Early in 2011, Ablene Cooper, a sixty-year-old black woman who worked as a maid to Kathryn Stockett's brother, sued Stockett for $75,000 based on the complaint that one of the book's principal characters named Aibileen Clark, was an unpermitted appropriation of her name and image.[33] Stockett filed for summary judgment, citing a one-year statute of limitations on the lawsuit. Just after the film's release in August 2011, a Mississippi judge agreed and threw out Clark's suit.[34]

Both the film and book concentrate on the relationships between the lead character and White Savior Eugenia "Skeeter" Phelan, played by Emma Stone, and her efforts to "save" black female domestic servants by interviewing them about their lives under the brutal conditions of racist, white housewives and publishing these interviews as a kind of tell-all exposé. *The Help*, like many a White Savior film, trades explicitly on this careful parceling of good and bad whites. By scapegoating the character Hilly Holbrook played by Bryce Dallas Howard as the evil racist housewife of the film, audiences are free to sanction Skeeter to usurp control of black women's voices under the guise of freeing them from their state of economic and racial servitude. Skeeter is then easily framed as the savior that breaks free of the constraints of white normativity, and her winning of a job offer from a New York publishing company is thus seen as her deserved reward. This story then tells a powerful mistruth: "To suggest that bad people were racist implies that good people were not."[35]

It would seem that the White Savior motif is commonly used to retell stories in forms palatable to US mainstream consumption. Such imposition allows for the negative stereotyping of a nonwhite character or culture as essentially broken, marginalized, and pathological while an ideal white person emerges as possessive of messianic characteristics that can fix the previously hopeless nonwhite pariah. These stories construct and glorify the ideal white person as a paternalistic administrator of people of color, and consistently portray nonwhite people as biologically or culturally broken and in need of salvation. This inter- and intraracial boundary construction, again, assists with the rationalization of asymmetrical relations across the color line, naturalizes social relations of violently unequal resources, and valorizes paternalistic forms of white supremacist rhetoric and practice.

THE GOOD, THE BAD, AND THE COMMON IDEAL OF WHITENESS

In an ethnographic comparison of a white nationalist and white antiracist organization,[36] I found that members of both supposedly politically opposite and ideologically antagonistic organizations constructed an ideal white identity via two distinct symbolic boundaries. First, an ideal whiteness is set apart from a set of fictional black and brown behaviors thought endemic to those racial groups. Second, the white ideal is removed from those whites that fail to acknowledge and orient themselves in opposition to the aforementioned dysfunctional behaviors.

The white nationalist organization that I call "National Equality for All" (NEA) and the white antiracist organization I call "Whites for Racial Justice" (WRJ) represent seemingly opposite ends of the spectrum on race. NEA advances both biological and cultural arguments about the natural inferiority, common immorality, and hyper-violent character of black and brown people for the purposes of rationalizing their defense of a white nationalist political platform. WRJ makes arguments about the emasculation of black and Latino men and the overall dysfunction of nonwhite communities because of the historical effects of targeted racism. In either case, such rhetoric obscures white deficiencies and problems, reproduces a racist worldview in which nonwhites are one-dimensional masses whose essential differences separate and arrange them in a social hierarchy, and leaves whiteness unchallenged as a hegemonic ideal that all should rationally emulate. The claim that pathological people of color are a threat to the social order makes either NEA or WRJ (depending on your leanings) appear functionally necessary and as a force for good. In some ways, these different positions are like two sides of the same coin.

While a tenet of NEA logic is that blacks, especially black men, are both culturally and genetically hardwired to act in dysfunctional and immoral ways, WRJ argues that the pathologies of people of color are the result of racist maltreatment and discrimination. Regardless of intention or pathway, a crucial similarity remains. In both worldviews, the existence of immoral, flawed, and unfit group-level characteristics among people of color is taken for granted, a common-sense "truth" that evokes a kind of white moral panic. As a result, a white supremacist vision of people of color is juxtaposed against whites as the antithesis of such behavior.

To NEA members, racial and gender differences are simply inherent and immutable, and it is rather fruitless to attempt to change them. Those that attempt to do so are engaging in little more than a pipe dream. As NEA member Mason told me:

> I used to be just like you, I did. . . . I wanted to believe that with enough social engineering that we could make the country a harmonious place, that we could have a real equality. It's an attractive and seductive proposition, I know. It still kind of pulls at my heart. . . . Look throughout history, the communists and Marxists tried to make it happen and failed. . . . I finally got to the point where I realized it was a child's dream, I mean no offense, but really, I can show you biological evidence that refutes any claim for racial equality. . . . I'm not going to put myself or my future family at risk by trying to make something work that just can't . . . Black men are violent . . . especially in regard to sexual violence . . . You can't fight your genes, you know?

Unlike NEA, members of WRJ often advanced the argument that black women, because of the oppression and emasculation of black men, were forced into an unnaturally masculine identity and made to unfairly play the role of the black man—as providers and heads of household. To WRJ, such matriarchy is unnatural and unfair to black women, unfairly burdening them with the responsibilities that only a man should, and can, handle.

The idea of black family role reversal is firmly embedded in mainstream logic and pop psychology. What is most insidious about the claim of sexual and gender role reversal is that it acquiesces to patriarchal and white normative notions of domesticity, sexuality, and gender politics. In the end, the thesis results in a picture of black masculinity that is inextricably tied to the social and sexual control that men think they should have over women. Accordingly, WRJ often spoke of black woman as incomplete, as in need of man to fill a void in her life. For example, as I sat at the kitchen table of WRJ member Sean and his wife, while three of his four children milled about the house, Sean stated:

> We don't have a lot of the issues that black, or Native, or Latino fami-
> lies possess. That's white privilege. We don't have to worry about, well,
> she [referring to his wife] doesn't have to worry about taking care of
> the children *and* [said with emphasis] working. She can work, or stay
> at home, or put the kids in day-care, or whatever we decide is best.
> She, and I too, are not discriminated against when we leave the house.
> So we have a rather healthy family. . . . Blacks can't, unfortunately, say
> the same. . . . I'm fortunate to be white. That's privilege. I can be a man,
> and my wife sees me as that. The attraction, the relationship, the way
> she sees me, *and hopefully looks up to me and respects me* [said as
> he turned and looked adoringly at his wife] is constant. . . . If I were
> under the constant barrage of racism, how could she respect me? . . .
> I don't have a mind that makes habitually bad decisions like so many
> men of color. I mean, it's not their fault, you know?

Later in the conversation Sean told me:

> Look, sure, there are many white families that have problems too. It
> could be because they are poor, or gay, or what-have-you. . . . This
> will sound a bit callous, I know, but really, there's no excuse for white
> families. They have a huge advantage. Their development has not been
> stunted, or retarded, like that of black families in a white supremacist
> environment. *They have no excuse!* [said with a raised voice]. . . . If
> you're white and not making it, while not all whites have the same
> advantages, I know, still, there's really something wrong with that
> individual.

Sean's words illuminate the collusion of inter- and intraracial boundaries and narratives in the making of white racial identity. First, Sean is clear in his demarcation of white and black characteristics. White families, and white men in particular, do not acquire the dysfunctions that men of color possess. To Sean, white men do not have minds that make "habitually bad decisions." Rather, whites differ fundamentally from people of color because they do not reproduce the social and moral dysfunctions that result from racist discrimination. Second, if whites are not successful, the cause is not a group characteristic or group effect but is because "there's really something wrong with that individual."

While no one can fully embody all the dimensions of the ideal or hegemonic form of whiteness, those who claim a socially dominant status can more easily define the standards and the intraracial distinctions between them and the whites who are "something less." Hence, NEA members made frequent efforts to claim a hegemonic status and avoid a subordinate and marginalized status. Members failed in their intraracial boundary work when they were unable or unwilling to adequately demarcate the difference between them and the negative traits thought characteristic of people of color. One NEA member I call Will told me:

> We had to kick a member out a few years ago. . . . We started sending a couple of folks to these interracial discussion groups that some city committee was sponsoring. It was to facilitate learning across and trust across the color line. . . . [laughing] I mean, I wouldn't say we were going there to "spy." That would be too harsh a word. But we didn't want good white people duped by that nonsense. . . . She became friends with a few black women in the group. . . . Next thing I know, she's doing drugs with them. Like heroin or something. . . . It was clear to us that she had no clue as to her heritage, who she was really. I mean, it's very sad. When white people lose their way like that. They can't be a part of NEA. . . . She strayed too far from our ideals. . . . She stopped believing in our ideology. . . . She stopped aiming for our ideals.

As further indication of intra-white boundaries, Josh, a first-year NEA member and an artist, told me:

> I don't want to say I don't get a lot of respect here, but, okay, I guess I just don't get a lot. . . . I don't really buy that black folks are all that bad. I just don't think we can successfully get along, so the nationalist approach just seems pragmatic. Does that make sense? I mean, I have a couple black friends that are black nationalists . . . They wouldn't

identify like that, but they don't believe that black and whites can get along either, so until that day, we're friends. . . . They're intelligent people, I think one has a master's or doctorate or something like that. She's raised smart kids. Her husband is a nice guy too. There's nothing wrong with them, so what's the big deal? . . . I can't really say that around the office, you know? [laughing] I mean, that's not kosher to say, I mean, unless we're talking to a TV camera, that blacks are intelligent. . . . I think they are, so there's a limit to how far I can go here.

It should be clear that the dominant meanings of white racial identity are not formed in relation to a paramount racial "other" but also in relation to forms of whiteness deemed other. The presence of simultaneous inter- and intraracial boundaries demonstrates that NEA and WRJ actors cannot simply claim a white status but must perform the right type of whiteness as inter-subjectively understood by others. NEA and WRJ shore up the meanings of an ideal white identity vis-à-vis (1) the pathologies of people of color and (2) whites who do not view people of color as pathological or those individual whites who embody dysfunctions of their own. In a hegemonic white regimen in which demonizing people of color achieves common-sense status, unjust racial arrangements are internalized and endlessly reinforced in not only the identities that overtly rationalize such relations (white nationalists) but also within the identities of those who have been delegated to fight against these relations (white antiracists).

GREAT EXPECTATIONS: RACIAL IDENTITY ALLEGIANCE

In any given setting, an ideal of whiteness emerges alongside many other ways of "being white" that are complicit, subordinate, or marginalized in relation to that ideal. This ideal remains grounded in the everyday reproduction of, and appeal to, both inter- and intraracial distinctions. Hegemonic whiteness is formed through a process of marking the meanings of "whiteness" as (1) essentially different from and superior to those marked as "nonwhite" and (2) through marginalizing practices of "being white" that fail to exemplify those differences.

From historical examples and everyday racial code words to "white savior" films and white activists, evidence suggests that whites possess similar and shared definitions of an ideal white self that functions as an implicit ideal against which one's worth, behavior, and ultimately one's identity are measured. While very few whites may actually attain or measure up to the ideal white racial identity, those who hold a dominant status have greater ability to define the standards and distinctions. To successfully pursue this ideal, one must continually engage in inter- and intraracial boundary work in order to demarcate both nonwhite "others" and specific "lesser" forms of whiteness.[37]

Because there are infinite contexts and situations in which people find themselves, the dominant meanings of white racial identity—as primary categories—provide a way of navigating everyday life regardless of context. Racial categories (like that of gender, age, and some socially perceivable markers of class or sexuality) transcend contextual limits and local definitions of the self and "others." Shared understandings of race allow one to act quickly within the structural constraints of quick and unexpected interactions. The primacy of social categories like race, then, enable the process of self–other interactions by affording what sociologist Cecelia Ridgeway calls "an all-purpose starting place, an initial frame for figuring the other out, whether we encounter that other in a familiar institution or in an utterly unfamiliar context."[38]

Within the contemporary sociological study of white identity, "structure" models of whiteness examine how differently stratified resources affect white worldviews and political persuasions; "agency" models analyze how whites employ various discourses and attitudes to navigate the world. Hence, it is common for "whiteness" to be used as a variable to explain or predict certain inequalities. For instance, one might ask, "What effect does whiteness have on income?" Or, one might ask, "What racial attitudes do lower-class whites hold?" From these points of departure, one can demonstrate how being white increases the probability of a higher income for someone relative to another of a different race, or how whites in the lower class understand their racial world.

In either case, labels like "whiteness" are often labor-saving reifications of something deeper going on in the social world. We would be better served to move away from linear causal models in which whiteness is a fixed and static identity already in place, to examining white identity as an ongoing social process in which structural forces and acts of volition convene and synthesize. That is, the situational processes of identity formation attempt to fix the meaning of the self in relation the social world to provide a set of expectations for white action and order. As sociologist and cultural theorist Stuart Hall writes:

I use "identity" to refer to the meeting point, the point of *suture* [emphasis in original], between on the one hand the discourses and practices which attempt to "interpellate," speak to us or hail us into place as the social subjects of particular discourses, and on the other hand, the processes which produce subjectivities, which construct us as subjects which can be "spoken." Identities are thus points of temporary attachment to the subject positions which discursive practices conduct for us. . . . The notion that an effective suturing of the subject to a subject-position requires, not only that the subject is "hailed," but that the subject invests in the position, means that suturing has to be thought of as an *articulation* [emphasis in original], rather than a one-sided process.[39]

Whites "invest," in the words of Hall, in the dominant and inter-subjectively shared meanings of what whiteness is, and more importantly, what it should be (ideal white racial identity). These meanings are far-reaching or what we can call "transposable." That is, ". . . they can be applied to a wide and not fully predictable range of cases outside the context in which they are initially learned. . . . Knowledge of a rule or a schema by definition means the ability to transpose or extend it—that is, to apply it creatively."[40]

By arguing that the dominant meanings of race can transpose local or specific contexts, one could too easily misinterpret my argument that I see "racial meanings" as free-floating norms and values to which actors latch on and apply befitting their utilitarian needs. Rather than take this misstep, I implore the reader to think of racial meanings as powerful, implicit, and far-reaching expectations to which people are socially accountable as members of their particular racial group. While meanings are certainly situational, they are never disconnected from extra-local concerns.[41] Rather, the relationships between white actors in any locale or context depend on a larger "net of accountability" that is shared with people outside of the particular setting. Sociologist Michael Schwalbe argues:

Often when we are called to account, it's as a member of group or social category. And usually this is because we're not behaving the way someone thinks we should, as a member of that group or category. We are thus vulnerable to being ignored, discredited, shamed, or otherwise punished for behaving in a way that others deem wrong in light of who we claim to be or who they think we are. One way to put it is to say that identities carry accountability obligations.[42]

Elsewhere, Schwalbe and his colleagues argued:

> ... the power to hold others accountable in one setting depends upon relationships—that is, a larger *net of accountability*—with actors outside the setting. The general point, again, is that to understand the reproduction of inequality in one setting, we need to see how social actors in that setting are enabled and constrained by what actors elsewhere have done, are doing, or might do.[43]

This accountability is not a matter of individual choice. Rather, it is "a feature of social relationships . . . drawn from the institutional arena in which those relationships are enacted."[44] While actors in divergent settings certainly navigate the meanings of race in different ways, dominant expectations constrain and enable actions in similarly recognizable patterns and in ways that produce similar pursuits of an ideal white racial identity, what we might think of as "hegemonic whiteness." Sociologist Amanda Lewis writes:

> Hegemonic whiteness thus is a shifting configuration of practices and meanings that occupy the dominant position in a particular racial formation and that successfully manage to occupy the empty space of "normality" in our culture. Collectively, this set of schemas functions as that seemingly "neutral" or "precultural" yardstick against which cultural behavior, norms, and values are measured. . . . It is also something people may well have only partial access to and that regularly is contested. For example, colloquial references to blacks "acting white," to Jews being "too Jewish," and to whites behaving as "wiggers" all are examples of people partially crossing borders in and out of hegemonic whiteness, with varying degrees of reward or penalty. Undoubtedly, hegemonic whiteness is not merely an ideological or cultural artifact but carries material rewards.[45]

I do not argue that all whites engage in the practices of inter- and intraracial "othering" at all times. Rather, my argument is that whites, by virtue of their membership in that racial category, are not immune to the pursuit of the white racial ideal. They are, simply put, "white bound."[46] The dominant racial meanings that guide white racial identity formation are not simply local matters but are a changing configuration of inter- and intraracial boundary-making practices that occupy the dominant position across varied social relations. One's pursuit of that ideal, and allegiance to white racial identity expectations, varies in relation to very real material relations, rewards, interests, and punishments. With this understanding in play, we can better understand the identity compulsions that simultaneously constrain and enable the formations of white racial identity, and thus, white action and order.

NOTES

1. David R. Roediger, *Colored White: Transcending the Racial Past* (Berkeley: University of California Press, 2003).

2. France W. Twine and Charles Gallagher, "The Future of Whiteness: A Map of the 'Third Wave,'" 31.1 *Ethnic and Racial Studies* (2008): 4–24.

3. Woody A. Doane, "White-Blindness: The Dominant Group Experience," in J. P. Myers, ed., *Minority Voices: Linking Personal Ethnic History and the Sociological Imagination* (Boston: Allyn & Bacon, 2004).

4. Twine and Gallagher, "The Future of Whiteness," 4–24.

5. Matthew W. Hughey, "The (Dis)similarities of White Racial Identities: The Conceptual Framework of 'Hegemonic Whiteness,'" 33.8 *Ethnic and Racial Studies* (2010): 1289–1309; Hughey, "The White Savior Film and Reviewers' Reception," 33.3 *Symbolic Interaction* (2012): 475–96; Hughey, "Stigma Allure and White Antiracist Identity Management," 75.3 *Social Psychology Quarterly* (2012): 219–41.

6. Matthew W. Hughey and Sheena Gardner, "Film Reviewers and Framing Race: Recuperating a Post-Racial Whiteness," 9.2 *Darkmatter* (2012); Hughey, "The (Dis)similarities of White Racial Identities," 1289–1309; Hughey, "Stigma Allure and White Antiracist Identity Management," 219–41; Hughey, "Color Capital, White Debt, and the Paradox of Strong White Racial Identities," 9.1 *Du Bois Review: Social Science Research on Race*, 169–200; Matthew W. Hughey, "Black Guys and White Guise: The Discursive Construction of White Masculinity," 41.1 *Journal of Contemporary Ethnography* (2012): 96–125; Hughey, "Racializing Redemption, Reproducing Racism: The Odyssey of Magical Negroes and White Saviors," 6.9 *Sociology Compass* (2012): 751–67; Hughey, "Backstage Discourse and the Reproduction of White Masculinities," 52.1 *Sociological Quarterly* (2011): 132–53.

7. Amanda E. Lewis, "What Group? Studying Whites and Whiteness in the Era of Colorblindness," 22.4 *Sociological Theory* (2004): 623–46.

8. Hughey, "The (Dis)similarities of White Racial Identities," 1289–1309.

9. Denisce DiAnni, *The Deadly Deception* (PBS/WGBH NOVA documentary video, 1993).

10. Ibid.

11. Allan M. Brandt, "Racism and Research: The Case of the Tuskegee Syphilis Study," *Hastings Center Magazine* (New York: Hastings Center; Institute of Society, Ethics and the Life Sciences, 1978).

12. DiAnni, *The Deadly Deception*.

13. Brandt, "Racism and Research"; Patricia A. King, "The Dangers of Difference," 22.6 *Hastings Center Report*, (1992): 35–38.

14. R. A. Vonderlehr, Taliaferro Clark, O. C. Wenger, and J. R. Heller Jr., "Untreated Syphilis in the Male Negro," 107.11 *Journal of the American Medical Association* (1936): 856–60.

15. King, "The Dangers of Difference," 35–38.

16. Jessie Washington, "NHL fans let loose with racist comments after loss," Boston .com, April 26, 2012, http://articles.boston.com/2012-04-6/sports/31412623_1_boston -fans-wayne-simmonds-tweets, retrieved July 13, 2012.

17. "Joel Ward's Game-Winning Playoff Goal Sets off Barrage of Racist Tweets," *Huffington Post*, April 26, 2012, www.huffingtonpost.com/2012/04/26/joel-ward-goal-sparks -racist-tweets_n_1455975.html, retrieved July 13, 2012.

18. Eduardo Bonilla-Silva, "The Linguistics of Color Blind Racism: How to Talk Nasty about Blacks without Sounding 'Racist,'" 1.2 *Critical Sociology* (2002): 41–64.

19. Jon Hurwitz and Mark Peffley, "Playing the Race Card in the Post–Willie Horton Era: The Impact of Racialized Code Words on Support for Punitive Crime Policy," 69 *Public Opinion Quarterly* (2005): 99–112.

20. John E. Farley and Gregory D. Squires, "Fences and Neighbors: Segregation in 21st-Century America," *Contexts* 4.1 (2005): 33–39.

21. Hurwitz and Peffley, "Playing the Race Card in the Post–Willie Horton Era," 99–112.

22. Hughey, *White Bound*; Hughey, "Taking Culture (and Race) Beyond Dichotomies: A Reply to Gans," 19.5 *Identities: Global Studies in Culture and Power* (2012).

23. John F. Dovidio, Samuel L. Gaertner, Yolanda Flores Niemann, and Kevin Snider, "Racial, Ethnic, and Cultural Differences in Responding to Distinctiveness and Discrimination on Campus: Stigma and Common Group Identity," 57.1 *Journal of Social Issues* (2001): 167–88.

24. Judith A. Howard, "Social Psychology of Identities," 26 *Annual Review of Sociology* (2000): 367–93.

25. Hughey, "Taking Culture (and Race) Beyond Dichotomies"; Gardner, "Film Reviewers and Framing Race."

26. *Cry Freedom* (1987), *Mississippi Burning* (1988), *A Dry White Season* (1989), *Glory* (1989), and the *Indiana Jones* trilogy (1981, 1984, 1989); Hughey, "Taking Culture (and Race) Beyond Dichotomies."

27. See *Dances with Wolves* (1990); *Dangerous Minds* (1995); *Sunset Park* (1996); *Ghosts of Mississippi* (1996); *Amistad* (1997); *Music of the Heart* (1999); *Monster's Ball* (2000); *Finding Forrester* (2000); *Hardball* (2001); *The Last Samurai* (2003); *The Constant Gardener* (2005); *Crash* (2005); *Half-Nelson* (2006); *Freedom Writers* (2007); *Gran Torino* (2008); *The Blind Side* (2009); *Avatar* (2009).

28. *The Last Samurai*.

29. Ibid.

30. *The Blind Side: Evolution of a Game* (New York: W. W. Norton, 2006.)

31. Michael Oher, *I Beat the Odds: From Homelessness, to The Blind Side, and Beyond* (New York: Penguin, 2011).

32. Oher, *I Beat the Odds*.

33. Campbell Robertson, "A Maid Sees Herself in a Novel, and Objects," *New York Times*, February 17, 2011, www.nytimes.com/2011/02/18/books/18help.html?_r=0, retrieved September 30, 2012.

34. Campbell Robertson, Arts Beat Blog, "A Victory in Court for the Author of 'The Help,'" *New York Times*, August 16, 2011, http://artsbeat.blogs.nytimes.com/2011/08/16/a-victory-in-court-for-the-author-of-the-help, retrieved September 30, 2012.

35. Patricia A. Turner, "Dangerous White Stereotypes," *New York Times*, August 28, 2011, A23; www.nytimes.com/2011/08/29/opinion/dangerous-white-stereotypes.html?_r=0, retrieved on May 20, 2014.

36. Matthew W. Hughey, "Stigma Allure and White Antiracist Identity Management," 219–41; Hughey, "Racializing Redemption, Reproducing Racism," 751–67.

37. Carla D. Shirley, "'You Might Be a Redneck if . . .': Boundary Work among Rural, Southern Whites," 89.1 *Social Forces* (2010): 35–62.

38. Cecilia L. Ridgeway, *Framed by Gender: How Gender Inequality Persists in the Modern World* (New York: Oxford University Press, 2011), 37–38.

39. Stuart Hall, "Who needs 'Identity'?" in Stuart Hall and Paul du Gay, ed., *Questions of Cultural Identity* (London: Sage, 1996), 1–17.

40. William H. Sewell Jr., "A Theory of Structure: Duality, Agency, and Transformation," 98.1 *American Journal of Sociology* (1992): 1–29.

41. Erving Goffman, "The Interaction Order," 48 *American Sociological Review* (1983): 1–17.

42. Michael Schwalbe, *Rigging the Game* (New York: Oxford University Press, 2008), 171.

43. Schwalbe Sandra Godwin, Daphne Holden, Douglas Schrock, Shealy Thompson, and Michele Wolkomir, "Generic Processes in the Reproduction of Inequality: An Interactionist Analysis," 79.2 *Social Forces* (2000): 419–52.

44. Candace West and Sarah Fenstermaker, "Doing Difference," 9.1 *Gender and Society* (1995): 8–37.

45. Amanda E. Lewis, "What Group? Studying Whites and Whiteness in the Era of Colorblindness," 22.4 *Sociological Theory* (2004): 623–46.

46. Hughey, *White Bound*.

9

THEORIZING WHITE RACIAL TRAUMA AND ITS REMEDIES

BECKY THOMPSON AND VERONICA T. WATSON

SOCIOLOGIST BERNARD GIESEN (2004, 114) ARGUES, IN HIS ESSAY "The Trauma of Perpetrators," that there is work to be done in recognizing the impact of racism on the perpetrators—those who commit direct acts as well as those who are collaborators, supporters, and silent witnesses. What does it mean to try to recognize, to acknowledge, the trauma of whiteness?[1] What do we surface when we consider that question? African American intellectuals have been saying for over a century that people of color are not the only ones who are traumatized by the politics of race in this country. Those writers—including W. E. B. Du Bois (1903, 1935), Charles Chesnutt (1905), James Baldwin (1998b), Kenneth B. Clark (1963), and Thandeka (1999)—have provided contemporary scholars a way to journey with the perpetrators, out of a spirit of love and concern, as they recognize their own pathology. One cannot speak of pathology, recognize the deep pain that whiteness has caused, without also seeing the loss of humanity that has attended those aggressions. This recognition does not mitigate or excuse white violence and repression; but it does require that those of us who serve as "disagreeable mirrors" (Baldwin 1998b, 320) to whiteness not lose sight of the bigger picture, their lost and denied humanity that we are journeying with them to reclaim.[2]

At the heart of racism are attempts of the perpetrators to deny knowledge of themselves as violent aggressors, morally destitute, even barbaric. In the United States, whiteness has rarely had to confront that image and knowledge of itself. Instead, it has worked hard to repress and discredit that history, which has continued the silence and deepened the trauma rather than opening avenues of accountability and healing. We might compare the need for public, interracial dialogue and historical accounting in the United

States to the reasons South Africa established the Truth and Reconciliation Commission at the end of apartheid, though its work was unfinished and uneven. As the former Minister of Justice Dullah Omar wrote, "A commission is a necessary exercise to enable South Africans to come to terms with their past on a morally accepted basis and to advance the cause of reconciliation."[3] But such effort and spirit have never found traction in the United States. Whiteness in the United States has been predicated on reinventing itself, of never looking back, of running from its own history, often under the guises of "progress" and "freedom." Thus, the violence and the trauma have continued. It shows up in the macabre fascination with unimaginable horrors that saturate both media and entertainment, and it shows up in the intransigence of racism. Attempts to give language to and visualize the unspeakable are the "haunting dreams" (Giesen 2004, 119) that evidence the trauma of whiteness.

Many activists, artists, and critical race scholars have established that racism has existed deep within the construction of white subjectivity and culture since the founding of the United States (Mills 1997; Morrison 1992; Roediger 1991; Feagin 2013). That exclusionary spirit was then actualized in the political and social institutions of the fledgling nation, even as elaborate systems of justification, myths, and evasions were also invented to maintain whiteness's sense of itself as moral, upright, and just. White Americans have not had to honestly confront racial oppression and violence as symptomatic of and central to whiteness because they have been told that the violence was committed by a few outliers, a fringe group of racists who acted in ways incommensurate with mainstream white America. Acknowledging that, instead of being "heroes," members of one's community are "perpetrators," necessitates a reckoning, an accounting that recognizes the distance between the egalitarian ideals and oppressive practices of a people.[4] Most will try to avoid this damning self-knowledge through "collective schizophrenia, ... denial ... decoupling or withdrawal" (Giesen 2004, 114). White racial trauma is the white response to its own racism and moral failures, and as such can be triggered by a range of individual acts and social conditions that intersect with racism, including the refusal to acknowledge and atone for the social world that whiteness has created.

We believe that white people carry with them memories and experiences that tell them that something is desperately wrong, that racism is not natural or inevitable. White racial trauma may occur from witnessing or being responsible for extreme acts of violence such as police brutality, for example, or from the mundane, everyday violence of racism such as refusing to interact with people of color or to acknowledge their contributions in professional or educational settings. Often, such exposure involves repeated witnessing of damage done without intervention or cessation—repeatedly watching children of color being bullied on the school bus, recognizing that your education has included no real attention to realities or histories other than that of white people, or hearing justifications meant to rationalize the mass incarceration and murder of people of color. Rather than stay present to feel the pain of brutalized bodies and psyches, and then act from that knowledge, most white people deny, justify, and then reproduce the very violence that was the source of their own dis-ease, often leading to a range of affects that counseling psychologist Lisa Spanierman and education researcher Nolan Cabrera outline as the emotions of white racism in their article "The Emotions of White Racism and Antiracism." White apathy, fear, and rage, and perhaps more that have yet to be recognized, we believe are usefully thought of as evidencing white racial trauma. The multilayered reality of this trauma—of enacting and/or supporting the violence done to people of color in a racist society, and of benefiting from the denials of what is seen and known—has significant implications.

In *Trauma Stewardship: An Everyday Guide to Caring for Self While Caring for Others*, activist Laura van Dernoot Lipsky (2009, 3) recognizes that "bearing witness to others' suffering" has an effect on those who are witnesses, and outlines sixteen "warning signs" of trauma overexposure.[5] While van Dernoot Lipsky identified these symptoms to describe people triggered or exhausted by taking care of people, these secondary trauma symptoms have an eerie resonance with what can happen to white people as part of a racist society. Though whites so affected are reluctant witnesses to the pain of others, what is striking are the parallels between the coping mechanisms of secondary trauma exposure of those trying to alleviate suffering and, in our analysis, those who are consciously or unconsciously enabling the suffering of people of color through their silence and inaction. What van Dernoot Lipsky describes as coping mechanisms that alleviate the pain of "staying in touch with the heart that was breaking" (3) look a lot like normative white culture in the United States.

Of the sixteen symptoms van Dernoot Lipsky describes, four are particularly revealing to our discussion of whiteness: hypervigilance, a sense of persecution, diminished creativity, and dissociation. Collectively, these signs of white trauma might usefully be thought of as a white schizophrenic subjectivity, which calls attention to the myriad ways that an investment in whiteness can distort how people think, act, and perceive reality.[6] It focuses us on the ways in which whiteness amplifies white fear and disconnection between people and the ways that it stifles the ability to discern the real from the imagined. Our interest is in naming the specificities of these traumas, how they manifest in everyday life, in culture, in psyches, and in the public imagination. Such naming then opens a way to consider antidotes to the trauma of racist domination and exclusion in ways that move us beyond the insanity of whiteness.

HYPERVIGILANCE AND A SENSE OF PERSECUTION

Van Dernoot Lipsky (2009, 64) describes *hypervigilance* as "a dynamic of being wholly focused on our job, to the extent that being present for anything else in our life can seem impossible." She continues, "It is often an attempt to restore safety and prevent any further victimization by anticipating and recognizing everything as a potential threat and acting accordingly." What an apt description of whiteness. When considered from the vantage point of racial trauma, whiteness can certainly be understood as having been "wholly focused on [the] job" of defining, policing, and protecting white privilege, space, identity, and culture. Collectively it has drawn boundaries, defined an inside and an outside to a presumed sacred space/identity, and aggressively ejected and rejected those bodies that fall outside of the ideological and social pale.

Policing those boundaries has resulted in the destruction and murder of innumerable people, from lynching victims in the nineteenth and twentieth centuries to civil rights workers of the mid-twentieth century to young men of color in the United States today,[7] including seventeen-year-old Trayvon Martin, an unarmed African American teenager killed in 2012 by a neighborhood "watchman" in the predominantly white community of Sanford, Florida,[8] after being described as "suspicious" by his attacker. Philosopher Sara Ahmed (2012, 2) astutely points out, however, that the act of "registering those who are out of place" actually serves to "*create* strangers and establish a direction toward them, as those who threaten the place of the 'in place,' as those who generate anxiety" (emphasis added). People of color are made into strangers by the act of policing whiteness, and whiteness becomes ever more anxious through its hypervigilant attempts to identify those who should not be part of the body, the community, of whiteness. But this obsessive behavior does not alleviate the trauma plaguing whiteness. Rather, it is a distraction from dealing with the real knowledge and disregarded emotions that are causing whiteness to feel out of control, threatened, and at risk, even as it continues to maintain almost exclusive control over contemporary social, political, and economic sources of power.

This racialized hypervigilance often leads white people to a false sense of persecution, another warning sign of trauma overexposure identified by van Dernoot Lipsky (2009, 93). In the context of whiteness, the *sense of persecution* is about believing that it (whiteness) is always threatened, victimized, and under attack. Whiteness sees enemies everywhere but in its midst: in its communities and in its homes. So, the myth of the black rapist still has white women clutching their purses while walking toward black men even as these women head to homes where they may, in fact, be among the epidemic of women abused by their domestic partners. White flight and segregated communities still provide white enclaves of living, but that does not prevent troubled white teens and adults from rampaging through schools in search of easy victims and a release from the pain of their lives. Those who are invested in whiteness believe that reverse racism is a truism rather than an oxymoron; they believe affirmative action programs are taking "their places" in jobs or education, adding fuel to their sense of displacement and endangerment. Much like the rhizomatous spread of white supremacist ideology described by Adela Fofiu in the Romanian context,[9] this sentiment is held, repeated, amplified, and given credence in discourse as well as legal suits that deny white entitlement and the overwhelming evidence that there are few black and brown bodies in positions of power, or often even present, in most institutions.

The myth of the black and brown job robber becomes a distraction from organizing against the perils of a post-industrial, neoliberal society where dignified living-wage and middle-class jobs are eliminated by the ever-growing search for corporate profits. Whiteness has long kept workers across race from supporting each other (Du Bois 1935; Roediger 1991), encouraging white laborers to be ever vigilant about being skipped over in favor of a black hire even as bosses increasingly hire neither. Instead, NAFTA-supported economies where there is nothing "free" about trade proliferate. In focusing on a perceived "black or brown threat," however, whiteness is able to ignore the larger, more imminent threat to individual and collective well-being, the threat of its own making that is not so easy to dislodge. In refusing the more difficult task of societal regeneration, whiteness abdicates the responsibility of "transform[ing] [its] circumstances" (van Dernoot Lipsky 2009, 93) in ways that benefit both self and others.

DIMINISHED CREATIVITY

Along with a sense of persecution, van Dernoot Lipsky (2009, 67) lists *diminished creativity* as a trauma response in which originality and innovation take a back seat to just getting the job (meal, holiday, funeral, garden, hiring, firing, life) done. Overwhelming signs of diminished creativity in white culture include the loss of originality in popular culture, including the endless recycling of film and television programs under prequels, sequels, and remakes. It also includes an increasingly noisy culture in malls, stadiums, and public gathering spaces as more and more of us conduct our daily lives with electronic appendages, seemingly fleeing from any moment of quiet that could lead to self-reflection. This noise keeps white culture from acts of contemplation that can be sources of transformation and drowns out the still, small voice that can be a seed of creative inspiration and originality. This shrinking of creativity can be heard when the jazz of Miles Davis and John Coltrane is stripped down to a Muzak track in a grocery store. It is evident in mainstream public school curricula that bore everyone, and a culture of standardized testing that de-emphasizes unique thought and creative problem solving. It can be seen in the dumbing down of political campaigns and a corporate culture where a Marriott hotel looks the same whether it is in New York City, Tunis, Amsterdam, Cairo, or Singapore. These corporatized cultural sites represent whiteness as a homogenized culture, reinforcing the elimination of ethnic and religious diversity among whites. It is a whitewashing that robs people of knowing who they are and where they come from.

The diminished creativity that results from homogenization makes people tired, lethargic, bored by everyday life, and susceptible to reaching for the next quick fix. It also leads to an inability to have a nuanced, holistic, and realistic understanding of one's history, a rush away from truths that fuel creative output. Alice Walker's *In Search of our Mother's Gardens* provides a model for the excavation of African American history leading to rich, creative work that reflects the past, present and an imagined future. The same willingness to search needs to take place among white people in order to find full and honest expression as citizens, activists, intellectuals, and leaders. That searching takes people to a place of recovery and innovation. Creativity—personal, cultural, and social—is forward-looking; it is creating something in the present that we believe will endure. Creativity nurtures moments in which we are able to envision the future and to communicate with people we hope we will meet.

Instead, white people have practiced a long history of historical amnesia, an aggressive "disremembering"[10] of historical realities that are replaced by fictitious versions of history that promote whiteness. Janet Koenig calls these historical fictions—nostalgic celebrations like the Fourth of July, Columbus Day, and oft-repeated contemporary notions of a "post-racial" world—"an advertisement for the state."[11] Enacted in and through legislation, taught in the school system, and incorporated into the lives of those who know them to be untrue,[12] historical amnesia coupled with advertisements for the state lead to an unclaimed sense of one's history and an unwillingness or inability to tap into one's creative potential. This is why feminist poet Adrienne Rich (1986, 141) refers to historical amnesia as "the imagination's sugar rush, leaving depression and emptiness in its wake."

One problem, of course, with such advertisements is that without an accurate sense of history, white people are unable to imagine a future that is fundamentally different from the present. A scant or misinformed understanding of history makes it easier to pretend that the past did not happen or that it has little meaning for today, which makes it possible to deny responsibility for what has happened and for enacting new ways of being. White people may be able to identify their geographical origins (in general terms, somewhere in Europe), but they typically lack a comprehensive understanding of whiteness's relation to slavery, genocide, land stealing, and other daily, less grand forms of racial oppression and exclusion. In this void, white folks flee to platitudes like "My family did not own slaves," "We are X, we were oppressed too" (where X equals an immigrant group who was discriminated against when first arriving in the United States), and "I have friends who are Y" (where Y equals a racial/ethnic group that is asserted to be unassimilative by mainstream standards).

White ideology provides flattering, nostalgic renderings of white history in place of nuanced, multicultural retellings of American history that would demand critical thinking and questioning from teachers, students, and citizens. Both issues—a nostalgic view of the past and a vague or nonexistent sense of one's future—erode one's creative potential, and in particular, the potential for seeing a world that is not based on hierarchy and division. This may be one reason that Henry Louis Gates refers to racism as "a profound failure of the imagination."[13]

DISSOCIATION

Another characteristic common to trauma exposure, according to van Dernoot Lipsky (2009, 92), is *dissociation*, a protective response in which "we cut ourselves off from our internal experience in order to guard against sensations and emotions that could be overwhelming to our system." It occurs when trauma is so severe that awareness cannot stay fully present. With dissociation a part of the psyche splits off from the rest of consciousness, separating from the trauma itself. This separation may manifest as vacating one's body during exposure to trauma (when witnessing racial shaming, exclusionary practices, police brutality, etc.), which renders the individual white person unable to remember the specifics of the event while carrying the emotional trailings associated with the event: untethered guilt, shame, panic, anxiety, a sense of betrayal, and/or a feeling of abandonment. As a traumatic response of whiteness at the individual level, dissociation runs on a continuum, from momentary unhinging to long-term and sustained fleeing of one's consciousness and conscience. It can be seen among those who appear not to reside in their bodies—no smiling, no dancing, no laughing, no gesticulating, no distinctive walk—and among white people in positions of power who have so separated themselves from reality that they cannot see their own entitlement even as they are benefiting from it. It often appears as seemingly free-floating, overwhelming anger and cynicism. Addictions are a common response to dissociation, an adaptation that, while immediately comforting, adds to depression, anxiety, and sense of persecution.

Dissociation can occur when trying to undo racism as well as when working to uphold it. Momentary splits can be experienced, for instance, by a white person who calls attention to a racial injustice in a personal or professional setting. Typically this truth telling in predominantly white settings is met by silence as the audience becomes flat-eyed, disengaging from the naming that is occurring in its midst. Such a response positions the truth-teller as the problem, as the one who is causing the argument.[14] In that moment, the witness is not only silenced, but also is made a nonperson by the nonengagement, an actual threat to the white family, organization, or institution. With such rendering, the chance for creative engagement with the issue gets reduced to moments of non-action and apathy. For the person who has spoken, the message is clear. Being shut down can produce a visceral sense of not being safe or not being seen, and of being erased, which can result in lifting a part of oneself out of the room, out of the trauma, as a means of protection. White traumatic disassociation is one reason why white people are often afraid to confront racism; as Thandeka (1999) persuasively illustrates in *Learning to Be White*, the possibility of being isolated and expelled from the body of whiteness is scary enough to keep them silent.

Momentary dissociation can also be triggered, as seen in the previous example, in the audience who is present at the moment in which personal, structural, or institutional racism is named. In educational settings, for instance, when students are encouraged to confront racial constructions, racism, and their own whiteness, they often experience fear, guilt, and sometimes shame.[15] Predictably, given our earlier discussion of the sense of persecution as a traumatic symptom, white students assume the position of victim. Their body language reveals their defensiveness; they lead their comments with familiar disclaimers such as, "I hope no one misunderstands what I am about to say. . ." and "I am not a racist, but . . . ," even as their contributions seek to dismiss, deny, or delegitimize the knowledge that is being shared. Just as often, however, they become broodingly silent, as if their refusal to speak, to engage, can stave off whatever they might hear, see, feel, and come to know in these moments. Silence prohibits their careful listening rather than creating a space where sympathetic, empathetic involvement with the perspectives of another human being can occur.

While dissociation is largely thought of as an individual response to trauma, with regard to whiteness it is also a collective cultural response with social implications. Sustained dissociation among white people is evident when racist ideology is repeatedly performed to the point where racism becomes seemingly "automatic," inescapable, and/or justified. This is the shift where whiteness, and the trauma associated with it, becomes hegemonic. Here, signs of trauma are evident in whiteness's unwillingness to acknowledge its "appallingly oppressive and bloody history" (Baldwin 1998b, 320), both in the United States and globally. It can be seen, for instance, in whiteness's refusal to be accountable for the removal and slaughter of native people on this continent, which makes it easier to continue national policies that ignore their sovereignty, colonize their lands, and keep them economically dependent on the "beneficence" of their colonizing government. In the place of accurate historical awareness and honest moral reflection, whiteness feeds itself stultifying myths of Native Americans being "dead," an inaccurate reframing that removes responsibility for the legacy and contemporary practices that continue to oppress Native American communities. This dissociation refuses to recognize the "open season" on black men, in particular, that has characterized US history (past and contemporary) and turns its back on the desperation of millions of people in their home countries and immigrants to western nations who have been set adrift by US economic policies (Martinez 1998; Alexander 2012; Alexander and Mohanty 1997; Grewal and Kaplan 1994). Ultimately, this dissociation is most clearly present in an unwillingness or inability to see people of color as fully human. Delegitimizing the experiences and perspectives of people of color—which is fundamentally dehumanizing—serves as both a mechanism for maintaining white supremacy as well as a disassociation that removes whiteness from the violence it is enacting.

With long-term dissociation comes an unwillingness to see oneself as responsible for one's actions, since the acts of the perpetrators are removed from the story itself. A devastating example of this form of dissociation is evident in the German government's dominant reference to the Holocaust as "the immense suffering of the Jewish people" (Giesen 2004, 119) with no mention of the perpetrators. The subjectivity and agency of the oppressors is lifted out of the story, a removal that parallels the dissociation (psychically removing oneself from the scene of the crime) on the part of many German citizens during World War II. Dissociation, then, is closely associated with historical amnesia; it is often the result of, but can also be triggered by, this white cultural practice.

Another chilling example of this lifting of a part of one's psyche away from the scene of the racialized terror is documented in Martha Collins's *Blue Front* (2006), a book of poetry where the author seeks to find the consciousness of a young white boy (her father) when he and 10,000 others viewed or otherwise participated in the lynching of a black man, and then a white man, in Cairo, Illinois, in 1909. Collins gives us clues of the five-year-old's daily life—a seller of fruit, a counter of money, a child who went to school—and then provides bone-crushing details of the fact of lynchings as a public spectacle. What Collins's poems show the reader is what is missing—the emotions, sensations, and memories of the five-year-old witness. There is a void where feeling and language should be. This is racial dissociation: the missing psyche, the missing emotion, a protective response to trauma that produces fragmentation, disorientation, and denial. Racial dissociation leaves a hole in its wake, a hole that might be filled with shame, guilt, loss of self or a "ruined moral identity" if the perpetrator engaged the emotional response that was suppressed (Giesen 2004, 116). This is the hole of unabiding hunger, of unspoken fear and repression, which leads to an insatiable desire for stimulus, noise, and distraction. Collins's poetry is a recent contribution that challenges us to better understand the triggers for and consequences of racial dissociation.

While underexamined in contemporary critical whiteness scholarship, dissociation is a white racial trauma and way of being that has been signaled. African American intellectual James Baldwin (1998a) wrote of it in his powerful short story "Going to Meet the Man." In the contemporary moment of the narrative, Jesse is a southern police officer actively working to suppress black activism in his community. After a day in which he had participated in the torture of a "ring-leader" spearheading a voter registration drive (258), he returns to his wife agitated and sexually impotent. As he lays next to her recounting his day of brutality, remembering that he felt "very close to a very peculiar, particular joy" (259) when he beat his victim, he slowly recovers a repressed memory of a lynching that he and his family attended when he was a child. He had buried the memory so deeply that only when he was participating once again in the brutalization of a black man, repeating an act that he had witnessed as a child, did the sources of his pain, confusion, silence, and fear return to him. Left unnamed and untreated, as Baldwin highlights in his story, dissociation leaves people at risk for repetition and at risk for the mentality of a mob. Alternatively, dissociation precipitates a radical withdrawal from others, an unacknowledged fear that association within whiteness might introduce additional trauma and pain. This refusal to connect with others leaves whites unable to strategize collectively and inhibits the mortar and brickwork needed for long-term social change.

ORIGINAL TRAUMAS

Where does whiteness learn to separate heart from head, body from spirit, and humanity from living? What are the original traumas that have only begun to be excavated, examined, and recovered from? While there is room for much theorizing about these early traumas and a promising roadmap has been provided by theologian Thandeka (1999) in her groundbreaking *Learning to Be White: Money, Race and God in America*, our sustained work over the years with white people struggling to understand white identity and racism has confirmed a common theme: a sometimes unconscious, often dogged return as adults to first encounters when whiteness was indelibly taught in across-race interactions. Our belief is that for many white people, especially in our contemporary moment,[16] the trauma of whiteness originates from the time when a child initially "sees" racism enacted. This "seeing" may come in the form of witnessing a parent or other relative lying, being condescending, insulting, or cruel to a person of color, which is often coupled with pretensions of kindness. In that moment the white child, who has not fathomed that distinction, may be so aghast that she/he cannot find her/his tongue; the level of betrayal is often overwhelming as well as unbelievable. Nothing seems safe anymore. In overwhelmingly white environments, this betrayal may be especially devastating because the individual person of color (the Chicano gardener, the African American domestic worker) is alone. They do not come with their kin. Their solitude makes them appear defenseless, unable to fight back. The child has no knowledge that the person of color has a family or community of protection. To see your kin in the role of the perpetrator is to be forever homeless.

As Baldwin (1998a) also highlights in "Going to Meet the Man," that vulnerability is recognized by white children because it is mirrored in their own life experiences. Like Jesse who finally remembers the castration of the black victim before he is burned alive, white children are just as likely to see themselves in the person of color who is being threatened and violated as they are to see themselves in the white adult who wields complete power over their lives, too. In the moment before the man is castrated, Jesse screams as if he is the one being dismembered, but he recognizes that he cannot ask his father why this violence is happening. He wonders helplessly, and silently, "What did he do?" (270). Thandeka (1999, 24) argues that this childhood trauma is the moment when the white person comes to know how fragile and tenuous their acceptance is within whiteness. Fear of being expelled from home and community, of being even more adrift and unprotected, leads to an embracing of the very thing—whiteness—that has alienated the white child from her/his sense of self. For in that moment, the hierarchy of race eliminates room for human bonding both within and outside of whiteness, resulting in devastating separations and loneliness—and guilt—for the white child. The slight, insult, pointed condescension, or reprimand done in the name of whiteness now implicates the white child.[17] While people of color may go back to a space of possible belonging and safety, the white child has no place in which to retreat, except to her white skin. The trauma becomes a source of alienation from what Marx (1964, 112) refers to as "species being," the ability to see oneself as connected in physical, spiritual, and artistic ways to other human beings.[18]

Perhaps this is why we often see the trope of the one black witness in so many white movies, such as Morgan Freeman in *Driving Miss Daisy* and Whoopi Goldberg in *Ghost*. That one black presence brings white people back to the original scene, compelled to go back to the trauma of which they have no conscious awareness. Without words, they are drawn back to that moment, even as they are unable to resolve the source of their uneasiness. However, the machinery of modern entertainment, while providing an archetype, does not help whites recover the trauma. In place of language that might connect the memory with an understanding of white violence, the industry instead provides comforting images of racial reconciliation and forgiveness, as if the forgiveness is all that is needed to heal the trauma. But forgiveness by the victim is a source of healing for the victim. The perpetrator has a separate journey to travel. That journey has to do with recognizing and becoming accountable for the violence they have done, and continue to do, out of their fear, greed, and apathy.

There is something about betrayal done at the level of skin—the largest, most unprotected, and most visible organ of the body—that makes a child feel especially defenseless, caught off guard, and then forever seen as the perpetrator even though she/he was not initially guilty. We hear this sense of being exposed in the fevered denials of white college students who are terrified of being perceived as racists, as if the very fact of their skin implicates them in something, accuses them of something, before they have a chance to speak. This is why many white children and adults throw themselves so unreflectingly, obliviously, into whiteness. They have a sense of there being no escape from this recognition, and the only protection they can imagine in their historically amnesiac, traumatized states, is a greater embrace of the white ideologies and ways of being that have prevented them from feeling anything too deeply.

This distorted dynamic typically gets stored in the unconscious where there are no words, a location that Freud has helped us understand leads us to repetition compulsion, a doubling back to the scene of the crime, each time trying to make sense out of it through reenactment. We know from trauma scholarship that trauma victims are in the same day every day, stuck in place, without the questions or resources to recover the memory not yet explored. But without the possibility of the reenactment being consciously tethered back to the original trauma, white people get stuck—the white child who witnesses his first racial affront, the white teen or adult who represses the initial trauma but internalizes the lesson of whiteness, the white society that denies its continued investment in whiteness even as it purposefully or inadvertently teaches another generation of white children what it means to be white. In the process, the meaning of whiteness and the emotional connection to that meaning are severed. While white folks may be aware of a vague sense of guilt, foreboding, or shame, they cannot necessarily connect these feeling to a source. They are free floating, haunting and painfully persistent.

Of course, not all white children are subjected to an "original trauma" as they see a loved one insult or violate someone of color. In fact, some white children have the fortunate chance to witness egalitarian, respect-driven relationships across race that affirm a sense of themselves as part of a larger world community. Unfortunately, however, this modeling does not protect them from exposure to racist ideology practiced in the larger world—in the media, at school, in their neighborhoods, in the military, through religion, to name but a few places where white ideologies are communicated. The dissonance between egalitarian modeling they may see in their families and what they witness in other social institutions can be equally devastating for white children, often without the language or skills to make sense of the contradictions they experience. The reality is that even children who are spared the personal betrayal of racist violence still witness racism around them and carry the knowledge of racism done in their names. Escaping an original trauma done at the hands of a loved one does not protect against the white racial trauma that white people experience, often in fits and starts, often without direct teachings. Those lessons seep into the bloodstream, reminding us, often without name, of the damage whiteness has caused.

Perhaps this unrecognized trauma at the heart of whiteness accounts for why people of color often say they are not able to "get anywhere" with white people in terms of having reasonable discussions about race. Instead of honestly confronting legacies of whiteness, many white people get frightened, driven, mean. The frustration, from the person of color's point of view, is that there is no way to call white people out from their spell, to be able to ask: "Why are you so frightened? Why are you lying again? Why are you denying the benefits of whiteness?" For people of color, it is unfathomable that white people do not know themselves and the world they have created well enough to engage these questions. But when one is chronically traumatized, much of life is lived in the land of hypersensitivity, if not outright delusion.[19] From the white perspective, nothing is so risky, so frightening, as acknowledging that whiteness is not neutral, not free of racism, not innocent. It would mean not only taking stock of one's own self, but reconnecting with the alienation that white folks might feel from their kith and kin.

This conversation about whiteness as racial trauma necessitates an awareness that, in the twenty-first century as in the past, whiteness is a tie that binds and blinds. Whiteness often makes people more susceptible to external reinforcements and guides, to not being able to listen to their own voices. Groupthink easily becomes the lay of the land. Seeking external reinforcements leads to a rabid grasping for things as indicators of personal and social success. Few pause to ask, "For what are you grasping?"[20] and the unchecked desire for endless growth and prosperity become the hallmarks of the nation. Investment in whiteness inhibits whites from recognizing the common ground that most of them share with most people of color in the United States: that job and housing markets are stacked against us, that the educational system is preventing more of us from aspiring to greatness, and that the political system serves the interests of a narrow and powerful few. Still in denial, white people will use many excuses to avoid responsibility. People get crazier and crazier; the violent binges get worse, seemingly willing to destroy the world before coming to their senses.

CRITICAL WHITE DOUBLE CONSCIOUSNESS

In Sara Ahmed's (2012, 14) "Whiteness and the General Will" she argues, "To stand against the world can require willfulness. . . . You have to become insistent to go against the flow and you are judged to be going against the flow because you are insistent." We take this as a political call to action. It requires us to recognize that the healing that is needed within whiteness will not come without concerted effort, without the will to reimagine what is possible. It will require people to acknowledge, then teach one another of the traumas of whiteness. The cessation of this white schizophrenic subjectivity will necessitate that allies and friends challenge the echo chamber of voices that tell the same twisted story of white innocence on the one hand, and victimization on the other. We need the histories that have been flattened, marginalized, and dismissed, and the complicated stories of antiracism activists who have dedicated themselves to living wholly and reconnecting all parts of themselves (see Thompson 2001). Whiteness must take responsibility for the injuries it has and continues to cause, and white folks must find ways to reimagine and reinvent themselves, authentically and in good faith, in the multiracial, multiethnic world that is, and always has been, our reality.

One of the many contributions of Marx's (1964) dialectical materialism is the recognition that dynamics of oppression (in this case, racial oppression) carry within them the seeds for their own transformation. Neuroses can be turned into resistance. Hypervigilance carries within it the seeds of its reduction; dissociation carries within it the seeds of its own reintegration; and the antidote for diminished creativity can be found in the creative energy that can come from working with people who are themselves doing antiracist work.[21] Building on Du Bois's concept of black double consciousness, we believe that the remedy to white schizophrenic subjectivity is the cultivation of a critical white double consciousness.[22] This consciousness, unlike its debilitating counterpart, seeks to rejoin the heart and head, body and spirit, and the humanity of whiteness to the social world that it both inhabits and creates. An antidote for the trauma of whiteness is a critical white double consciousness; it is a spirit of atonement that seeks to acknowledge and recover that which has been lost to whiteness through violence and oppression. Thus, critical white double consciousness is a resistant subjectivity. It is one that demands a fuller, multi-voiced narrative of the past and present, which it then utilizes for honest self-reflection and accountability. It seeks out multiracial, multiethnic interactions as an antidote to the monologues of whiteness, and learns the twin disciplines of silence and close listening as antiracist praxis. It commits itself to remaining a fully present and vocal *witness* in the face of white lies, denial, and aggression. It retools liability and trauma into assets for coalition building and organizing across race and other socially constructed differences. Critical white double consciousness nurtures the spaces that make the personal and social transformation of whiteness possible.

Thankfully, there are examples of this healing currently taking place. We are struck, for example, by a recent campaign to help organize a union among food service workers, most of whom are women of color, at a private women's college. Hypervigilance on the part of the food service workers and their allies was needed to learn the workplace conditions and to maintain the confidentiality and secrecy needed to lay the groundwork for organizing. To be the keeper of secrets for those who have been exploited and victimized can feel very risky—it can remind you of secrets kept when damage was first done (if you tell I will fire, kill, not love, disown you). Once that original betrayal has been committed, it can feel like everyone is lying, that there is no truth. But the workers' safety depended upon hypervigilance. For several months the momentum grew, culminating in a significant number of students, alumni, and faculty standing up in support of the workers' rights to organize. The energy garnered standing with people who were speaking truth to power, to telling their own stories of exploitation and resistance, fueled new energy among white allies to stay vigilant in their secrecy until it was safe to make the union demands public.

In this work we can also see the counter to white dissociation. Participants had to remain present for the sharing of difficult truths from people who are marginalized by race, class, and gender in their workplace. These were voices and perspectives not typically heard, not often welcomed, and difficult to reconcile with the privilege of college faculty and students. The desire to "check out" on the part of white people who were trying to support the food service workers was enormous. The responsibility of those participating in the process was to resist the urge to retreat to denial or to feel attacked or persecuted by the life stories being shared during the process. To choose to remain present physically, emotionally, and psychologically, to become an investigative journalist about the dynamics and complexities of race in a particular context, can be a powerful antidote to dissociation. It is a choice to stay in one's body and then speak out with clarity when racism and other injustices are being (re)enacted.

As for overcoming the original white traumas, there may be no substitute for getting to the bottom of the emotional legacies such scenes left us to carry. Just as people of color run the risk of carrying scarring memories from early racial traumas with them into adulthood, white people carry memories of when whiteness was first performed in their names, often at the expense of those they wanted to know, trust, and love. Making space in social movement organizing to do this deep psychological work together becomes a crucial piece of creating new scripts that are not based on hierarchy and exclusion.

Certainly, our sustained conversations over the past two years while writing this chapter, as a black and a white woman both seeking to understand white racial trauma, has required a willingness to do this work, with many intellectual and emotional bridges to build and cross over in the process. For people of color, a willingness to name and confront whiteness speaks both to a deep desire for social change as well as to a generosity of spirit. White people wanting to do antiracist work must come to understand that this commitment is essentially about saving their own souls. Confronting and healing the traumas of whiteness—hypervigilance, diminished creativity, a sense of persecution, and dissociation—is essential to developing a white racial identity that is not based on subjugation and alienation. Our charge, then, is to nurture the multiple ways that this can be embodied and passed on.

NOTES

1. Our shared experience based on decades of teaching in overwhelmingly white universities, of wanting to understand what keeps white students stuck, the role of fear and shame in the white psyche—and our need to know when breakthroughs do happen, what made that possible—laid the groundwork for the theorizing we offer in this paper. The authors want to thank Diane Harriford and Susan Boser for their generous conversations on various drafts of this chapter.

2. Throughout the chapter we use the term "they" and "them" in reference to white people, while recognizing that the "them" is actually "we" for one of the two authors (Thompson). Our pronoun gives example to how race necessarily bifurcates the English language—making divisions inevitable even at the level of words.

3. Truth and Reconciliation Commission, 2009. www.justice.gov.za/trc/.

4. James Baldwin implicitly makes this argument when he outlines the stammering responses of white Americans to their "black conscience, the black man in America"; see "Going to Meet the Man," in David Roediger, ed., *Black on White: Black Writers on What It Means to Be White* (New York: Schocken, 1998), 322.

5. While attending to all sixteen signs of trauma is beyond the scope of this paper, Lipsky does map out a comprehensive list: feeling helpless and hopeless; a sense that one can never do enough; hypervigilance; diminished creativity; inability to embrace complexity; minimizing; chronic exhaustion/physical ailments; inability to listen/deliberate avoidance; dissociative moments; sense of persecution; guilt, fear, anger and cynicism; inability to empathize/numbing; addictions; and grandiosity.

6. We use the term "schizophrenic" here to invoke the recognized symptoms of the genetic illness of schizophrenia. However, we diverge from the medical discourse of the disease most notably in our assertion that white schizophrenic subjectivity is a social construct that can be healed through specific knowledge and actions (i.e., it is not genetic or incurable). For additional discussion of white schizophrenic subjectivity, see also Veronica T. Watson, *The Souls of White Folks: African American Writers Theorize Whiteness* (Jackson: University Press of Mississippi, 2013).

7. Another tragic instance of the assault on black men in the United States occurred on July 17, 2014, when Eric Garner, a New York City resident and father of six, was killed by a New York City police officer. Garner, who was heard saying "I can't breathe" on video footage of the nuisance arrest, was subdued using a chokehold, a maneuver prohibited by New York Police Department regulations. The medical examiner who autopsied Garner's remains ruled his death a homicide.

8. According to the 2010 US census, there were 53,570 residents in Sanford, Florida. This population consisted of approximately 57.3 percent white and 30.5 percent African Americans. United States Census Bureau (2010), http://quickfacts.census.gov/qfd/states/12/1263650.html retrieved December 17, 2014.

9. In "Stories of a White Apocalypse on the Romanian Internet," Adela Fofiu borrows the term "rhizome" from the field of botany to describe the potential of apocalyptic narratives from the Romanian New Right blog to reinforce the panicked narratives of other

white supremacist websites as well as to spread to mainstream media outlets both in Romania and beyond. Her deployment of this term is useful for thinking about the ways that neoconservative and neoliberal sentiment gain popular traction and ascendency in purported nonracial states.

10. Toni Morrison coined the term "disremembered" in one of her novels. It is used in the last pages of the novel to describe the complex relationship the community has to the character Beloved after she has been exorcised. Beloved is both known and unknown, remembered and disremembered. The lack of memory the community has is active and deliberate, not a forgetting so much as a willful rejection of memory because of the fear that it animates in those who remember. As Morrison writes, "Remembering seemed unwise . . . They can touch it if they like, but don't, because they know things will never be the same if they do." See *Beloved* (New York: Alfred A. Knopf, 1987), 275.

11. Janet Koenig, "Commemorative Stamp Series," *Heresies: A Feminist Publication on Art and Politics* 4, no. 3 (1982): 8; cited in Rich 1986, 140.

12. Definition created by Celeste Lockhart, an undergraduate at the University of Massachusetts at Boston (Fall 1988), based on her reading of Adrienne Rich's (1986) essay "Resisting Amnesia: History and Personal Life."

13. Cited in Alexis Pauline Gumbs, "Communique to White Ally Heaven," *Sinister Wisdom* 87 (Fall 2012): 48.

14. For fuller discussion, see Sara Ahmed (2012).

15. In *Being White: Stories of Race and Racism*, Karen McKinney (2005, 2) argues that "whiteness is a *prompted identity*," a racial identity that is not thought of "in any depth" until people are asked to do so. This finding aligns with Thandeka's (1999) work, wherein she concludes that when white people *do* connect with the meaning of whiteness in their lives, they often tap into the emotions named above.

16. We stress the traumatic response that might be triggered among white youth in the twenty-first century because, unlike in previous historical moments, flagrant racism in language and action is not generally condoned by mainstream white America. That is, the social norms have shifted enough in this "post-race" era such that there is little support for outright acts of racism. We argue here therefore, that witnessing racist acts in the formative years creates irreconcilable dissonance in white children who grow up being fed a narrative about a post-race America. Though the conflict was always present (Clark signaled a similar psychological response in white children in 1963), it is heightened in this age that so vocally claims human equality, which is perhaps why we see these traumatic symptoms so pervasively now when we arguably did not before.

17. In more mixed-race environments, this initial scene may be slightly different. If the person of color is not alone, has community support, and/or the white child has access to more people of color (i.e., one person of color is not the initial stand-in for a whole people), there may be some buffers to the white loneliness, or at least less chance for the white child to equate white pain with black pain, to merge the two lonelinesses and alienations into one.

18. See also Diane Harriford and Becky Thompson, *When the Center Is on Fire: Passionate Social Theory for Our Times* (Austin: University of Texas Press, 2008): 122–25.

19. Interestingly, in yogic philosophy there are three states that cause suffering: delusion, aversion, and craving. All three are psychic states of whiteness—the delusion that racism does not exist, the aversion to people of color (as the original witness), and craving (for a belonging severed in the original scene).

20. This question is a recurring one in African America. It echoes Ethiop's (1999, 64) 1860 query, "Whither are this people tending?," voiced in his satirical essay "What Shall We Do with the White People?," and Baldwin's (1998b, 325): "To what, precisely, are you headed? To what human product precisely are you devoting so much ingenuity, so much energy?" There are many other examples, indicating a sustained African American critique of capitalist values and the dehumanization it fosters when it is embraced as a core national identity.

21. This is an example of what Douglas Kellner refers to as "'immanent reversal'—a flip flop or reversed direction of meaning and effects, in which things turn into their opposite." Douglas Kellner, "Baudrillard, Globalization and Terrorism: Some Comments on Recent Adventures of the Image and Spectacle on the Occasion of Baudrillard's 75th Birthday," *International Journal of Baudrillard Studies* 2, no. 1 (January 2005).

22. See Veronica Watson (2013), *The Souls of White Folks: African American Writers Theorize Whiteness*, for a conceptualization of white schizophrenic subjectivity and critical white double consciousness. Our work here is a fuller exploration of the psychological, social, and ethical/moral implications and possibilities of those terms. For additional discussions of white double consciousness, see also George Yancy, Introduction to *Look, a White! Philosophical Essays on Whiteness* (2012); Steve Martinot, *The Machinery of Whiteness* (2010); Linda Martin Alcoff, "What Should White People Do?" (2009); Shannon Sullivan, *Revealing Whiteness: The Unconscious Habits of Racial Privilege* (2006).

REFERENCES

Ahmed, Sara. 2012. "Whiteness and the General Will: Diversity Work as Willful Work." *philoSOPHIA: A Journal of Continental Feminism* 2 (1): 1–20.

Alcoff, Linda Martin. 2009. "What Should White People Do?" *Hypatia* 13 (3): 6–26.

Alexander, Jacqui, M., and Chandra Talpade Mohanty, eds. 1997. *Feminist Genealogies, Colonial Legacies, Democratic Futures*. New York: Routledge.

Alexander, Michelle, 2012. *The New Jim Crow: Mass Incarceration in the Age of Colorblindness*. New York: New Press.

Baldwin, James. [1965] 1998a. "Going to Meet the Man." In *Black on White: Black Writers on What It Means to Be White*, ed. David Roediger, 255–73. New York: Schocken.

———. [1965] 1998b. "White Man's Guilt." In *Black on White: Black Writers on What It Means to Be White*, ed. David Roediger, 320–25. New York: Schocken.

Chesnutt, Charles. 1905. *The Colonel's Dream*. New York: Harlem Moon.

Clark, Kenneth, B. [1963] 1988. *Prejudice and Your Child*. Middletown, CT: Wesleyan University Press.

Collins, Martha. *Blue Front*. Minneapolis: Graywolf Press, 2006.

Du Bois, W. E. B. 1935. *Black Reconstruction in America, 1860–1880*. New York: Simon & Shuster.

———. [1903] 1986. *The Souls of Black Folks*. In *W. E. B. Du Bois Writings*, compiled by Nathan Huggins, 357–548. Des Moines, IA: Library of America.

Ethiop. [1860] 1999. "What Shall We Do with the White People?" In *Black on White: Black Writers on What It Means to Be White*, ed. David Roediger, 58–66. New York: Schocken.

Feagin, Joe. 2013. *The White Racial Frame: Centuries of Racial Framing and Counter-Framing*. New York: Routledge.

Fofiu, Adela. 2014. "Stories of a White Apocalypse on the Romanian Internet." In *Unveiling Whiteness in the 21st Century: Global Manifestations, Transdisciplinary Interventions*, ed. Veronica Watson, Deirdre Howard-Wagner, and Lisa B. Spanierman, 29–47. Lanham, MD: Lexington.

Giesen, Bernhard. 2004. "The Trauma of the Perpetrators: The Holocaust as the Traumatic Reference of German National Identity." In *Cultural Trauma and Collective Identity*, ed. Jeffrey Alexander, Ron Eyerman, Bernhard Giesen, Neil Smelser, and Piotr Sztompka, 112–54. Berkeley: University of California Press.

Grewal, Inderpal, and Caren Kaplan, eds. 1994. *Scattered Hegemonies: Postmodernity and Transnational Feminist Practices*. Minneapolis: University of Minnesota Press.

Kellner, Douglas. 2005. "Baudrillard, Globalization and Terrorism: Some Comments on Recent Adventures of the Image and Spectacle on the Occasion of Baudrillard's 75th Birthday." *International Journal of Baudrillard Studies* 2 (1).

Martinez, Elizabeth. 1998. *De Colores Means All of Us: Latina View for a Multicultural Century*. Cambridge: South End Press.

Marx, Karl. 1964. *The Economic and Philosophic Manuscripts of 1844*, ed. Dirk J. Struik. New York: International Publishers.

McKinney, Karen. 2005. *Being White: Stories of Race and Racism*. New York: Routledge.

Mills, Charles. 1997. *The Racial Contract*. Ithaca: Cornell University Press.

Morrison, Toni. 1987. *Beloved*. New York: Alfred A. Knopf.

———. 1992. *Playing in the Dark: Whiteness and the Literary Imagination*. New York: Vintage.

Rich, Adrienne. 1986. "Resisting Amnesia: History and Personal Life." In *Blood, Bread, and Poetry: Selected Prose, 1979–1985*, 136–55. New York: Norton.

Roediger, David. 1991. *The Wages of Whiteness: Race and the Making of the American Working Class*. London and New York: Verso.

Spanierman, Lisa, and Nolan Cabera. 2014. "The Emotions of White Racism and Antiracism." In *Unveiling Whiteness in the 21st Century: Global Manifestations, Transdisciplinary Interventions*, ed. Veronica Watson, Deirdre Howard-Wagner, and Lisa B. Spanierman, 9–28. Lanham, MD: Lexington.

Sullivan, Shannon. 2006. *Revealing Whiteness: The Unconscious Habits of Racial Privilege*. Bloomington: Indiana University Press.

Thandeka. 1999. *Learning to Be White: Money, Race, and God in America*. New York: Continuum.

Thompson, Becky. 2001. *A Promise and a Way of Life: White Antiracist Activism*. Minneapolis: University of Minnesota Press.

van Dernoot Lipsky, Laura, with Connie Burk. 2009. *Trauma Stewardship: An Everyday Guide to Caring for Self While Caring for Others*. San Francisco: Berrett-Koehler.

Watson, Veronica, T. 2013. *The Souls of White Folks: African American Writers Theorize Whiteness*. Jackson: University Press of Mississippi.

CONTRIBUTORS

SADHANA BERY is assistant professor of sociology at the University of Massachusetts at Dartmouth. Her scholarship is focused on white supremacy—the systemic structures of racialized white rule over nonwhites. She addresses the ontologies and epistemologies of whiteness and the spectacular and routine white practices that exercise and re/produce dominance. She advances a case for making white supremacy *analytically* central to our study of society and social processes. Her current research agenda centers on an examination of the suturing of global spaces of whiteness, comparative studies of representations and performances of black slavery and American Indian conquest in museums, and the epistemic violence of black discourses that incorporate the racial logics of white supremacy.

ERICA COOPER is associate professor of Communication Studies at Roanoke College. She earned B.A. and M.A. degrees from the University of Wisconsin at Milwaukee and a Ph.D. from Indiana University. Her teaching and research areas include critical race studies, the rhetoric of social movements, critical theory, intercultural and interracial communication, and race, law, and rhetoric. In her dissertation, "One 'Speck' of Imperfection—Invisible blackness and the one-drop rule: An interdisciplinary approach to examining *Plessy v. Ferguson* and *Jane Doe v. State of Louisiana*," she identifies the techniques that were used within a rhetoric of jurisprudence to marginalize and oppress groups of people. She also has published meta-analyses that examine the relationship between race, gender, and teacher-student interactions in primary classrooms.

TIM ENGLES is Professor of English at Eastern Illinois University. His primary research and teaching areas include critical whiteness studies, multiculturalism, and contemporary United States literature. His publications include numerous articles and chapters, as well as *Towards a Bibliography of Critical Whiteness Studies* (editor), *Approaches to Teaching DeLillo's White Noise* (co-editor), and *Critical Essays on Don DeLillo* (co-editor).

MATTHEW W. HUGHEY is Associate Professor of Sociology and Affiliate Faculty in the Africana Studies Institute and the American Studies Program at the University of Connecticut. His research agenda centers on the examination of (1) racial identity formation, (2) racialized organizations, and (3) the production, distribution, and consumption of mass media racial representations. His scholarly articles have appeared in *Social Problems, Social Psychology Quarterly, Symbolic Interaction, Journal of Contemporary Ethnography, Critical Sociology, Sociological Quarterly, Du Bois Review, Ethnic and Racial Studies,* and *Ethnicities,* among many others. His books include *The White Savior Film: Content, Critics, and Consumption* and *White Bound: Nationalists, Antiracists, and the Shared Meanings of Race,* which was a finalist for the Society of Social Problems prestigious C. Wright Mills Book Award in 2013. His co-authored works include *The Wrongs of the Right: Language, Race, and the Republican Party in the Age of Obama.*

STEPHEN MIDDLETON received his B.A. from Morris College (*cum laude*), M.A. from Ohio State University, and Ph.D. from Miami University (Ohio). He completed the first-year curriculum in law at New York University School of Law, where he was a Samuel I. Golieb Fellow in Legal History. His research interests are race and the American legal system. His last book is *The Black Laws: Race and the Legal Process in Ohio, 1787–1860.* He is also the editor of *Black Congressmen During Reconstruction: A Documentary Sourcebook.* Middleton's research on whiteness has appeared in *Freedom's Conditions in the U.S.-Canadian Borderlands in the Age of Emancipation,* edited by Tony Freyer and Lyndsay Campbell, and in *Traces of Indiana and Midwestern History.* He is also working on a biography of Judge Robert Heberton Terrell, the first African American to be appointed to a judicial office by a U.S. president. He is currently the director of African American Studies and Professor of History at Mississippi State University.

DAVID R. ROEDIGER teaches American Studies at University of Kansas. He was born in southern Illinois and educated in public schools in that state, with a B.S. in education from Northern Illinois University and a Ph.D. from Northwestern, where he studied under Sterling Stuckey and George Fredrickson. Roediger has taught working-class and African American history at the University of Missouri and University of Minnesota. He has worked as an editor of the Frederick Douglass Papers at Yale University. His many books include *The Wages of Whiteness, How Race Survived U.S. History, Towards the Abolition of Whiteness,* and *Working Toward Whiteness.* His *The Production of Difference* (with Elizabeth Esch) won the International Labor History Association Book Prize. His edited books include the Modern Library edition of *W. E. B. Du Bois's John Brown* as well as *Black on White: Black Writers on What It Means to Be White.*

DONALD M. SHAFFER earned his undergraduate degree in English (magna cum laude) from Jackson State University, M.A. in English from the University of Illinois at Chicago, and Ph.D. at the University of Chicago. He is Associate Professor of African American Studies and English at Mississippi State University. Shaffer's research examines the socio-historical construction of race in African American and southern literature. His most recent article, "African American Folklore as Racial Project in Charles W. Chesnutt's *The Conjure Woman,*" appeared in the *Western Journal of Black Studies.* Along with Pearson and Gloria Liddell, Shaffer published "Is Obama Black? The Pseudo-Legal Definition of the Black Race: A Proposal for Regulatory Clarification Generated from a Historical Socio-Political Perspective," in *The Scholar: St. Mary's Law Review on Minority Issues.* He is currently working on a book manuscript examining the racial project that ideologically structures the writing of African American essayist and novelist Charles W. Chesnutt.

BECKY THOMPSON is a poet, activist, and scholar whose work focuses on antiracism and social justice. She is the author of several books, including *A Promise and a Way of Life: White Antiracist Activism; Mothering without a Compass: White Mother's Love, Black Son's Courage; When the Center is on Fire: Passionate Social Theory for our Times;* and *A Hunger So Wide and So Deep: A Multiracial View of Women's Eating Problems.* Her poetry can be found in her book *Zero is the Whole I Fall into at Night* as well as in the *Harvard Review, Tidal Basin Review,* and *Sinister Wisdom.* Her most recent book, *Survivors on the Yoga Mat: Stories for Those Healing from Trauma,* is the first multiracial vine on the subject of trauma, yoga, and healing. She is Professor and Chair of the Sociology Department at Simmons College and has taught at Duke University, Wesleyan University, the University of Colorado, Bowdoin College, and elsewhere. She has been awarded a number of prestigious fellowships and teaching awards (including from the Ford, Rockefeller, and National Endowment for the Humanities Foundations).

VERONICA T. WATSON is professor of English and faculty in the Graduate Program in Literature and Criticism at Indiana University of Pennsylvania. Watson received her M.A. and Ph.D. from Rice University. She publishes and presents a range of literary works focusing on twentieth-century African American literature, southern American literature, race and gender, geography, place and race, and critical race and whiteness studies. Her work has appeared in the *Mississippi Quarterly*, *Journal of Ethnic American Literature*, and a number of books and critical editions. Watson's recent book is entitled *The Souls of White Folk: African American Writers Theorize Whiteness*, which is the first study to consider the substantial body of African American writing that critiques whiteness as social construction and racial identity.

ROBERT WESTLEY earned his B.A. with honors distinction from Northwestern University; his J.D. from the University of California at Berkeley; and his M.A., M.Phil., and Ph.D. degrees from Yale University. He is currently the LOCHEF Professor of Legal Ethics and Professional Responsibility at Tulane University. His dissertation topic was on "Fourteenth Amendment Jurisprudence: Race and the Rights of Groups." His fellowship awards include a Mellon Foundation Fellowship in the Humanities and a President's Postdoctoral Fellowship at the University of California, San Diego. His research and teaching interests are in the fields of critical race theory, constitutional law, philosophy of law, law and literature, and the legal profession. His publications include "Many Billions Gone: Is It Time To Reconsider the Case For Black Reparations"; "The Accursed Share: Genealogy, Temporality, and the Problem of Value in Black Reparations Discourse"; and "First Time Encounters: 'Passing' Revisited and Demystification as a Critical Practice," in addition to numerous other articles.

INDEX

CPSIA information can be obtained
at www.ICGtesting.com
Printed in the USA
BVHW03s0926150618
518918BV00003B/20/P

9 781496 818294